AMERICAN IDEOLOGIES TODAY

SHAPING THE NEW POLITICS OF THE 1990s

AMERICAN IDEOLOGIES TODAY

SHAPING THE NEW POLITICS OF THE 1990s

Second Edition

Kenneth M. Dolbeare
The Evergreen State College

Linda J. Medcalf

McGraw-Hill, Inc.

New York   St. Louis   San Francisco   Auckland   Bogotá   Caracas
Lisbon   London   Madrid   Mexico   Milan   Montreal   New Delhi   Paris
San Juan   Singapore   Sydney   Tokyo   Toronto

American Ideologies Today
Shaping the New Politics of the 1990s

1 2 3 4 5 6 7 8 9 0 DOC DOC 9 0 9 8 7 6 5 4 3 2

ISBN 0-07-017411-3

 This book is printed on recycled, acid-free paper containing a minimum of 50% recycled de-inked fiber.

This book was set in Aster by Better Graphics, Inc.
The editors were Peter Labella and Fred H. Burns;
the production supervisor was Richard A. Ausburn.
The cover was designed by John Hite.
R. R. Donnelley & Sons Company was printer and binder.

Library of Congress Cataloging-in-Publication Data

Dolbeare, Kenneth M.
    American ideologies today: shaping the new politics of the
1990s / Kenneth M. Dolbeare, Linda J. Medcalf.—2nd ed.
    p.   cm.
    Includes bibliographical references and index.
    ISBN 0-07-017411-3
    1. Political science—United States—History—20th century.
2. Right and left (Political science)—History.   I. Medcalf, Linda.
II. Title.
JA84.U5M44   1993
320.5'0973—dc20

92-16441

ABOUT THE AUTHORS

Kenneth M. Dolbeare teaches political economy at The Evergreen State College in Olympia, Washington. He has taught at the University of Wisconsin, the University of Washington, and the University of Massachusetts at Amherst, and is the author of several research monographs and books on American politics, public policy, and political thought. He has served as a Guggenheim Fellow, as president of the Policy Studies Organization, and as a Fulbright Lecturer in Denmark.

Linda J. Medcalf earned her Ph.D. at the University of Washington and has taught American politics, public law, and political thought at the University of Massachusetts at Amherst, South Puget Sound Community College, and The Evergreen State College in Olympia, Washington. She is the author of several books and articles on American politics and currently serves as County Commissioner of Thurston County, Washington.

CONTENTS

PREFACE

This is a basic book about American politics and government. The political values and beliefs that have sustained and given direction to American political institutions and practices for generations are changing in fundamental ways, because the world has changed. American politics and government are being reshaped by these changes.

But neither scholars nor participants yet have been able to define what is happening or where we are heading. One reason is that we are in the very midst of a major economic, social, and political transformation, with only outmoded concepts and obsolete labels for our political thinking. The distinguished political scientist Robert Dahl offers this sweeping characterization:

> The most powerful ideologies of our age all suffer from having acquired their shape and substance in the 18th and 19th centuries, or very much earlier, before the world in which we live had come fully into view. They are like medieval maps of the world, charming but dangerous for navigating unfamiliar seas. . . . Liberalism, conservatism, capitalism, socialism, Marxism, corporatism, anarchism, even democratic ideas, all face a world that in its form and thrust confounds the crucial assumptions, requirements, descriptions, predictions, hopes, or prescriptions they express.[1]

In 1991 the scholar-journalist E. J. Dionne published a much-noted book, *Why Americans Hate Politics*[2], which blamed the "false choices" of outmoded ideologies for the growing American distaste for politics. Dionne flatly declares:

> The categories that have dominated our thinking for so long are utterly irrelevant to the new world we face. Most of the problems of our political life can be traced to the failure of the dominant ideologies of American public life, liberalism and conservatism. . . . to hold ideologies responsible for our troubles is . . . a way of saying that ideas matter, and that ideas, badly formulated, interpreted and used, can lead us astray.[3]

This book is an attempt to analyze what is happening to American political ideas, why, and what difference it makes for American politics. Although our focus is on what these changes mean for the future, we must first understand how we got where we are. No country can shake off well-established values and beliefs and start entirely afresh. The United States is certainly no exception in this respect. The political premises, goals, and

programs now taking shape may be the equivalent of a whole new generation of ideologies, but they build on a base of the old.

For these reasons, we grant as large a role to history as to any other way
of understanding the ideas that we explore. Although we employ everyday
American meanings for such terms as *liberal* and *conservative* in the text
(with explanations), we recount their classical origins and evolution in a
historical glossary. Our emphasis, however, is on the substance of the
emerging ideologies, as put forward by their leading authors and
spokespersons. That is, we try to let the reader judge each of the competing
American belief systems on the basis of its own merit.

In this second edition, we have found it necessary to make extensive
revisions and significant additions in order to follow the development of
American ideologies into the 1990s. We have also sought to make our
analysis accessible to beginning students of American political ideas
through a thematic organization and a continuing focus on the impact of
ideas on our politics.

We would also like to thank the following reviewers for their many
helpful comments and suggestions: Frank Colcord, Tufts University;
Robert Grafstein, University of Georgia; John Hughes, St. Michaels College; Steven Koven, Iowa State University; Joseph Kunkel, Mankato State
University; and Jeff Sedgwick, University of Massachusetts.

Kenneth M. Dolbeare
Linda J. Medcalf

PART I

IDEOLOGY AND POLITICS IN THE UNITED STATES

CHAPTER 1

AMERICAN IDEOLOGIES: THEIR ORIGINS AND IMPORTANCE

Every person alive goes through life with *some* mental images and expectations—whether fully formed or fragmentary—about how the world is and should be organized. The images come from often unexamined assumptions, values, and notions about what is good or bad, right or wrong, natural or inevitable. That collection of images, expectations, values, and assumptions constitutes an *ideology*. An ideology simplifies, organizes, evaluates, and gives meaning to what otherwise would be a very confusing world. Particularly in times of uncertainty and change, some people cling desperately to old values, images, and expectations while others reach eagerly for new ones. Americans are no exception to this rule.

In other words, ideology is pervasive. Often it is unrecognized as such, because it is so deeply embedded in people's lives and so widely employed in everyday life that it is misunderstood as reality. Sometimes it serves to unite people to seek changes in their world. For both these reasons, ideology is a crucial factor in politics. American politics is no exception to this rule either. Indeed, the United States today is a huge laboratory in which various ideologies, some unrecognized but most quite explicit, are contending for the opportunity to shape our future.

To understand American politics one must understand what Americans *think*—about themselves, their world, and their future—and *why* they think that way. Of course, depending on their cultural background, life experiences, and current policy preferences, Americans espouse different ideologies. This book is an attempt to understand the rich variety of American ideologies today and where they may be taking the United States tomorrow.

We start with brief descriptions of the nature and sources of ideology. Then we explore the ways in which ideologies link up with American politics.

THE NATURE OF IDEOLOGY

An ideology is a more or less coherent set of values, beliefs, and hopes (and sometimes fears) about how the world *does* and *should* work. This set of images and expectations operates as a kind of map in people's minds, telling them what they are seeing and how to understand and interpret what is happening. Because it rests on deeply rooted values and often unconscious assumptions, an ideology also provides cues for judgment about whether something is good or bad.

An ideology thus affects perception, understanding, *and* evaluation. We see a "fact" in a certain way, fit it into a context of meaning, and evaluate it as good or bad—all in terms of the ideology we hold. In effect, ideology intervenes between so-called objective conditions and events and the people who see and evaluate them. It is a socially generated and transmitted screen, or lens, through which people view themselves and their social world.

Ideology may be understood and analyzed at two distinct levels. The most *fundamental*, or *core*, level is that of basic values and assumptions. In the United States people share six core values to a very great extent—at least in the abstract. These core values are individualism, property, contracts and law, freedom, equality, and democracy.

These values are so important to the understanding of all American ideologies that we devote the entire next chapter to describing and analyzing them. There we shall see that although the values themselves are strongly held and widely shared, Americans differ about how they should be defined and what the priorities should be among them. These differences have been and still are at the heart of much of the ideological conflict in American politics.

Ideology may also be analyzed at an *applied* level of concepts, definitions, images, expectations, beliefs, and cues for action. All of these are grounded in the core values and extend from them to connect with the world of perceived reality. They make up a more or less integrated whole, or a *system* of (related) beliefs, by which a person organizes and interprets reality without conscious effort. Whether they are accurate or inaccurate portrayals of reality does not matter; what is important is that they operate to give shape and meaning to what is perceived "out there" in the world.

Ideologies are more distinctive at the applied level, because the process of translating "reality" into terms that fit into people's real-life situations tends to emphasize what is different rather than what is shared. All Americans do not have the same cultural backgrounds, life experiences, or present advantages and preferences. To the extent that these factors have shaped people's beliefs and expectations, therefore, their ideologies will differ from those of others.

These differences often take regular, repeated, or patterned forms, such that a distinctive (ideological) view of the world comes into being among many people at roughly the same time. After decades, the differences in ideologies get larger. Despite the fact that all share the same fundamental values, at least in the abstract, they have sharp differences about how those values should be defined or applied.

At the outer limits of ideology lies the activity of taking positions on issues of the day. A person's position on an issue may or may not have anything to do with his or her ideology. One may be *for* a particular policy for several very different reasons; some of those reasons might stem from ideology, and some not. Moreover, people of very different ideologies may be on the same side of any given issue; there is not always a liberal or conservative position on every issue. Thus, it is vital to understand that positions on issues do not *necessarily* connect to ideology, although clearly sometimes they do. Sorting out the relationship between ideology and issue positions is a major part of our analytical task.

Finally, ideologies do not just organize and interpret the world for people. They also serve as guides to action, as a means of self-expression, and as the "glue" that holds social groups together. Ideology is a powerful means of social control and is deliberately used as such in every society, the United States included. The particular ideology conveyed is the one preferred by those who have the power and influence to decide what is taught. For example, the reverence urged for the Constitution is a form of ideological indoctrination. It teaches people what to think and why and that the document is right and good, in ways that foreclose independent critical analysis.

THE SOURCES OF IDEOLOGY

There are a great many sources of ideology, some quite obvious and some much less so. They share the task of inculcating the elements of the dominant ideology. In the United States such sources seem particularly powerful and successful. However, their success is not constant or comprehensive. Some people develop ideologies that differ from the dominant one. How people acquire and change ideologies is one of the key questions of political analysis. In this section we shall identify some of the major sources of ideology and speculate about how ideology is developed or changed.

Probably the two most important sources of ideology are the history and culture of the society. Values and ideas that have worked in the past and have become symbols of the nation and its greatness have an imposing longevity. In the United States the values associated with the Declaration of Independence and the Constitution are almost impregnable. They are givens. If they are challenged, the challenge is one of redefinition within the most limited range that will meet current needs.

As may be expected, history, culture, and most other sources of ideology as well stress the rightness and goodness of things as they are. The United States is celebrated as the embodiment of (good) American values, which in turn are presented as universal and inevitable—in tune with human nature and the aspirations of people everywhere. Of course, some people benefit by this spirited defense of the status quo and have an interest in seeing that it is continued; others do not but are not always aware of the power of ideology.

History not only determines the givens with which the present is confronted and the apparent range of the possible, but also teaches that some alternatives are unworkable, undesirable, or utterly unacceptable. In the United States, for example, individualism and private property are virtually unquestionable values; capitalism and religion are close seconds. In contrast, Marxist socialism is beyond serious discussion.

Culture has many subtle effects as well. The meanings of concepts and words, buried in the everyday language that people use, can carry ideology across generations. Even colors carry ideological meanings. Black, red, and white all have different meanings, for example. Music, folklore, art, and literature all reflect and transmit dominant values from the past and suggest the range of socially acceptable beliefs and expectations. Most of all, the way of thinking that is characteristic of a society sets limits to what people can think *about*. In the United States, for example, it is far easier to think about tangible, demonstrable "things" than about what might happen if today's conditions were to change markedly.

History and culture provide the background, but the educational system and the mass media are the contemporary vehicles for inculcating the ideology. In the United States compulsory public education has long been a means of indoctrinating people (particularly immigrants) in proper American middle-class values and beliefs. Textbooks and teachers are carefully screened to assure orthodoxy and adherence to conventional interpretations.

The mass media repeat versions of the same basic images of the world, values, and benevolent interpretations of things American. Consider, for example, the ideology in one standard plot: a white American military hero struggles against overwhelming odds, often employing miraculous technology to destroy the enemy, who usually appears to be of a different race and infected with communist ideology. For more mundane examples, one has only to identify the values and assumptions that shape any TV news broadcast.

The teaching of ideology occurs in many other equally unobtrusive but effective ways. Events are interpreted by the media or seen by the public in ways that confirm or (much less frequently) question the dominant ideology. Sometimes an event is so dramatic that it carries an interpretation of its own. The Great Depression of the 1930s, for example, sent a message to many people that the American economic system did not work any longer—and had the effect of reshaping ideologies.

Similarly, a large popular movement or a major public policy may draw forth a new or revised ideology in support. The Populists of the 1890s initially rallied around a specific program of reform, for example, and when they were unsuccessful, many adherents ended up a decade or so later as Progressives or Socialists. Anticommunism and the cold war with the Soviet Union served as central components of conservative ideology for several years after World War II. More recently, the abortion issue played a major role in the rise of the New Right.

In short, a number of continuing culture-teaching sources and many more obviously political factors are at work to communicate ideology to people. How the individual integrates these messages with other aspects of his or her life, however, is more problematic than any simple communication-acceptance model would suggest.

As youngsters, children acquire basic political values and beliefs from their families and schools; often it may seem that there is no end to the public school effort to teach the propriety, inevitability, and utility of all things American. But for some children, the conditions of everyday life effectively deny these benevolent interpretations. Others go through experiences that cause them to question what they earlier accepted. Sustained deprivation and dramatic events often are necessary before large numbers of people break away from a dominant ideology.

In general, once inculcated, ideology tends to resist change. We cling to the familiar, in part, because a whole web of other beliefs—or even our basic identity—may depend on maintaining established ideologies. Changing conditions may cause ideologies to adapt so as not to lose their adherents. However, despite the power of the dominant ideology and all the forces that hold people to it, the fact is that many people develop different and often directly challenging ideologies. When and why there are shifts from one ideology to another or change in a given ideology are vitally important questions in politics.

THE IMPORTANCE OF IDEOLOGY IN AMERICAN POLITICS

Ideology fulfills many functions within a society. Ideology drives political action, mobilizes people, explains and justifies what elites have done—or it rallies the opposition, offering new ways of seeing and doing in politics—or it tells people to withdraw and wait passively for others to decide on the future directions of the society. In other words, ideology shapes politics and in turn is shaped by it. Ideology justifies what has happened in politics, and from it movements are organized in support of new alternatives. No ideology, no politics.

Some eras in the history of a country are more important than others. Social, economic, political, and cultural changes occasionally converge and reshape the way a society understands itself and sets its future course. In such periods, both the dominant ideology and newly developing ideologies that challenge its dominance undergo substantial change, struggle for impact in politics, and seek to shape the future in their preferred image.

Our premise is that the United States is in the midst of just such a period of significant change—perhaps as fundamental as any in our history—which began in the mid-1960s and has yet to run its course. Our ideologies, both the dominant liberalism and its many challengers, are in a process of reconstruction that will drive our politics in yet-unrecognized directions. This new political context and the potential for ideological reconstruction require some further comment.

The New Context of American Politics

The context of American politics is being reshaped by rapid changes in global ecology, economic relations, and political alignments. The scope of air and water pollution, the depletion of finite resources, and the threat to life posed by the continuing deterioration of the natural environment have given environmental issues unprecedented prominence. These factors fundamentally challenge long-established assumptions about the imperative of economic growth.

Economically, the United States has declined in several key measures, and a growing number of other nations are outperforming us in international competitiveness. The American economy appears to be in an unprecedented and dangerous situation, lending a new urgency to finding solutions. The apparent end of the cold war removed a long-standing threat and calls into question the military expenditures and world policing role that shaped U.S. government structure and policies for half a century.

At the same time, continuing trends in domestic conditions are changing the fundamental givens of American politics and raising wholly new issues to compelling stature. The U.S. government, for example, has run up a huge new debt, with deficits looming for years ahead. The economy seems unable to support the investment needed to cope with today's social problems. Millions of blue-collar manufacturing jobs disappeared, some replaced with high technology positions but more with lower-paid service-sector jobs. Declining real wages and sustained underemployment have, for the first time, become characteristic of the aging U.S. economy.

The largest cities have become predominantly nonwhite, with serious housing needs, declining quality of public education, and high crime rates. Racial polarization heightened while the nation appeared to retreat from the gains of the civil rights era. Related to these last two trends, the population moved steadily west and south during the last four decades, changing the political weight of states and regions. Education and health care are increasingly recognized as vital but unserved long-term needs. The lack of capability, hope, and purpose among a near majority of Americans casts a brooding cloud over the whole political context.

Perhaps the most salient change in American politics was the rupture of the long-standing Democratic party coalition. The New Deal, Harry Truman's Fair Deal, and even Lyndon Johnson's Great Society, were products of a tacit electoral alliance between trade union members, urban white ethnics, African-Americans, and white southerners. This coalition, however, collapsed under the combination of growing affluence, Democratic party support for civil rights legislation, and reaction against the changes of the 1960s associated with big and Democratic government. White southerners began to leave the party; white ethnic voters, many newly moved to the suburbs, were not far behind.

Other factors also contributed to the remaking of American politics. In little more than a single generation, the rise of television helped reduce the role of *both* political parties and make money much more important to campaigns. Media, both news and commercial, require information that can be compressed into thirty- or sixty-second messages. Basic cultural values and symbols—the essence of ideology—are much more amenable to thirty-second spots than to detailed discussion of issues and qualifications.

Simultaneously, voters have lost confidence in political institutions and leaders and in their own ability to hold them accountable. Turnout at elections has dropped steadily, to the point where barely half of the eligible electorate actually votes, even for presidential candidates. Moreover, white and middle-class voters disproportionately account for the actual voting electorate. A much sharper decline in voting exists among the very people who once were thought to be the primary beneficiaries of government assistance. A large body of potential voters sits on the sidelines at each election; when, or if, sufficiently motivated to vote, they could determine the outcome of any given election.

The context of American politics is thus one of great economic and political change, giving rise to many new issues and problems. Existing ideologies contain neither explanations nor solutions for many of these conditions and problems. The fundamental structure of the economy and long-standing political traditions have eroded; a new and little-understood kind of politics is taking shape. In this new American political context, new and changed ideologies will play major roles.

The Potential Reconstruction of American Ideologies

In a period of profound change in all dimensions of social life, formerly dominant ideologies may lose their grip on people and/or undergo adaptive change; alternative ideologies, once ignored, may rise to a governing role. Of course, a deeply imbedded ideology may no longer serve its original purposes but still control the range of political thought and effectively block change for a long time. This book explores what is happening to once dominant American liberalism, what the major challengers for ideological impact are, and what their chances for reshaping our politics may be.

There is clearly a great impatience among Americans today, not only with liberalism but also with the whole range and character of political ideas that have defined our politics for the last several decades. However, there is as yet neither agreement on new political ideas nor an effective reconstruction of the key terms of political debate in the United States. In the meantime, the old categories endure, our politics atrophy, and Americans pull away in revulsion.

This argument may be found in the current work of many political thinkers, but it is the major theme of a recent political history by E. J. Dionne, *Why Americans Hate Politics*. Dionne speaks for those who share his view when he argues first, that liberalism *and* conservatism now serve to block needed and desired changes and second, that we must go beyond left and right as they are presented in our current political debate. On the first point, he says:

> liberalism and conservatism are framing political issues as a series of false choices. . . . liberalism and conservatism *prevent* the nation from settling the questions that most trouble it. . . . We are still trapped in the 1960s. . . . By continuing to live in the 1960s, conservatives and liberals have distorted their own doctrines and refused to face up to the contradictions within their creeds.[1]

In a particularly thoughtful essay on the imperative for the United States to come to terms with race relations, the black thinker Cornel West makes much the same point:

> The first step is to reject the narrow framework presupposed by public discussions of race. This debilitating framework, pitting liberals against conservatives or Great Society Democrats against self-help Republicans, reinforces intellectual parochialism and political paralysis.[2]

Dionne's second point, that the United States must "go beyond left and right," is becoming a widely shared slogan. His image of what is required is put in the form of an existing demand from the American middle class. It is

> an inchoate demand for a new center that will draw on the lessons and achievements of the last thirty years by way of moving the country forward—and ending . . . the "screaming." It is a demand for an end to ideological confrontations that are largely irrelevant to the 1990s.[3]

The rejection of old frameworks on behalf of ideas that represent a genuinely new kind of political dialogue is stated somewhat more pungently by two libertarian democrats from Vermont:

> First of all we believe the liberal/conservative definition is a black hole in the universe of ideas. . . . The new movement afoot in America is . . . an ideological bridge to a new future.[4]

The black perspective is similar, but with a sense of foreboding:

> America needs a new framework, a new language, and a new leadership to talk about race in America. There is a deep hunger across the country for this new level of discourse about race—yet there is also a warranted fear that if we fail to make this jump to a higher ground, an ugly xenophobic backlash will fill the vacuum.[5]

The early feminist thinker Betty Friedan makes much the same point:

> We need to bridge the old conservative-liberal chasm and leave behind fixed positions of ideological purity . . . eliminate the false polarities and appreciate the limits and true potential of women's power.[6]

Given such broad agreement among contemporary American thinkers, why is there so little apparent change in the range and character of our political debate? The real question may be whether, despite all the recognized need and contextual opportunity, Americans are willing and able to develop a new or significantly modified set of terms for our political debate. We shall return to these questions in our final chapter, after exploring the changing and emerging ideologies of the 1990s.

The process of crystallization of new ideologies, as well as that of adaptation or replacement of old ones, will take place in response to the basic values of the broadly shared American belief system. These basic values define the way Americans think about politics. We must start our analysis with careful examination of these building blocks.

ADDITIONAL READINGS

Baradat, Leon P. *Political Ideologies: Their Origins and Impact*. Englewood Cliffs, N.J.: Prentice-Hall, 1979.

Dionne, E. J., Jr. *Why Americans Hate Politics*. New York: Simon & Schuster, 1991.

Dolbeare, Kenneth M. *American Political Thought*. 2d ed. Chatham, N.J.: Chatham House, 1989.

Hoover, Kenneth R. *Ideology and Political Life*. Monterey, Calif.: Brooks/Cole, 1987.

Love, Nancy S. *Dogmas and Dreams: Political Ideologies in the Modern World*. Chatham, N.J.: Chatham House, 1991.

Lustig, R. Jeffrey. *Corporate Liberalism: The Origins of Modern American Political Theory, 1890–1920*. Berkeley: University of California Press, 1982.

Rejai, Restafa. *Political Ideologies: A Comparative Approach*. Armonk, N.Y.: M. E. Sharpe, Inc., 1991.

Sargent, Lyman Tower. *Contemporary Political Ideologies: A Comparative Analysis*. 6th ed. Homewood, Ill.: Dorsey, 1987.

CHAPTER 2

AMERICAN IDEOLOGIES: THE BASIC VALUES

The readily identifiable values and assumptions that have characterized American political thinking since prerevolutionary days include five building blocks—individualism, property, contracts and law, freedom, and equality. In addition, there is another summarizing "supervalue"— democracy—and some surrounding beliefs, or "cultural baggage."

These values have been and are widely shared, but chiefly in a general and abstract sense. Before they can be seen as actually realized in social life, values must be (1) defined with some clarity and (2) ranked according to priorities, establishing which shall be striven for first or how to settle conflicts among them. Vigorous disagreements about proper meanings *and* the proper priorities have been continuing features of the American political dialogue.

Superficial consensus, in other words, has masked serious conflict. There is no one "true" American ideology or belief system. Despite the appearance of agreement stemming from the use of a common set of terms, distinct mainstream ideological traditions have always competed with each other. At the margins of this mainstream tradition, lesser known alternatives have ebbed and flowed in strength over the years.

In the following sections, we first take up the five building blocks, each of which has a long and revered history. By now, these components of our thinking are thoroughly fused; it is neither possible nor necessary to draw sharp boundaries between them. Locked in a mutually supportive system, they appeal powerfully to all of us. Next we explore democracy, our supervalue. Americans set democracy on a pedestal because it summarizes all our other values and symbolizes our political achievements and goals. However, democracy too is a contested concept whose meaning has always been in dispute. The nature of that dispute and its implications tell us much about the history and prospects of American ideologies. Finally, we note several American premises and assumptions not explicitly political, but which surround and shape the way our political values and ideologies are understood and applied in our politics. We call these premises and assumptions cultural baggage because they are such deeply grounded elements and have been carried forward from generation to generation and from place to place in American thinking.*

THE FIVE BUILDING BLOCKS

Individualism

Probably no country in the world has as deep a cultural commitment to individualism as the United States. Our individualism is widely cele-brated ("I did it my way," "The Lone Ranger," "a nation of Robinson Crusoes," and so forth), and it seems utterly natural to us. We all carry images of splendid isolation, of the fulfillment to be found in not having to depend on anyone for anything.

In the United States the individual serves as the self-evident starting point for thinking about the nature and purposes of social life. We have no image of society as an independent organism with a life of its own and with the right to ask certain behavior from the individuals who happen to make it up at any given time. We do not even have a historical memory of such an image; it is truly foreign to our thinking. Instead, we start with the notion of the necessity and propriety of each person seeking individual survival and satisfactions. All other individuals naturally do the same; the inherent nature of all human beings is to seek to serve their own self-interest first and foremost.

To prevent this self-seeking from becoming mutually destructive, how-ever, individuals are said to have certain rights, and a government is instituted to preserve such rights. Both society and government are the creations of individuals and are subordinate to the rights of those individ-uals. They merely maintain the context in which individuals pursue their important private goals.

The availability of all these private opportunities also carries the ex-pectation that individuals will make good use of them. People should advance themselves in the terms that they and others value—chiefly money, land, and jobs with status and security. If they do, they will be satisfied and receive the respect and envy of their fellows. If they do not, they will be judged wanting—even failures—as individuals. Moreover,

---

* We must note, even at this early stage, that the values and beliefs about to be examined are uniquely American. Not even the European countries from which the United States was initially settled hold these values in the way that Americans do. Europeans start from quite different social histories and political principles. As a result, Europeans have developed a much wider range of ideologies and a different set of labels for them. We look at the American ideological experience, using a European perspective, and the classical labels of political theory derived from it, in the extended Glossary at the end of this book. In the main body of the text, however, we use familiar American labels. Readers should make conscious use of the comparative and analytic perspective that the Glossary offers but be alert to possible confusion in these descriptive labels.

because they share the same criteria as other individuals, they will judge *themselves* as failures.

These dimensions of American individualism have profound and double-edged implications. On one hand, all individuals are expected to work hard to achieve their goals. They should not rely on anyone else. Self-reliance is a mark of character, an indication that one is truly an individual. Everybody carries personal responsibility for his or her standing on the social ladder. One's prestige and property reflect personal effort, character, and achievement. When realized, social mobility marks the individual achiever as a worthy and successful person.

On the other hand, many individuals do not achieve their goals. They do not gain money, land, or high-status and secure jobs. They do not rise on the social ladder. In this case, the American assumption is that they have only themselves to blame. Responsibility for the individual's eventual place in the world lands squarely on his or her own shoulders. In this way, the work ethic and the belief in self-reliance and personal responsibility can combine irretrievably to burden the individual. Failure to achieve material success and social mobility readily translates into a character flaw or a lack of personal effort.

Such attitudes have powerful stabilizing effects in American society. Those at the top of the social pyramid often credit their own personal character and effort for their success. They may claim special status for that reason, including, for example, the right to make decisions for less favored members of the society. And many people may accept their claim, granting them deference and respect and perhaps even the power to govern. Moreover, strong belief in rugged individualism may cause those at the bottom of the social pyramid proudly to reject needed assistance or to blame themselves for their failure to succeed.

However, not everyone shares these attitudes and beliefs. With respect to those at the bottom of the social pyramid in particular, shared assumptions begin to diverge and become disagreements. For some people, the responsibility for an individual's inability to fulfill his or her wants and needs does not rest entirely with that individual. Some part of the explanation is seen as lying outside of the individual's control. It is related, instead, to aspects of the larger social and economic system, such as discrimination or lack of educational opportunity. How much of the responsibility is attributable to individual versus systemic factors thus becomes the subject of heated debate—and the basis for different belief systems.

Moreover, our individualism is much stronger in rhetoric than in our lived reality. Only a few Americans actually live isolated, purely self-seeking, ruggedly individualistic lives. Parents routinely sacrifice their own interests for their children. People share many scarce resources with each other, particularly in times of crisis, disaster, war, or economic hardship. People generously give money, time, and energy to community causes and organizations, often at genuine cost to their own interests. Our individualism fills our abstract social and political judgments even as it contradicts our day-to-day world. Some people recognize this and explicitly call for more in the way of sharing and collective action; others hold firmly to the purer form of individualism. Thus individualism is both a shared value and a continuing subject of disagreement.

Property: Paramount among Rights

Although the concept of property always has been highly valued in the United States, its meaning has changed considerably over time. In seventeenth-century England, the source of many of the basic elements in our thinking, *property* primarily meant land but also included people's capacity to improve or cultivate that land. Soon the term included money derived from the sale of crops and livestock, and then goods made for sale or trade. It was not long before *property* also meant various certificates of investment or indebtedness convertible to money at some future time. Whatever its form, property was taken to be a vital goal of any individual. The rights to hold property, be secure in its possession, and be free to use it as one wished came to be thought of as natural rights of individuals, fully equivalent to the paramount rights of life and liberty.

From the colonial period well into the nineteenth century, free or very inexpensive land lured settlers to the American continent and to its westward expansion. Land meant the prospect of growing food and of being able to support one's family. In some cases the production of enough surplus to generate investment capital meant the ability to rise above one's origins. The concept of ownership carried with it the possibility of economic independence and permitted participation as a citizen in the affairs of government.

Thomas Jefferson linked ownership and citizenship on the level of political principle. He argued that land ownership was the only way of assuring the independence necessary for people to act as free and thoughtful citizens in public affairs. If possessed of such a stake in the society, citizens would inform themselves and exercise their best judgment in the public interest. A landless population working in urban factories would be subject to too many economic pressures and, in Jefferson's eyes, would lose first its independence and then its capacity for self-government.

Alexander Hamilton, on the other hand, accepted the ownership-citizenship link, but he explicitly supported another form of property ownership. Stocks, bonds, and creative uses of indebtedness, Hamilton believed, would spur trade and eventual industrialization. Such a commercial base was necessary if the United States was to gain power and independent stature among the nations of the world. Hamilton thus argued for creation of a stake in society for bondholders, financiers, and other commercial and manufacturing property holders.

From George Washington's administration well into the nineteenth century, this conflict between *forms* of property and their associated models of economic development continued. Jefferson and his followers supported rural agricultural development; Hamilton's camp looked to a political economy with manufacturing, commerce, and finance at its base. Similar conflicts reverberate within our concept of property today as we try to come to terms with such innovations as instantaneous computer transmission of billions of dollars and multinational corporations and banks. We also continue to seek ways to give propertylike rights to public goods, such as clean air and water, to protect those aspects of our environment from the rights of certain owners to do as they wish with their pollution-producing property.

The essential idea of property ownership remains very strong, however. It may be most visible in the symbolic aura that surrounds owning one's own home. In real terms, home ownership is encouraged by government subsidies and tax concessions. The strength of the belief in property ownership certainly helps explain the fact that most Americans feel threatened by those who advocate social ownership of the means of production. People who are believed to be in favor of "destroying private property" seem truly far-out to most Americans. Property ownership is more to Americans than just a widely sought material achievement. The ownership-citizenship link supports democratic participation in certain enduring ways, and ownership and the taxpaying obligation that accompanies it may in turn benefit from the high value placed by Americans on democracy.

Contracts and Law

In American thinking, bolstered by actual colonial practice that culminated in the making of the Constitution, both collective social obligations and governments are created by contracts among people. It is not only public life that rests on the principle of contract; business transactions of every kind are carried on through contracts. This, too, traces back to colonial practice. Reliance on future performance of all such contracts was so utterly necessary for commerce and investment that there soon developed the legal principle of the sanctity of contracts. The notion of many binding contracts is fundamental to development of the modern commercial and participatory society made up of many individuals, corporations, governments, and so forth.

More specifically, colonial experience fixed two important principles in American minds. One was the idea that governmental powers were controlled by some form of contract that could be found somewhere. The second was that the origins of this set of controlling limitations lay somewhere outside of and above the ordinary reach of people in power, whether kings, legislatures, or popular majorities. These limitations were truly superior to the everyday acts of public authorities; they were rooted in the natural rights of individuals, that is, in the law of nature itself.

This link to natural law is far from the only way in which the notion of contract is interwoven with the value attached to law generally and to the neutral, procedural "rightness" of legal mechanisms in particular. To begin with, the American Constitution of 1787 is in effect a contract. It sets forth the powers of government as well as limitations on that government. These provisions have the force of law but flow from a level superior to that of ordinary lawmakers. The idea of a higher law was hardly a new one, but in the Constitution it was for the first time combined with the notion of contract to produce an explicit set of governing powers and limitations.

The new republic thus emerged with a written contract-constitution embodying higher (natural) law. It soon became a symbol of things good, unique, and even God given about the United States. There developed something akin to a civil religion or religiouslike faith and sense of mission about our Constitution and the institutions it had created. Faith in the American future, in contracts and constitutions, in natural law and higher law, and in ourselves as individual citizens all came to be tightly fused together. In this context, it was but a short step for everyday positive law (the statutory enactments of legislatures and the steadily accumulating mass of judges' decisions) to claim some of the same elevated status. Law seemed to offer a neutral set of rules, appropriately concerned with the protection of property, by which individual striving for private goals could be refereed.

Contracts are, of course, written documents. As such, at least arguably, they require interpretation by people with appropriate skills and experience, namely lawyers. When contracts make up the basis for a society's daily transactions, the people who assert the capacity and right to be the interpreters become very important. Legal skills lead to vital roles as facilitators and adjudicators. And when, moreover, a society uses a written contract as the embodiment of a higher law to limit public use of power, law and lawyers will pervade all its affairs—public and private.

As lawyers come to predominate, so does their defining institution, the court. In the American case, the United States Supreme Court has become the operative symbol of the Constitution. It provides most people's understanding of proper government conduct according to the Constitution. Public issues involving profound value choices are systematically shaped and reshaped into legal questions. Thus they can be taken to court and, if significant enough, eventually controlled by the value preferences of a majority of the nine justices. What results over time is a very special role for law, lawyers, and courts in the government of the society.

This very assertiveness on the part of law and the legal profession leads to the major disagreements surrounding the generally shared values of contracts and law. Though derived from the general commitment to contracts, the emphasis on law and legal means of decision making can impinge on the capacity of citizens to make choices and implement their preferences in a democratic manner. Just how much public decision-making authority should be given over to the law and lawyers, therefore, has been a source of dispute throughout American history.

Similarly, there have been constant disputes over the extent to which the law and its workings are in fact neutral. Value choices of profound importance lie in such assertedly neutral or mechanistic acts as the interpretation of words and phrases in the Constitution; far from always being readily accepted, the Supreme Court's decisions often have proved highly controversial. It is easier to insist on the fair and neutral procedures of the law when they are working in one's favor than when they appear to be manipulated by others for their private advantage. American legalism, strong as it is, thus barely conceals vigorous disagreements about the nature and proper role of law and lawyers.

Before leaving these three key values, it might be useful to note how thoroughly individualism, property, and contracts and law support the concept of the economic free market. All individuals are and should be free to make their own arrangements for their private advantage. Property is the focus of individual striving. Contracts both limit government's interference with private activity (the laissez-faire, or hands-off, principle) and facilitate any number of private transactions. The free market is thus not just an image of how an economy might work for the greatest good, but one that takes on the quality of something good in its own right from the way that it fits with these basic values.

Freedom and Equality

We take up the values of freedom and equality together because they are so fully complementary that it becomes difficult to discuss one without the other. Historically, the two values have often stood together, twin pillars in the foundation of American social order. On examination, the pairing turns out to be much more than mere habit. The definition or implementation of one often, though not necessarily, affects the definition or implementation of the other.

Sometimes freedom and equality appear to be in direct conflict, so that one or the other must be given priority. In other words, the more of one, the less of the other. Having to choose one over the other troubles all and can lead to bitter divisions among people. Many would prefer not to choose, but given the often unavoidable tension between the usual definitions, the luxury of not choosing merely transfers the choice to others.

Why is there sometimes a conflict between freedom and equality? The definition of freedom has seemed relatively straightforward. Perhaps that is part of the reason it usually has been granted priority in cases of conflict. Generally, freedom means the absence of restraints on an individual. More specifically, it means freedom from government's interference with one's personal liberty or economic activities. Freedom finds its strongest expression in the Bill of Rights and in state constitutions, both of which amount to long lists of prohibitions against arbitrary acts. Under all circumstances, governments must follow a host of procedural requirements before individual life, liberty, or property can be affected.

Recently, another version of the notion of freedom has arisen. If the dominant definition just described is understood as "negative" freedom, in the sense that freedom means the absence of restraints by government, the newer version can be termed "positive" freedom. It involves affirmative actions on the part of government to increase the opportunities for individuals to realize their human potential. *Freedom* thus has begun to mean the chance to accomplish some things that would not be possible without government help, even if that help is only in the form of keeping others from preventing such accomplishments. This twentieth-century development is still clearly subordinate to the dominant notion of "negative" freedom.

By contrast, the definition of equality has been complicated from the start and grows more so every year. Hardly anybody argues that people are or could be made equal in physical strength, intelligence, personality, or talents. Our notion of equality ("all men are created equal . . .") concerns entitlements with respect to *social* life. There is, however, little consensus about what these entitlements should be, and some care is needed even to identify the issues involved.

Two major dimensions or areas of life need to be taken into account when defining equality. One is the social and economic area. It involves the social status and economic well-being of people and the general social and economic conditions of their lives. The second is the political and legal area. People enjoy equal rights before the law and as citizens, particularly with respect to participation in public decision-making processes.

Attention usually focuses on the second of these areas. Political and legal rights are more formal, visible, and are basic to practically everything else. They have their roots in the basic contracts that create governments. Yet even here conflict and problems abound. Those entitled to certain rights of citizenship in principle, such as the right to vote or appear in court, may have to struggle to convert such formal provisions into practical reality. Those outside the range of citizenship struggle for admission to full political and legal status.

In the early years of the republic, full citizenship extended only to white males who owned property of a certain minimum value. Even some who met those criteria were obliged to document their entitlement and to assert their right vigorously amidst a variety of physical and social obstacles. White males without property (particularly former indentured servants), black males, and women all engaged in more or less lengthy struggles simply to obtain the franchise. Other entitlements of full citizenship necessary to achieve equality solely in the political and legal sense were slowly and painfully won.

All this attention to the formal side of equality tends to overshadow the social and economic dimensions of the principle. In the early years of the republic, however, conditions of rough social and economic equality actually existed among the great bulk of the population. Most people either were or could become economically self-sufficient through small-farm ownership. A lively spirit of social egalitarianism had been furthered by the shared experience of the movement for independence. Social and economic equality seemed to be a fact. It was the exercise of equal legal and participatory rights that required further development.

This situation was specific to those times, however, and actually underscores a crucial point. *Without* social and economic equality, political and legal equality may not mean as much as appearances first suggest. When conditions of social and economic life are highly unequal, for example, some people possess so much wealth that they can influence actions in the political-legal world and ensure that these actions favor them. If for some reason they are unsuccessful in getting what they want through politics, they can use their wealth to achieve their goals in other ways—even in opposition to public decisions.

The moment that numbers of people try to use their equal-participation rights to prevent influence through wealth or to gain greater social and economic equality through the use of government, the conflict between freedom and equality erupts. Those who have the most in the unequal social and economic world validly claim that their freedom is being limited. In fact, their use of their property *is* being limited. The prices they can charge may be limited, some of their profits may be taken away in taxes, and so forth. Social and economic regulations appear necessary to assist less advantaged people who need greater opportunities. Freedom seems to lead to social and economic inequality, particularly in an industrial society, but efforts to reduce that inequality through exercise of equal political-legal rights seem inevitably to reduce freedom. Having to choose between the two important values therefore seems unavoidable. And seen in this way, the choice can be agonizing.

Related to this issue of choice are three different versions of equality that have developed, each embodying a distinctive mix of the social-economic and political-legal dimensions just discussed. *Formal equality* is the most basic and narrow version. It limits equality to the political-legal dimension and does not even address the social-economic dimension. By now, almost nobody in the United States challenges others' right to vote or to equality before the law. Some oppose making voting easier for people, for example, by scheduling elections on weekends or easing registration or language requirements. Also, opposition exists to helping some to exercise their legal rights, for example, by providing lawyers to criminal defendants or to poor people generally. However, the formal principle of political-legal equality seems firmly established as a minimum. The question is whether equality should mean anything *more*.

A version of equality with broader implications is *equality of opportunity*. This second version assumes that equality entitles people to equal opportunities to compete with others. Individuals should start equal in the race for the goals, economic or otherwise, that they seek in life. This requires and legitimates a variety of government programs, including educational assistance, vocational training, small-business loans, and affirmative action boards. Such programs compensate for existing inequalities or discrimination. They give everybody an equal start. The idea is that equality can be balanced with freedom, with no real conflict ensuing between the two principles.

The problem with this approach is not only that it often requires substantial limits on the freedom of some people or even that it helps some with financial aid drawn from taxes paid by others. More fundamentally, the problem lies in agreeing on when to stop trying to compensate for accumulated social and economic disadvantages in what has become over time a highly unequal society. Equality of opportunity, taken literally, promises to provide genuine equality at the starting gate of life, but it cannot truly do so. The attempt to do so often incurs the resentment of those whose freedom has been limited in order to provide opportunity for others. At the same time, those whose disadvantages were not effectively compensated for by government action often cry "fraud."

The version with the greatest scope is *equality of condition*. This third version frankly and completely includes the social and economic sides of equality. Equality takes precedence over freedom. Alternatively, freedom is simply redefined to express the need for all people to have certain levels of both opportunity *and* achievement, something like the positive form of freedom noted earlier. Equality of condition means that public (and governmental) concern focuses on the actual conditions people experience in their everyday lives. Governmental action should provide at least a floor of substantive equality for all. To be sure, this version of equality involves a major alteration of the organization of our social order, including the way that many Americans think, but equality of condition remains an ideal dimly visible on the horizon.

Each of these three contemporary versions of equality poses a particular conflict with received understandings of freedom. The conflict can be solved by openly granting one or the other principle complete priority, or by redefining one to fit with a preferred version of the other. As we shall see, both strategies have been employed throughout American history. Perhaps no final victory for one or another combination is possible, but the evolution of the American political belief system cannot be understood without grasping the conflict between contending versions of these two central principles.

DEMOCRACY: SUPERVALUE
AND CONTESTED CONCEPT

Democracy is the American supervalue; as such, it is the absolute center of American ideology. To truly understand democracy as Americans understand it is to see three centuries of history, the present, and the future all in one blinding insight. However, our aspirations in this book are much more limited. We seek only to begin exploring the part that democracy—seen as the key value in the American ideological tradition—has played in the evolution of American political thinking.

The concept of democracy *summarizes* the five building blocks: when they are all in place, democracy is the result. It depends upon and stands for, or *symbolizes*, all of the others. The idea of democracy is also a symbol for all that is good in politics and particularly the American political system.

Yet, and perhaps most importantly, democracy itself is a contested concept. Its meaning is in dispute, and because of democracy's importance, much is at stake in this dispute. Whoever succeeds in defining this most revered value and symbol (presumably in ways that reflect their preferences) will draw the support of many Americans to their side. Democracy is an unequivocal good or right thing, and if a group can convince others that democracy requires a certain action, it suddenly will have many new allies. Not surprisingly, the dispute over the meaning of democracy has gone on for centuries, sometimes explicitly but more often covertly or by implication from what has been argued and decided about other values, institutions, or public policies.

In the paragraphs that follow, we shall begin to see how democracy has served as summary, symbol, and contested concept as American ideologies have evolved over the years. Literally, *democracy* means "the people rule." In practice today, democracy means that people participate in public affairs and exert at least some degree of control over what governments do. However, the meaning of democracy has been elusive and changing ever since it came into public favor at the end of the eighteenth century.

How Democracy Became "Good"

A fundamental change in the meaning of democracy necessarily occurred in the nation's early years. As late as the framing of the Constitution, not only people of property but also ordinary citizens looked with disfavor on democracy. Democracy implied mob rule; that is, rule by the people meant rule by the rabble. Obviously, for democracy to become widely accepted and to attain specially valued status as *the* defining characteristic of American government, something had to change.

The framers of the Constitution carefully designed a republic. As such, there were many bulwarks against popular majorities and against democracy as it was then understood. The claim of ordinary people to participate in government grew in the last decades of the eighteenth century and the opening decades of the nineteenth. Spurred by the egalitarianism of the French Revolution and, indeed, of the American Revolution itself, the appeal of democracy spread. Jefferson rode to power as head of the Democratic-Republican party in 1801. Contrary to Federalist expectations, he did not dismantle the Constitution or its institutions. Instead, he began the process of attaching the (now good) label of democracy to the (good) Constitution and national government. The years that immediately followed saw a general franchise expansion and democratization of state constitutions within the original republican framework. Both the property-defending nonmajoritarian Constitution and the popular-rule notion came to be understood as American democracy.

Democracy became a "good" word and a supervalue, willingly embraced by almost all people, only *after* the first five building blocks were fully accepted and institutionalized in the Constitution. Thus, the American version of democracy has always been grounded in individualism and holds a specially inviolate regard for property, contracts, and law. Similarly, freedom, in the sense of freedom from government, took precedence over various claims for equality. Thus, limits have always existed on what the popular, or majority, rule adherents of democracy could hope to accomplish. Within these limits, however, room was left for disagreement about how far popular rule could go in seeking to promote equality. This disagreement led directly to one of the enduring conflicts over the meaning of *democracy*.

Two Versions of Democracy

If understood in terms of the five building blocks as expressed in the Constitution, democracy is limited almost entirely to the political-legal world of voting, due process, and fair procedures. This is *procedural*, or, to employ a classical label from political theory, *liberal*, democracy.* It assumes that politics is a sphere of activity separable from economic and social life; therefore, equality should be understood only in formal terms or as a very limited equality of opportunity.

If understood in terms of a full and adapting expression of the five building blocks, however, democracy broadens to include the economic and social conditions of peoples' lives. *Substantive*, or *social*, democracy* assumes that politics, economics, and social life are inextricably integrated. Therefore, equality must be understood in comprehensive terms— that is, equality of opportunity must be expanded to include aspects of equality of conditions.

---

* In this instance, the classical labels are essential to our analytic and comparative purposes. For reasons set forth in detail in the Glossary, the five building blocks are the essence of classical liberalism, and their version of democracy is meaningfully identified as liberal democracy. Equally meaningful is the recognizable contrast that emphasizes the social and economic conditions of peoples' lives, social democracy.

The liberal definition focuses on the rights and mechanisms for participation that citizens have, in theory and in practice. If these opportunities are in place and working properly, then all the requisites of democracy have been fulfilled. This definition connects, of course, to the political-legal side of equality in which formal rights, such as the right to vote and equality before the law, fulfill the principle of equality.

Liberal democracy promises nothing about results. Instead, the essence of democracy lies in the process by which public decisions are made. When opportunities for participation are open and a fair set of rules for goal seeking is enforced, the results—whatever they are—can be taken as the expression of popular will. This is true whether or not most people actually do participate in voting or in any other political activity. Those who do not participate can be safely assumed to be either satisfied or too apathetic to matter.

The social definition acknowledges the great social achievement of procedural democracy. Fair and open processes can enable people, when they are thoroughly mobilized to do so, to gain many important goals. However, social democracy insists that democracy also should include concern both for the social and economic conditions of people's lives and for the results of the policy-making process. Advocates of the social definition argue that gross inequality in social standing and economic possessions make fair and open procedures in the political-legal arena more appearance than reality.

The bottom line of this argument is that a social system cannot have genuine political equality together with great social and economic inequalities. The latter condition effectively dominates and therefore denies the former. Wealth, status, and social power will overawe less advantaged people and cause them either to support whatever the "better people" offer them or to accept quietly what they do not want. The weight of dominant opinion, shaped in the image of those who hold wealth, status, and social power, will almost inevitably cause others to fall in line and often even to participate in discouraging opposition or punishing dissidents.

Advocates of social democracy insist that the sense of fairness and social justice basic to the democratic idea ought not to be compartmentalized in the political-legal sphere. It should apply as well to the social and economic conditions under which people live. In other words, democracy should mean some minimum standard of living for everybody. To understand democracy solely in terms of the right of the people to participate in the decision-making process stops short, missing the point of the whole enterprise of democracy. After all, the underlying reason for all this political activity is the desire of people to gain control over conditions that affect their lives. People also participate in order to achieve a goal, for example, to change something about their circumstances that is bothering them. They become involved in politics for a *purpose*, not just for the exercise.

Finally, we should note some continuing implications of the liberal-social tension. Today in particular, the root of the tension, and the underlying reason for two quite different versions of the definition of democracy in the United States, is to be found in the great social and economic inequality in our country and in the major cause of this inequality. By its very nature, an industrialized capitalist economy consists of great aggregations of wealth that are owned and managed by a relatively few people in order to produce private profit. The great majority of people are dependent on them for work and income. Inevitably, the result is a highly unequal society.

As we know, this system also strongly endorses the principles of equality and democracy. The key to having *both* inequality *and* the conviction that equality and democracy are in full effect lies in making a sharp distinction between the social-economic world and the political-legal world. Somehow, the concept of a wall of separation between the two worlds must be developed and sustained. This wall is necessary so that people can believe that democracy and equality can be fully served in the political-legal world alone, while the basic structure of the social-economic world is left essentially untouched by government action.

The liberal version of democracy insists that freedom from interference with property rights is paramount. Further, the distinction between the political-legal world and the social-economic world is right and proper. Equality and democracy can only be defined in terms that are consistent with these first principles.

The social definition of democracy starts from broader notions of, and higher priority for, the principle of equality. It simply denies the separability of the political-legal world from all other areas of social and economic life. The conflict between procedural and substantive definitions remains unresolved, regularly recurs, and is likely to last well into the future.

The continuing nature of this conflict shows how vital it is for people who believe in the liberal definition to find ways to maintain its predominance. If they don't maintain the fiction of separation between the two worlds, they will have to defend existing social and economic inequalities and the political power disparities that go with them on their own merits. This task would be difficult and possibly a prelude to open conflict. By and large, the liberal definition *has* been maintained. Some people even find it difficult to understand how any other version of democracy could be imagined. In other words, what *is* in the United States is the right, only, and universal definition of democracy. However, the notion persists that democracy could or should mean more, and so the conflict endures, sometimes unrecognized and in a variety of forms.

OTHER CULTURAL BAGGAGE

Several other deeply grounded premises and assumptions round out the basic American belief system. Though not explicitly political, they surround the political values and shape their applications to social life generally and to politics particularly. Derived from European origins, these premises and assumptions go unacknowledged except by the affected few, even though consistently acted out and powerful in their effects. They are often applied covertly or euphemistically while being explicitly denied. Others are developed as uniquely American and are much celebrated even when not much evident in reality.

Prominent among the first category is *racism*—the conviction that one race is superior to all others. In the American context, this has meant the belief that Caucasians are superior to all other nonwhite peoples. Racism helped justify the appropriation of Indian lands and the near extermination of native Americans. Of far greater importance to today's politics, racism helped to justify slavery in the United States until 1865 and legal limitations on Asian immigrants well into the twentieth century. The residue of slavery remains today in the form of continuing racial discrimination and tensions, particularly with respect to African-Americans. Racism constitutes perhaps the single most important factor in our politics.

Also evident is *patriarchy*—the belief in the propriety of male domination over women. Although most legal distinctions and impediments have been removed, cultural traditions and practices, shaped by male assumptions, continue to impose effective limits on women's educational, occupational, and social opportunities. Patterns of gender-based assumptions and expectations run through the society and the social relationships within it, giving special meaning to the basic political values.

Among the uniquely American, much-celebrated concepts, perhaps the most prominent assumes an economic *free market*. We noted earlier how directly the basic building blocks of American thinking led to and supported the notion of a free market. It is no coincidence that Adam Smith's *An Inquiry into the Nature and Causes of the Wealth of Nations*, published in 1776, was of such importance to Americans. The principles and assumptions underlying the idea of a free market precisely mirror those articulated as dominant political values by Americans.

For most Americans, economic thinking begins with the idea of the free market. Despite ample evidence to the contrary, its conditions of perfect competition, perfect knowledge of competing products, and equal access by informed consumers are all assumed to be more or less in effect. Also assumed is that any action by government, by definition, "interferes" with the (good) workings of the market. Those who end up losing in the actual practice of economic activity, therefore, are perceived as individually failing and not quite deserving.

This set of assumptions surrounding the idea of a free market helps to emphasize the distinctiveness of the economic and political worlds. Indeed, politics should be a totally separate sphere of activity and should stay clear of "intervention" in the mechanical workings of economic life. Otherwise, the market cannot produce the (mythical) greatest good for the greatest number—the appropriate definition of the public interest. Those who are doing well in the private world of economics benefit by convincing others that their private world should remain free of public intervention. In other words, the notion of separation of politics and economics is itself part of the free market image, and thus it becomes part of the *ideological* debate between liberal democrats and social democrats.

One of the reasons for the staying power of the market imagery in American thinking lies with the undoubted success attending the American economic enterprise for its first two centuries. Helped by a faith in science and the conviction that new inventions serve the cause of unending progress, American affluence was attributed to ingenuity and institutions rather than to vast available resources and a favorable geographic setting.

Another uniquely American cultural commitment is special zeal for *religion*, meaning Christianity in the general sense. The American sense of mission (to build the city on the hill, to fulfill the dream of the promised land, to Christianize the Indians, to do good unto others, and so forth) draws on this generalized Christian ethos. Our national political language and symbols are full of Christian images.

Grounded in the American sense of mission, but drawing on a belief in "republican virtue" and experimentalism, the early settlers saw themselves as a model for the Old World. From the Pilgrims through the Declaration of Independence to today, Americans speak and act as if the world were not only watching but also depending upon the American example for guidance. A special sort of patriotism follows from this, holding that the United States is and by right ought to be number one in the world.

SUMMARY

We first identified and analyzed the five basic building blocks of American political values: individualism, rights and particularly property, contracts and law, freedom, and equality. We discussed how the original idea of democracy emerged as a "good" term in the light of these values as institutionalized in the Constitution, and then how it became a contested concept. A principal conflict over the true meaning of democracy continues between the procedural (or liberal) version and the substantive (or social) version. A good part of the significance of the five basic values and democracy, however, derives from the more general cultural concepts and assumptions surrounding them in the context of American life. How these values and beliefs fuse into political ideologies and begin to shape our politics and how we can make sense of all this is the subject of the next chapter.

ADDITIONAL READINGS

Boorstin, Daniel. *The Genius of American Politics*. Chicago: University of Chicago Press, 1953.

Commager, Henry S. *The American Mind*. New Haven: Yale University Press, 1950.

Dolbeare, Kenneth M. *American Political Thought*. 2d ed. Chatham, N.J.: Chatham House, 1989.

Ekirch, Arthur A. *The Decline of American Liberalism*. New York: Longmans Green, 1955.

Gabriel, Ralph. *The Course of American Political Thought*. New York: Ronald Press, 1940.

Girvetz, Harry K. *The Evolution of Liberalism*. New York: Collier Books, 1963.

Grimes, Alan P. *American Political Thought*. New York: Holt, Rinehart Winston, 1960.

Hofstadter, Richard. *The American Political Tradition*. New York: Alfred A. Knopf, 1948.

Mason, Alpheus T. *Free Government in the Making*. Englewood Cliffs, N.J.: Prentice-Hall, 1965.

Reolofs, Mark. *Ideology and Myth in American Politics*. Boston: Little, Brown, 1976.

CHAPTER 3

AMERICAN IDEOLOGIES
AND AMERICAN POLITICS

Americans start thinking about politics from an apparently shared commitment to the five building blocks and the supervalue of democracy. When these values are applied to actual political issues, however, disagreements erupt about specific definitions and priorities. Over time, these disagreements crystallize into distinct packages. For example, a nineteenth century railroad owner's strong belief in the primacy of the individual might be associated with a strong commitment to property rights and a definition of freedom that precluded all government regulation. On the other hand, a small farmer's resentment against railroad rates might lead that individual to feel that individual opportunity justified government regulations over the railroad's right to use its property.

In both cases, a major continuing issue became associated with a distinct package of quite specific but different definitions and priorities. These packages were not randomly constituted; rather, they were the natural expression of the economic interest of a substantial group or class of people. When several economic issues arise and are seen in roughly similar terms, the repetition of this particular set of definitions and priorities converges into a coherent ideology. Soon enough, an event or an image may be enough to call up all the associated values and beliefs. The ideology starts to function to mobilize people into political action.

Not all issues of importance are economic in character, of course, particularly in the 1990s. However, most of the major issues in American history have been in some way economic. Generally, they have divided Americans (and shaped ideologies) along lines of social class.

Two implications follow from this historical fact. First, we must understand how specific ideologies arose in the American historical context and what labels were applied to them by Americans. Those ideologies and labels possess a staying power that carries over into the present. Second, we must develop ways of organizing and comparing those ideologies that reflect both their initial economic origins and their current, more diversified character.

Accordingly, this chapter begins with a capsule history of the evolution of American ideologies in the context of American politics. It will be obvious that many of these ideologies and labels remain very much a part of today's politics.

Next is developed the traditional (economic) ideological spectrum, which specifies the distinctness of each ideology, identifies its social class base in a general way, and locates each with respect to its competitors. Also explored are some ways in which today's issues and problems are undermining or reconstructing the traditional spectrum.

Finally, we describe a framework for analyzing current American ideologies, which is used throughout the remainder of the book. This framework preserves the historical connections and insight provided by the traditional spectrum without losing sight of the fact that American ideological and political worlds today are undergoing fundamental change.

IDEOLOGY AND POLITICS IN AMERICAN HISTORY

A final word of caution about the use of labels. The labels for the consistent packages of values and beliefs that constitute ideologies often change over time. Ordinary people and media commentators tend to use such labels in ways that relate ideologies to immediate issues of the day. In contrast, scholars and other professional students of political philosophy use the same labels in ways that are grounded in their original, or classical, meanings.

For example, *liberalism* in everyday usage means the belief in governmental intervention in the economy for social purposes and the use of government to provide help for disadvantaged people. In classical terms, *liberalism* means serving the needs of the individual and freeing that individual from restraints—most of which were assumed to come from government.

In this book we use the everyday labels that Americans use. In the paragraphs that follow, we trace the development of those everyday labels in American history. They are different enough from scholarly use, however, that we encourage you to refer to the Glossary, which explains how many of the labels are used by scholars of political philosophy. Especially students who are new to the study of ideologies should read the Glossary carefully along with this historical account. The two will provide an integrated understanding of the evolution of American ideologies, as well as a contrast between everyday usage and scholarly precision.

From the earliest years of the movement for independence, Americans asserted their uniqueness and rejected old-world practices. The language of the Declaration of Independence reflects their sense of the need to explain American actions to puzzled Europeans. Following the ratification of the Constitution, the simultaneous feelings of uniqueness, rejection of Europe, and need to explain fused into a sense of a special mission among nations. America was to serve as a republican model. It would teach the rest of the world a lesson in the nature, simple virtues, and practical workings of (American) republican political institutions.

The label *republicanism* sufficed for the first fifty years after independence. Republicanism rested on the self-evident principles of individualism, freedom, and equality. It meant representative government with constitutional limitations on majorities on behalf of minority rights—property, that is, and the protection of other personal liberties. It was gradually replaced by a new label, *democracy*, which came to mean essentially the same thing. This was, for the most part, a procedural version of democracy, which, of course, fit comfortably with the developing privately owned, profit-oriented industrial economy. By the time of the Civil War, this economic system was celebrated as *capitalism*. This term included private ownership, profit orientation, the free economic market where sellers' supply would be equated with buyers' demand in a self-regulating manner, and the governing principle of laissez-faire.

Despite a large number of slogans, epithets, and colorful third-party names, *democracy*, *capitalism*, and *republicanism* were the only categories in wide usage that expressed general *sets* of ideas, or belief *systems*. They encompassed the economic and political order in the United States, except as equality and substantive democracy arose in the abolitionist and feminist movements, until late in the nineteenth century. For the most part, definitions of such key terms lay in the practice of American institutions at the state and national levels. Labels needed no elaborate definition when their referents were in plain view.

This situation began to change almost immediately after the Civil War ended, but surely by the threshold year of 1877. The Civil War marked a turning point in the American experience. First, a long-festering anomaly in the American self-image was removed. The commitment to equality no longer coexisted uncomfortably with its total refutation in the legality and practice of slavery. The Declaration of Independence was validated anew. Second, the war confirmed the country's evolution as a single continental power, united federally, rather than as a league of states. Finally, the war gave great impetus to the already burgeoning process of industrialization.

Two momentous events in 1877 mark the beginning of a new era, the one period in our history comparable in scope and character of change to our own. One of these events was the disputed Hayes-Tilden presidential election. The dispute was resolved only days before the scheduled inauguration in a political party bargain that also effectively ended Reconstruction. The other event was the great railroad strike that occurred a few months later. The most far-reaching and destructive strike in American history, it loudly proclaimed the arrival of a new set of issues on the agenda of an industrializing society. Before the era ended in 1920, the national government would be fundamentally reconstructed, a new kind of politics would be put in place, and changed values and beliefs would dominate.

In this brief forty-three years, the United States moved from a predominantly rural, agricultural society to an urban, industrial one; from a laissez-faire system to an active, purposeful national government; and from an insular nation to an imperial world power with far-flung colonies and other interests. Simultaneously, separate farmers' and workers' movements engaged in the most protracted and bitter period of protests, strikes, and general social unrest that the United States has known. Unable to join together electorally, these movements were repulsed in the election of 1896.

But a new and more middle-class movement, drawing support from some of their remnants, arose to press for substantial changes in government policies. New coalitions of "progressive" businessmen, bankers, lawyers, and the larger corporations sought similar ends. They used the threat posed by more aggressive reformers to gain approval for apparently moderate, but potentially dramatic, changes in the role of government. From this turbulence emerged a national government with wholly new powers and administrative capabilities. The product has often been characterized as a Hamiltonian government for Jeffersonian ends. It was a government capable of rationalizing and controlling the competitive excesses of the new national economy, of rendering it more stable, predictable, and efficient. Finally, the U.S. entry into World War I provided an opportunity to put these new mobilizing capabilities into practice.

By the end of the era, World War I was over, women's right to vote was finally established, and a president was elected with the slogan "back to normalcy." The contrast between the United States in 1877 and in 1920 was so stark that none could ignore it. The year 1920 seemed to begin a time when the pace and purposefulness of change slackened. The full implications of the changes of the era just ended awaited the New Deal, World War II, and the mid-century aftermath. Despite the gap in time, it is clear that the governing principles and beliefs of the mid-twentieth century were shaped in fundamental ways by the transformations of this Populist-Progressive era.

As indicated, the era gave rise to a number of new political beliefs and labels. The process of industrialization in the 1870s and 1880s was accompanied by frequent panics and depressions and sustained hardships for farmers, particularly those struggling under the crop-lien system of the south and southwest. Both workers and farmers began to cast about for explanations and remedies. Their search led them to deeper and deeper levels of analysis, until in many cases they identified the system of private ownership and profit taking by a few as the real culprit. Soon the term *radical* came into widespread usage.

The waves of immigrants that followed industrialization brought with them new categories and beliefs derived from the longer European experience in factories and labor movements. Many of them thought in terms of class conflict and the need for the working classes to organize against the capitalists. These immigrants too were promptly labeled radical. Thus, this term now acquired a second meaning: "foreign." In this second sense, *radical* specifically meant beliefs that denied the rightness of private ownership of the major means of production and transportation, such as steel mills and railroads. It also applied to any who sought to implement such beliefs. Indeed, many American radicals, both native born and immigrant, did advocate various forms of public ownership or control over the major units of the economy—particularly the railroads, banks, and steel plants.

The category of radical soon developed subcategories such as *socialist* and *anarchist*. To many Americans, these terms meant "foreign" at least as much as they did anything substantive. Gradually, however, the sustained arguments of (and disagreements between) socialists and anarchists won each some separate identity as proposed alternatives to the dominant American version of capitalist democracy.

Socialists were seen to advocate an organized political movement grounded in the working class and seeking social ownership and a planned economy. Particularly visible in the labor movement, socialists sought to establish industrial unions (organizations of all workers in a given industry, rather than of individual strategic and relatively well-paid crafts or skill groups) and to bring these unions into politics. Anarchists were never really understood. They continued to be viewed as rigid, bitter, and often violent individuals opposed to all forms of organized society. Slogans such as "property is theft" and "propaganda of the deed" (a euphemism for bombings and attempted assassinations) helped to build a quite misleading impression of anarchism.

The easy equation of radical with foreign was always belied by totally indigenous movements of workers and farmers and by native-born socialism. All such groups could quite legitimately claim American origins in the pre-independence period. Moreover, these various reform movements generated in the late nineteenth century a major surge of substantive democracy, fully in the American tradition. In particular, the Populist party's goals of public ownership of railroads and a new public banking system were both profoundly radical and utterly native. In part, the foreign image was a measure of the success of opponents in painting those who sought substantial change in non-American colors. In part, it was also accurate. Many immigrants brought with them visions of alternative ways of organizing society that would not have occurred to most Americans, and such immigrants did consistently support radical goals.

In this context of multiple demands for egalitarian change, Americans who defended the status quo came to be known as *conservatives*. Although used more precisely by some Americans, to most the term meant simply preservation of existing institutions and practices from the apparently growing threat of violent radicals of various kinds. Not the least of the principles that conservatives feared would be violated was freedom for corporations to use their property as they wished without government controls or restraints. Social-reform legislation, such as minimum wage and maximum hour laws or health and safety regulations, was opposed with special vigor. Conservatism was intent on preserving as much as it could of the status quo, even as that status quo drifted toward more and more government intervention in the free market economy.

Conservatives shared two important characteristics. One was a growing concern for defending the rights of property against what seemed like danger from all sides. The second, which was related to the first, was a deepening anxiety about the governing capacity of the majority of people. With so many new immigrants, it was felt, general popular participation in politics might become even less stable and constructive. From such a perspective, almost anybody who advocated changes seemed to pose a threat to property and the American way. Conservatives developed a theme that drew on many of the older versions of the basic values to celebrate wealth and impugn poverty as evidence of lack of character and effort. Their argument came to be called social Darwinism because of its analogies to Charles Darwin's point about the survival of the fittest in the natural world. Regardless of the aptness of the analogy, conservatives' insistence on protection of property and denial of social responsibility reached a shrill peak in the early 1890s.

The vigor of the conservative reaction to the essentially substantive democratic claims of workers, farmers, and socialists opened a wide gap between the two camps. Many Americans began to locate themselves in the expanding middle ground between the two. The traditional claim to equality seemed in their eyes to deserve some recognition. Circumstances *were* desperate for many of the unemployed. In the cities, the physical conditions under which many were forced to live were visibly a scandal. It seemed necessary to do *something* to reduce the human suffering generated by the economy. Many began to feel that corporations should be prevented from pushing freedom to the point where government could put no limits at all on the use of property.

However, they were unwilling to go as far as the farmers and others urged. They strongly respected the principle of private property and believed in the sanctity of contracts. They were united in the conviction that reasonable people could work together to improve the condition of all people. Poverty and disease could be eliminated through rational use of government and through modern technologies. Great progress already had been made in material terms. Further progress in raising standards of living and in improving the quality of life was entirely possible through the (open) channels of (procedural) democracy.

This balanced combination of traditional American values, humane concern for the disadvantaged, and faith in progress soon became known as *liberalism*. At a minimum, liberals argued for the use of government to prevent the economy from imposing major hardships on individuals unable to help themselves. In its larger vision, liberalism stood for the use of government to actively promote social reforms that would contribute to social progress. The Progressive era of 1900 to 1920 was an early high point of this type of middle-class liberal reform. Many of the Progressive reforms were opposed by conservatives. Enacted nevertheless, the reforms often had the conserving effect of undercutting the substantive democratic demands and reducing the pressure for greater changes.

Liberalism is thus a centrist position. It appeals to middle-class people, particularly professionals, because it seems to apply some of their knowledge and skills to the solution of social problems. It also attracts forward-looking ("socially responsible") businesspeople and the larger corporations that can afford the taxes to support government social services. With a bit of patching here and there in response to the worst side effects of a growing industrial economy, progress can be assured, stability maintained, and all major claims responded to in some fashion. Generally, this liberal balancing act has been successful, at least as long as the economy did in fact grow steadily so that the have-nots could be satisfied without taking current possessions away from the haves.

Liberals require time and space to work out the necessary accommodations between multiple and conflicting claims. The mechanisms of procedural democracy, when they are operating smoothly, provide this opportunity. Danger looms, however, when the economy contracts, profits and wages drop, and the conflicting claims can no longer be readily accommodated. The extremes increasingly appear to be on the verge of taking rights or property from the other. Under such circumstances, liberalism's middle ground is increasingly squeezed. The procedural mechanisms become paralyzed as the extremes close in to engage each other directly. For these reasons, liberalism has made preserving the procedural mechanisms a special cause in itself. Over time, liberalism has become almost synonymous with maintenance of the regular procedures of the political system, including both property rights and other civil rights.

Finally, first the Russian Revolution of 1917 and then its exportation by the Soviet army after World War II provided new content for the labels *socialism, communism,* and *Marxism.* These events gave specific meanings to what had been abstract philosophies with vague utopian connotations. To Americans, these labels now stood for the political-economic systems of the Soviet Union and the eastern European countries. They became interchangeable terms for austerity, militarism, and a one-party state that denied democracy, property rights, and other liberties. In a way, Americans returned to equating the umbrella term *radical* with the foreign and un-American nature of these subcategories.

American usage of the various political labels simply does not conform systematically to the deeper and more complex (and consistent) meanings that are given them in scholarly discourse. Nevertheless, it is the way we have come to understand each other's political values and beliefs, and it is reflected in the way that newspapers and magazines write about how changing conditions and events are affecting our political ideas.

THE AMERICAN POLITICAL SPECTRUM

Not all people are totally consistent thinkers, of course. For the most part, however, ideologies are internally coherent. A particular definition of one value leads to a definition of another that is consistent with the first, and so on through the full range of values and the images and expectations that flow from them. People gradually acquire a consistent package of values and beliefs, aided by an underlying set of assumptions about human nature.

This recognition of the tendency toward consistency is what makes possible the analytic device of a political spectrum. The word *spectrum* suggests a predictable pattern of colors, which always follow the same order from one end to the other and which fade into one another without sharp demarcations. This is a serviceable, if somewhat crude, image for the relationship among different definitions of basic values and even among various political belief systems. Americans usually visualize a horizontal continuum with conservatism located at the right-hand extremity, radicalism at the left-hand extremity, and liberalism in the middle. We shall add three further thoughts to make this notion of a spectrum a more useful analytic tool.

First, we should try to be more specific about what is being measured along this spectrum, or continuum. Beliefs about the distribution of wealth, status, and power are the obvious candidates, but beliefs about the distribution of any socially valued right or privilege might be involved. Those people who favor the narrowest distribution of the valued resource—where only a few would possess the most—are situated at the right-hand end of the continuum. The status quo (today's distribution pattern) is located to the right but well short of the end of the possible range of the imagined continuum. Some people, farther right, may yearn for an even tighter concentration of wealth and power, but probably many more people would be located at various points along the continuum to the left of the status quo.

More or wider distribution is sought the farther one moves to the left. Thus radicals seek the widest distribution to the most people, whereas liberals seek more modest departures from the status quo. Radicals are understood to some extent as merely calling for *more* of whatever is at stake than liberals do. Radicalism also is viewed as entailing a desire for greater or more rapid change and as a critique of fundamental values and social-economic structures. In this last sense, and derived from radicalism's original meaning of going deeper or to the roots in search of explanations and solutions, radicalism also has applications on the right-hand side of the continuum (as in the radical Right). In the United States, the term is used primarily to describe people on the Left whose ideas imply too much change to be practical or acceptable to the majority (and we shall try to note explicitly whenever we employ it otherwise).

Second, the continuum may shift over time, and people move back and forth along it over time. For most of the twentieth century, the center of gravity of American ideology seemed to drift gradually toward the left of the spectrum. Yesterday's radical often has ended up as today's liberal, without changing his or her own personal position very much. Formerly unimaginable or utopian claims have made their way toward the center. Times change, and people grow more conservative with age. To older people, the young seem ever more radical.

However, those shifts may have been only temporary or only in appearance. In another period people may cling grimly to the center, move together toward the right, or simply fragment in all directions. What if economic conditions are such that growth is neither great nor steady, and wider distribution to the have-nots is possible only at the cost of reduced distribution to the haves? The continuum might have to be reexamined for validity—which is exactly what we suggest is required in the United States today.

Third, other important assumptions and goals are associated with the continuum at *any* point in time. One example is the definition of democracy held by people of different belief systems along the continuum. Substantive democracy, as we have seen, includes the most comprehensive definition of equality. It clearly fits best with radical beliefs. Procedural democracy just as clearly is an integral component of liberalism, although it also is compatible with conservatism. Still more limited versions of democracy are conceivable, such as plebiscitary democracy (in which majorities essentially endorse what their rulers have done), but most American conservatives would stop short of advocating such methods.

Perhaps more revealing is the fact that assumptions about human nature and capabilities also seem to differ along the continuum. Most radicals believe that people are or can be cooperative and community oriented (to be sure, some do not always *act* that way). People therefore can be trusted with full power to govern in almost all matters, in a kind of ongoing participatory democracy. Liberals believe that people are by nature reasonable but also competitive and self-interested. Therefore, elaborate rules and channels for participation in politics are necessary to prevent them from doing bad things. With such procedures, however, people can rationally design improvements and expect to achieve progress for the society. Many conservatives believe that people are irrational, dominated by short-term and self-interested considerations, and not really capable of understanding their own true public interest. Therefore, conservatives believe that people need to be guided by those few who are knowledgeable and successful.

Figure 3.1 provides a summary of some major relationships that have become embedded in the traditional American political spectrum over time. Particular definitions of the key values and underlying assumptions about human nature are at the base. Each vertical column represents a consistent package of value definitions and priorities. Over time, each such package has become associated both with its major supporters from a given social class and with a label reflecting a pure or ideal version of its ideology. (Reality is, of course, much less consistent; these connections are crude and general. Moreover, variants in each category overlap to the right and left, shading into each other like colors on a spectrum.)

The labels for each belief system or ideology are given at the *top* of the spectrum in traditional terms, that is, as of the 1960s. *Under* the spectrum, more speculative and less widely accepted, are the labels we shall employ for the emerging packages of values and beliefs of the 1990s. Associated

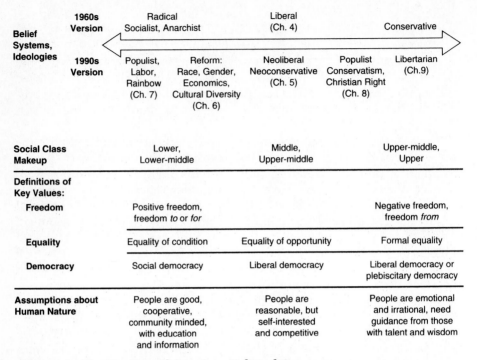

Figure 3.1   The Traditional American Political Spectrum

with the latter are the chapter numbers of this book analyzing each package. Laying out these relationships and selecting labels is *meant* to be provocative; debate and disagreement with Figure 3.1 is welcome.

As noted earlier, the spectrum requires two obvious caveats. First, it is strictly American. Other countries' political spectrums extend much further right or left, and often both. Scholars often describe the American spectrum as lacking both a far right and a far left. Over time, Americans have, if anything, tended to shorten their continuum rather than lengthen it. Sometimes American political debate, at least as reported by the news media, seems to be entirely between liberals and conservatives. Moreover, the call to rally against extremists from either side strongly appeals to Americans. This is undoubtedly another factor that has made for stability in our system. But the shortened continuum may be caused in part by the fact of steady leftward movement for most of the twentieth century. Because that movement no longer continues, the continuum may lengthen.

Second, the spectrum grows more outdated every day, but no clear alternative has yet taken shape. New and different issues, many of them noneconomic in character, have arisen since World War II. Foreign policy questions and the issue of race relations have frequently been more important than domestic economic matters. More recently, movements such as feminism and environmentalism have focused attention on wholly different relationships. The old ideologies either do not address these matters or do so in ways that cut across the old liberal-conservative divisions. Similarly, the old labels and their associated social class of supporters may not be consistent with the actual taking of positions on major issues.

Ideological confusion and change is normal during global economic and political change such as is occurring at the present. A basic political realignment may be underway in the United States, fueled in part by the crystallization of new ideological perspectives. The chief historical force for reconstruction of American politics from the bottom up (that is, by lower- and lower-middle-class people from outside of government) has been *populism*. Certainly, the major dynamic of the 1960s through the 1980s—from the civil rights movement to the New Left to the reaction of the New Right—was populist in its values and beliefs.

Among middle- and upper-middle-class people, however, the principal dynamic seems to be that of *libertarianism*—removing governmental restrictions from all aspects of individuals' lives. We therefore turn to the potential impact of, first, populism and then libertarianism for some illustrations of what a reconstructed American political spectrum might look like.

By *populism*, we mean people at lower-middle-class and working-class levels who are dissatisfied with their circumstances and blame the bigness of our institutions for their problems. They feel that recent years have cheated the "little people" (or the "silent majority" or the "forgotten people"), who work hard, pay their taxes, and seek nothing more than what America has promised them. This definition of populism is intended to have continuity with the class basis and political alienation characteristic of the original populists of the 1890s without prejudging the direction such protest might take. Many of today's populists are properly identified by Kevin Phillips as "populist conservatives," whereas those of the 1890s were seen as left-wing radicals. The fact is that today's populists can easily go in *either* direction, depending on their definition of problems and the nature of the offered solutions.

How many populists are there, and what are their politics? Two sources provide the bulk of our information. One is Donald Warren's *The Radical Center: Middle Americans and the Politics of Alienation*, the first study documenting the anger and volatility that swept through the lower ranks of Americans from 1968 through the 1980s.[1] Warren's work, based on 1972 survey data, established that there was a distinctive body of lower-middle-class people angry about their circumstances and determined to vent their anger. He termed this group "Middle American Radicals" (MARs) because their attitudes were so different from those of other middle-class people.

The distinctive feature of MARs was a profound alienation from the national government and such national institutions as welfare agencies, unions, and corporations. The essence of MAR ideology is best captured by its adherents' overwhelming endorsement of the statement "The rich give in to the demands of the poor, and the middle-income people have to pay the bill." No other category of middle-income people came close to this view, and most explicitly rejected it as false.

On the basis of his data, Warren estimated that there might be as many as 25 million MARs in the American electorate. His concern was their ideology, not their long-term voting potential. It has been left to others to project the political implications of such numbers of disaffected people. Phillips believes that there may well be an even larger body of MARs and that the support of voters among them was vital to Ronald Reagan's 1980 election. With the continued loss of blue-collar jobs and a declining standard of living for many in the lower ranks of the American social pyramid, it is reasonable to assume that the number of MARs has stayed at least stable, if not grown, in the 1980s.

The second source that contributes to an understanding of populism is actually primarily concerned with the emergence of libertarianism. The study, by William Maddox and Stuart Lilie, is aptly titled *Beyond Liberal and Conservative*.[2] The conceptual premise informing the work is that the cross-cutting effects of economic and social issues have produced four basic viewpoints, not two as shown in Figure 3.2. For example, "liberals" on economic issues may be either "liberal" *or* "conservative" on social issues. The four-celled matrix shown in Figure 3.2 portrays these relationships.

Maddox and Lilie define *populists* as economic liberals who willingly accept government regulation of corporations and aid to maintain their incomes but oppose such social innovations as abortion rights, banning prayer from public schools, affirmative action, and permissive life-styles. Based on the quadrennial Michigan voting studies, Maddox and Lilie classify American beliefs with greater precision than the traditional liberal-conservative dichotomy permits. Table 3.1 condenses their findings.

In the first row, populists emerge as the largest single ideological group, slightly outnumbering liberals. It is worth noting that when libertarians and conservatives are distinguished in this way, conservatives become the smallest classified group. The second row shows that populists are also quite likely to be nonvoters, as are liberals. Fully half of each of these groups did not vote in 1980. Perhaps liberals might have had a better record with a different candidate. Populists, by definition alienated from

Figure 3.2 Cross-Cutting Effects of Economic and Social Issues

Economic Issues

		Liberal	Conservative
Social Issues	Liberal	Liberal	Libertarian
	Conservative	Populist	Conservative

Table 3.1 Ideological Types—1980 Electorate (in percent)

	Libertarian	Conservative	Populist	Liberal	Uncla*	Total
Size of group	18	17	26	24	15	100
Minus nonvoters	6	6	13	12	9	46
Actual electorate	12	11	13	12	6	54

* "Unclassified." Includes those voters who have no strong or discernible ideological iden-tification. They are not likely to vote, but when they do, they vote in an unpredictable manner.

SOURCE: Condensed from William Maddox and Stuart Lilie, *Beyond Liberal and Conservative* (Washington, D.C.: Cato Institute, 1984), table 14.

politics, are probably the most likely nonvoters. Moreover, there is consid-erable turnover from one election to the next among the populists who actually do turn out to vote. People are likely to drop in and out of the regular voting electorate on rather casual grounds.

Only one-third of the libertarians and conservatives were nonvoters. This means that the actual voting electorate is much more evenly divided than Americans generally. When the breakdown of electoral choice among the ideological groups is analyzed, populists are the most evenly split between the candidates/parties. Their party loyalties appear to be the weakest and/or their tendency to choose according to their estimates of the candidate is the greatest.

Table 3.2, also condensed from Maddox and Lilie, breaks down ideolog-ical beliefs by political generations. Political scientists have long believed that voters are powerfully influenced by the politics, issues, and events occurring around the time of their coming of voting age. Those who came of voting age during the Great Depression, for example, were dispropor-tionately "fixed" in pro-New Deal and Democratic political beliefs and voting behavior. Each era seems to generate distinctive patterns of ide-ology in its generation of voters. These beliefs and voting tendencies remain fairly consistent over time. Thus, the New Deal generation can be traced through election after election.

Perhaps the most striking finding in Table 3.2 is the fact that conser-vatives represent so small a proportion of the electorate, particularly of the newer generations of voters (those who came of voting age in the 1960s and 1970s). Substantially more of these newer voters appear to be liber-tarians. The two types of conservatives taken together represent well below half of the general public in every generation, but, as we have just seen, more nearly half of the voting electorate. Liberals, in contrast, are numerous among the newer generations; there are more liberals among

Table 3.2 Ideological Support by Generations, 1980 (in percent)

Generation	Libertarian	Conservative	Populist	Liberal	Divided
Pre-New Deal	12	18	34	13	14
New Deal	15	21	32	16	12
War era	17	20	27	17	13
1950s	20	24	26	21	7
1960s	22	14	25	27	10
1970s	16	11	23	35	10

SOURCE: Condensed from William Maddox and Stuart Lilie, *Beyond Liberal and Conservative* (Washington, D.C.: Cato Institute, 1984), table 4.

the 1970s generation than among the two kinds of conservatives combined.

The data on populist as shown in Table 3.2, carries vital implications for our argument. When the numbers of eligible voters in each generation are combined, populism is the largest single ideological grouping. It appears to be declining with each generation, but its appeal remains strong. Populists are far less predictable than the other groups, however, in the two crucial decisions that an eligible voter makes at each election—*whether* to vote and *for whom*. Which populists will vote and for whom is determined by the particular appeal of a candidate or party program in each election. Conceivably, *a large share of populists might turn out on behalf of a particularly attractive candidate or program at any time, and if they did, it would completely control the outcome of that election.*

What factors might cause a sudden surge of populists to the polls to vote for a particular candidate or program—*and in which political direction would that support go?* Crisis conditions and a believable alternative would provide necessary ingredients for an unusual turnout, but the direction is far less predictable. It would depend to a great extent on the context of the times and the particular triggering events. Based on past experience, economic issues or events would bring populists to the side of the Democrats; national security threats or racial issues would send them to the Republicans. This assumes continuity of the major parties, of course, and does not take into account the possible creation of new parties in the process of electoral realignment. In more general terms, economic problems would lead populists to the Left, and threats of war or racial conflict would send them to the Right. In either case, populists might be expected to embrace a relatively dramatic solution.

There is no assurance that the American ideological spectrum will undergo these particular kinds of changes. We have sought only to illustrate, on the basis of some available evidence, how changes *might* occur and how they *might* affect our politics. The point is that the ultimate payoff from understanding emerging ideologies occurs in the insight provided about the possible directions of our politics and public policies. It also justifies the particular selection of emerging ideologies we have chosen to analyze in the rest of this book.

A FRAMEWORK FOR ANALYZING AMERICAN IDEOLOGIES TODAY

Let us try to distill all we have seen so far into an efficient way of looking at American values and beliefs. Clearly, the approach must be sensitive to history, focus on values and value definitions, be oriented to what is happening today as the American political spectrum is being reconstructed into a new and unprecedented form, and explore what that may mean for the future. We think it is possible to develop a four-part framework that will be responsive to each of these needs and yet be manageable when applied. We propose, then, to analyze each of the new political belief systems in terms of these four parts, and each chapter is divided accordingly.

Links to the Past

The historical origins and evolution of a political belief system carry crucial significance for two important reasons. One is that the past has powerfully shaped the language, logic, and habits of mind of everybody's political thinking. For tools of thinking and communicating, we all rely chiefly on what we have been given. It is very difficult to create entirely new words or to give new meanings to familiar words or concepts. Such acts often involve long and only partially conscious social struggles. Similarly, a belief system is powerfully shaped by the sources that led to its original coalescence and by the particular evolution that led to its present form.

Second, many contemporary belief systems define themselves in some way in terms of the past. Each set of beliefs seems to reach back for pieces of what it perceives to have once been important. Identifying with some part of an enduring tradition is a means of legitimating today's positions. Some sets of beliefs claim to be the only current valid versions of particular past principles. Others involve an explicit rejection of specific past beliefs or events as deviant or undesirable. In any case, the past perceptions and judgments associated with a political belief system reveal much about its present character.

Thus the past not only shapes the present but also influences our capacity to think about the future. It continuously affects what people understand as the range of the possible. The past does not control the future, but past values and ways of thinking play an important part in how people who subscribe to a belief system understand the present and address the future. Therefore, we try to trace the origin and view of the past of each belief system we examine, not only to see where it came from but also to begin to understand how it thinks about the past, the present, and the future.

Basic Values and Assumptions

By *values*, we mean beliefs about what is good or bad—for example, it is good to be a hard-working, self-reliant individual who succeeds in acquiring property and rising on the social ladder. By *assumptions*, we mean things that are taken to be true without the necessity or perhaps possibility of proof—for example, human nature is universally self-seeking and competitive.

Identification of the basic values and assumptions of each belief system will help us to see into the essence of that system as well as to compare various belief systems—new and old—at this basic level. Some belief systems may rest on consistent basic elements, while in others there may be tensions among these elements. Some values and assumptions are relatively constant, while others are in the process of adaptation and change. Most belief systems can be characterized primarily through analysis at this level.

Problems and Possibilities

Each belief system sees something different when it looks at the everyday world that makes up its present environment. In part, it sees things in ways affected by its basic values and assumptions. Conditions in the world sometimes seem to be in conformity with these values and assumptions but at other times seem to be in opposition. A belief system also may look at the world through particular concepts that fit with its values and assumptions. A *concept* is a mental construct that helps people to identify and organize relevant "facts" and understand their meaning. For example, the concept of a free market, unimaginable before the seventeenth century, has dominated our thinking ever since the American Revolution. Values and assumptions infuse concepts, and the resulting combination helps people to see and judge the world, all in one instant.

Problems and possibilities, too, are understood differently, depending on the perspective of the belief systems. Problems are identified and defined, and their causes and importance estimated, in totally different ways. We try to reconstruct what each body of beliefs sees as problems and how each depicts the causes, priorities, and solutions. From this we move to their respective images of what, under current circumstances, can and should be achieved in the way of programs and goals. In other words, according to each belief system, what are the *bad* possibilities if things continue as they are and what are the *good* possibilities that can be brought to fruition if its adherents come to power?

Implications and Prospects

In the final section of each chapter, we analyze the obstacles and opportunities that each belief system faces today. We explore the system's links with enduring themes in American political thought and try to assess what the results would be if its adherents were successful in mobilizing people or influencing public policy. This is the point at which our own criteria and judgments become applicable, and some indication of our purposes may be helpful.

Our goal in analyzing the new political belief systems now competing for acceptance in the United States is not primarily intellectual or academic. These are entirely valid purposes, of course; it would be very satisfying to understand what is happening for its own sake. However, our purposes extend further. We want to help people see where we are going as a nation, particularly when, as now, we are in the midst of profound changes. People must be able to act in politics before it is too late to affect the outcome. In other words, we want to help empower people not only to see the forms of the future as they first emerge in ideas but also to play a full role as citizens in shaping and choosing new beliefs and programs.

ADDITIONAL READINGS

Allen, Robert. *Reluctant Reformers: Racism and Social Reform Movements in the United States*. New York: Anchor Books, 1975.

Beard, Charles. *The Economic Origins of Jeffersonian Democracy*. New York: Free Press, 1935.

Bowers, Claude G. *Jefferson and Hamilton: The Struggle for Democracy in America*. New York: Scholarly Reprints, 1972.

Croly, Herbert. *The Promise of American Life*. New York: Dutton, 1963.

Destler, Chester. *American Radicalism, 1865–1901*. Chicago: Quadrangle, 1966.

Goodwyn, Lawrence. *The Populist Moment*. New York: Oxford University Press, 1979.

Hays, Samuel. *The Response to Industrialism, 1885–1914*. Chicago: University of Chicago Press, 1957.

Hofstatder, Richard. *Social Darwinism in America*. Boston: Beacon Press, 1944.

Kolko, Gabriel. *The Triumph of Conservatism, 1900–1916*. New York: Free Press, 1963.

Lasch, Christopher. *The New Radicalism in America*. New York: Random House, 1967.

Potter, David. *People of Plenty: Economic Abundance and the American Character*. Chicago: University of Chicago Press, 1955.

Weinstein, James. *The Corporate Ideal in the Liberal State, 1900–1918*. Boston: Beacon Press, 1968.

Wiebe, Robert. *The Search for Order, 1877–1920*. New York: Hill and Wang, 1967.

Williams, William A. *America Confronts a Revolutionary World*. New York: Norton, 1976.

Wiltse, Charles M. *The Jeffersonian Tradition in American Democracy*. Chapel Hill: University of North Carolina Press, 1935.

PART II

IDEOLOGY AND POLITICS IN THE 1970s AND 1980s

CHAPTER 4

LIBERALISM: THE TROUBLED MAINSTREAM

Liberalism emerged from World War II at the peak of its strength. It dominated both major political parties, all the institutions of the national government, and all but a handful of intellectuals and their journals. Its body of beliefs was so widely shared that the theme of a leading scholar's history of liberalism was regret that no credible alternative existed to force Americans to better understand the principles they so uncritically accepted.[1] Throughout the 1950s and into the early 1960s, liberal values and beliefs in action seemed to produce an affluent society. Social conflict was effectively smothered by the material achievements generated by economic growth.

Not two decades later, liberalism was widely perceived to be in almost total eclipse, bereft of creative ideas and leaders, and unlikely to again mobilize popular support. Now, almost no thoughtful political leader or socially engaged intellectual accepts the characterization of "liberal" without some exculpatory prefix or an extended qualifying explanation. This change cannot be explained solely by one or two or even several causes, yet it must be understood if we are to assess recent changes in American politics. New bodies of belief define themselves in terms of their differences from liberalism. Established values and beliefs are reconstituted in new combinations and sometimes given new definitions on the basis of judgments about what went wrong with liberalism. Old antagonists of liberalism, fresh and bold in their success, confidently offer answers that liberalism would never have considered. In short, the eclipse of liberalism has given rise to the present spectrum of political beliefs. All of our new belief systems owe something to liberalism in much the same way that an exploding star is thought to have created our solar system.

LINKS TO THE PAST

The Postwar Years

It would be difficult to exaggerate the effect that the great international conflict of World War II had on Americans. An entire generation was deeply marked by the unforgettable experience of massive mobilization

49

and collective national effort. Following the war, individuals' energies were poured into achieving success in civilian life to make up for the wartime loss of opportunities. One not insignificant result was a massive baby boom.

Another distinctive mark of this period was the sustained prosperity that soon took hold. Not only did the feared depression not recur, but the nation began to enjoy unprecedented affluence. The United States had emerged from the war as the world's leading military and economic power. It was able to profit substantially from this stature. The government policy of encouraging business enterprise while assuring at least minimum individual security seemed highly successful. Economic growth and real personal income rose steadily and seemed assured. Whether the dominant belief system and government practice was termed "welfare liberalism" or "corporate liberalism," it seemed to work and had few serious opponents. If it did not work for all, it did for most of the politically significant population.

The distinguishing feature of this period was the rise of the cold war between the United States and the Soviet Union. The United States believed the Soviet Union was determined to expand even beyond its newly extended borders. The United States moved to contain that expansion through military preparedness, including threats to use the American nuclear arsenal. An atmosphere of hostility and danger prevailed between the free world and the communist nations. To Americans, it was a "battle for men's minds," and the battle raged all over the world by a variety of means short of all-out war.

The anticommunist crusades of these years gave vent to energies long felt yet contained, and they also established lasting criteria of belief and practice for all Americans. Politicians and citizens alike across the political spectrum accepted the necessity of both foreign and domestic anticommunism. Any connection with principles associated however distantly with socialism or communism could destroy credibility and prevent serious consideration for one's ideas. The entire left side of the traditional political spectrum lay under a cloud of suspicion, and radicals virtually went underground.

If effect, a new theme in American political thought was created, one that reaffirmed traditional values and practices with expressions of resentment against changes of various kinds. When invoked effectively, many people responded to its appeal—often forsaking other values and commitments to do so. A similar effect is produced today when racist symbols are invoked, even covertly.

The 1960s and 1970s

This period began with strident reminders of the immediate past. John F. Kennedy ran for president on a characteristic cold war platform. He promised to close a missile gap later found to be nonexistent and generally to put us ahead of the Russians—on the moon as well as elsewhere. He defeated Richard Nixon, then chiefly known as one of the leaders of the anticommunist crusades of the 1950s. The Kennedy style and the re-awakening of national pride and sense of omnipotence that it promised occasioned much media attention. It was not long before the power of the civil rights movement, the rise of the New Left and militant feminism, and the chaos generated by the Vietnam War took over and defined the period. Sweeping cultural changes occurred, soon followed by a national trauma over the ending of the Vietnam War and the Watergate scandal.

On top of this came the worsening economic conditions of the post-1973 years. The status of the United States as the world's paramount economic power began to crack as early as 1968. At that point, the modernized European and Japanese economies became truly competitive, and the Vietnam War undermined the dollar as the standard of value in the world's monetary system. Trade deficits, inflation, and pressure on the dollar forced severe protectionist action in 1971. In 1973 the oil price increases began. The resulting drain of billions of dollars from the U.S. economy helped to spur the spiraling inflation of the decade. Contrary to all prior experience, high inflation and high unemployment began to occur together, sending shock waves of doubt and resentment through the society.

From about the mid-1970s, even these developments were over-shadowed by a massive new social phenomenon. Profound changes in cultural values, life-styles, and social practices had occurred with great media visibility in the 1960s and early 1970s. One of their greatest effects was the reaction of millions of other Americans who neither desired nor accepted the changes. Many of them blamed these changes on the liberal belief system and its predominance in the national government. A diverse but militant alliance of conservatives soon mobilized to defend the status quo and reassert "traditional" values. They took aim as much at liberal permissiveness as at radical presumptuousness. Particular targets were liberal social engineering and the arrogance of bureaucrats, planners, academics, social workers, and others who seemed intent on imposing their values on others.

BASIC VALUES

The liberal belief system rests solidly on centrist versions of the six basic values set forth in Chapter 2. Liberalism, as a matter of principle, seeks the moderate versions that mark the middle ground. It avoids extremes in any direction, delicately balancing competing interests within the parameters that result from adopting moderate versions of *each* of the major values. The issue inadvertently raised by this commitment is whether these centrist versions *can* be harmonized under present social, economic, and political conditions.

For liberals, the individual and his or her satisfactions are the major focus. The purpose of government is to provide the conditions whereby individuals may pursue their own rational self-interest. People are entitled to certain kinds of assistance to equalize opportunities, but personal effort remains vital to achieving one's ends. There is a point after which government aid is unjustifiable. Private-property rights are highly valued as necessary to individual well-being. However, the public interest may require reasonable regulations. Law and legal mechanisms are of paramount importance, especially in the protection of individual and minority rights. Given their objective and rational character, courts, almost in and of themselves, embody the proper solutions to problems.

Similarly, equality of opportunity is strongly supported, and, to the extent practical, liberals endorse a version that will compensate for past disadvantage. Freedom includes the right to use one's property as one wishes; however, it is subject to the limits that public health and welfare and equality of opportunity make appropriate. Civil liberties stand on higher ground as absolute areas of freedom, but here too courts (only) may impose limits based on the need for public stability. Liberalism's balanced version of freedom is summed up in the phrase, "My freedom to swing my arm ends at your nose."

Finally, democracy is understood in procedural terms, and the process is celebrated as capable of satisfying all legitimate needs. Once something has been enacted through the regular channels of procedural democracy, it is presumed to be the best possible approximation of the public interest—and one that all should accept. No other criteria exist by which to judge the output of the American political system. Questions of moral validity or of the adequacy with which the public interest has been served are not answerable or even appropriate within the liberal system.

Looking over these six specific versions of the major values, one may come to feel that they are not so specific after all. Indeed, they are so ambiguous that they can hardly be said to chart anything like a clear course. Words like *reasonable, appropriate, realistic,* and *practical* fill the crucial junctures in liberal principles, substituting ambiguity for definite standards of judgment.

This ambiguity is neither coincidence nor deliberate caricature on our part; it is the hallmark of mid-century liberalism. Intent on filling the middle ground and maintaining the flexibility to respond to steadily rising demands, liberals made virtue out of not being locked into any specific substantive position. Only procedures were fixed, and even these could be adjusted under heavy pressure. This combination of flexibility and lack of definite standards led to what is termed "interest group liberalism" or "special interest liberalism." Both terms refer to the same thing: a system with no definite standards of its own that seeks to respond to whomever and whatever applies the most pressure. Not suprisingly, when demands grew in number and began to conflict fundamentally, liberalism was in danger of becoming overloaded.

This is the feature of liberalism that triggered the impatience and then contempt of radicals and conservatives alike. From both sides, liberalism was assailed for failing to take principled stands. Once people begin to feel the rightness of a polar position, the wishy-washy middle draws their fire even more than their most hated opponents, who are at least principled as they are. Both radicals and conservatives have clear polar definitions of the basic values, as well as distinct priority rankings among them. They are not particularly interested in balancing or moderating them, as liberals would do. It is difficult to be passionate in defense of moderation and reasonableness, so liberals were in many respects unable to respond effectively.

Radicals argued that liberalism was interested only in cosmetic changes that would not threaten the stability of the capitalist economic system. They saw liberalism as so enmeshed in capitalism that it could function only within the range of what capitalism deemed acceptable. What radicals most resented was liberalism's sanctimonious rhetorical commitment to equality and democracy. They missed the fact that those terms had always meant something quite different to liberals and radicals.

The dominant commitment of many radicals was the expansion of equality toward something like equality of condition. Certainly radicals were clear that equality of opportunity was a never-to-be-realized illusion, continued invocation of which at some point amounted either to willful ignorance or deliberate hypocrisy. In contrast, most liberals still thought equality of opportunity was a realizable and worthy goal and that to expand it too much would be a truly unjustifiable infringement on the freedom of others. The gap between the radical commitment to social democracy and liberal inability to see beyond procedural democracy needs no further explanation. Nevertheless, the differences in definition of commonly used terms implied bad faith and hypocrisy to people on both sides.

Like radicals, conservatives adhered to a specific and internally consistent set of definitions of the basic values—and they were just as impatient with liberalism's failure to take a clear stand. They argued, for example, that the appropriate definitions of individualism, freedom, and property were the traditional ones—without qualifications. Constant efforts to expand equality, in their eyes, were not only unworkable but also actively destructive of individual incentive and, ultimately, character. Conservatives insisted that liberalism must give up its rhetorical endorsement of expanded equality of opportunity in the name of freedom. More dangerously, they claimed that liberals were creating unfulfillable expectations among the lower classes.

The conservatives' heaviest resentment focused on two major failings of liberalism: (1) its toleration of licentious behavior by so many people; and (2) its inability to assert a definite public interest that, if necessary, should be followed regardless of popular preferences. These twin defects, they felt, made liberalism unfit to govern. It was as if liberalism had no way to assert and defend any principles at all and now was merely a helpless spectator as the American social and economic system crumbled around it.

The question remains whether it would have been *possible* to harmonize moderate versions of all six values concurrently. The empirical answer seems to be that liberalism did not find a way to do so and for this reason drew attack from both Right and Left. Ironically, many liberals feel most comfortable when they are being attacked from both sides. It assures them that they truly must be in the middle. Was liberalism being attacked for having taken a principled stand on the merits of an issue or for failing to take any stand but one that said certain regular procedures must be followed? It is a critical difference.

PROBLEMS AND POSSIBILITIES

Liberals' perceptions of the problems they should address are, naturally enough, linked to their versions of the basic values and to their past experiences. Liberals take credit for effectively handling the depression of the 1930s, World War II, the cold war, and the postwar imperative of continued economic growth. These successes loom large in liberals' memory. What appeared to work as solutions then make up the storehouse from which to draw solutions today. It is difficult for a belief system to ease away from problem definitions and proven remedies of the past, particularly when it still holds power. Intellectuals, political leaders, and institutions like the Congress and political parties see some merit and certainly less risk in following previously traveled paths. Established policies often have a self-reproducing character; they become the equivalent of the old patent medicines—remedies for any problem that is troubling.

Many of the problems that liberals saw and sought to solve were real enough, but the more problems they addressed, the more seemed to blossom. Part of the liberals' difficulties was that they acknowledged a large number of problems as compelling. In attempting to respond, they applied temporary remedies to a great many problems without locating the fundamental causes. We shall take up only two important issues, but they illustrate the range of problems perceived and the kinds (and consequences) of the solutions applied.

One of liberalism's basic assumptions is that the private economy, in this case modern capitalism, provides a set of givens that serve as the background for all public decisions. Some liberals regularly complain that this makes for private affluence, leaving public needs poorly attended. However, such complaints have by no means ruptured the basic complementarity of capitalism and liberalism. The concept of the free economic market is also a powerful element in liberal thinking, shaping approaches to understanding and the ability to act. It is within this context that liberals seek to solve the problems they see.

Two Leading Problems

Liberals perceive one of the greatest problems to be the excesses and hardships of the free market. It was a response to problems such as this that brought the current version of liberalism into being in the first place. In the early twentieth century, the national government, at the urging of the corporate and banking communities, accepted responsibility for stabilizing the economy, regulating competition, maintaining some sort of floor of security under individual workers, and setting standards of health and safety for consumer products and workers. National government regulation of business practices, particularly after certain scandals and excesses were exposed during the depression, had become a thoroughly accepted principle. When consumer advocates and environmentalists urged greater protections, therefore, it was no basic change of direction for liberals to seek to achieve such ends through vastly expanded regulation.

Very close in importance to this first problem is the need for sustained economic growth. The ability to respond to new demands for expanded versions of equality and basic social services depended on expanding revenues. In turn, such revenues depended on the ability of corporations and the wealthy to pay increased sums in taxes, or, in other words, on steadily growing profits and incomes. The expansion of social services and retirement benefits is clearly redistribution from the rich to the poor. In the liberals' world, this redistribution is really practical only when the total economic pie is expanding. As long as the pie is growing, increments can be drawn off to serve new demands without incurring prohibitive resistance from the rich or other benefactors.

Thus, liberal success became intimately tied to sustained economic growth. For many liberals, the imperatives of growth threatened to dominate all policy considerations. Other liberals, however, began to lose sight of this imperative in their concern to respond to growing demands through increased regulations. As in other areas, liberal definitions and solutions to problems began to conflict.

The Liberal Solutions

The solutions that liberals offer in answer to these concerns are often contradictory, always require an expanded state bureaucracy and technocratic expertise for implementation, and in other ways contain the seeds of ultimate failure. This may seem a harsh indictment, but it is one that liberals themselves began to make in the 1980s.

The concern for softening the harshness of the free market, for example, led to extensive regulations and the administrative oversight capability to make them effective. Protection of the environment, the health and safety of workers, or the interests of consumers in safe and lasting products all are better achieved by monitoring activities at the workplace than by multiplying legal remedies to be pursued later in courts. This means either massive new reporting requirements for businesses or an extensive network of personnel for regular inspections and enforcement—or both.

At some point, such expansion in administrative oversight becomes counterproductive. Business costs rise and growth slows, regulations conflict, the technical expertise and required equipment place a heavy financial burden on the government, and political reaction is provoked. The prospect of effective resistance grows as efforts are increased to realize the goals that initiated the regulatory effort.

A similar dilemma arises in efforts to fine-tune the economy to accomplish steady growth. A vast body of data is needed, the collection and interpretation of which, although the ostensible province of experts, nevertheless is open to vigorous debate. The tool kit traditionally employed by liberals, at least since the depression, is known as Keynesianism, after the English economist John Maynard Keynes. The basic principle is that government should manage the business cycle, eliminating both too rapid upturns (inflation) and excessive downturns (recession) through its fiscal policies. When the economy seems headed up too fast, government should put on the brakes by reducing its spending and increasing revenues. When the economy is declining or not growing fast enough, government should stimulate it by running a deficit, that is, by spending more than it takes in through taxes.

There are several problems with Keynesian theory, as the 1970s made clear. One is that it cannot cope with periods when inflation and unemployment occur together. Its remedies are designed to cure one by causing the other. It also does not work when inflation is caused by factors other than too much demand (or money) in search of consumer products. For example, fiscal policies cannot compensate for oil price increases or corporate pricing in monopoly situations.

Another problem is that it is politically easier to increase government spending than to cut spending or increase taxes. Keynesian deficits worked well to stimulate the economy in times of low inflation and high unemployment, as occurred in World War II and again in 1983. They are so effective that nearly all presidents and Congresses tend to stimulate the economy in these ways prior to elections. But Keynesianism never has been purposefully invoked to prevent excessive expansion, and liberals were politically unable or unwilling to attempt it while inflation was at its peak in the 1970s. Thus the liberal tool kit was ultimately unequal to the new conditions of that decade. Both Keynesianism and liberalism suffered accordingly.

In short, liberalism's perception of problems and choice of solutions succeeded only in binding liberalism ever more tightly in bonds of its own making. None of the solutions to which it was drawn seemed to work, at least for long. Liberalism clearly faced increasing difficulties. It also faced new economic conditions—conditions that it probably could not cope with unless it departed in some basic way from its specific definitions and mix of values. Such a departure would require repudiation of some part of that mix—that is, a shift away from liberalism itself. Liberalism was trapped. Meanwhile, the reaction began to build.

IMPLICATIONS AND PROSPECTS

In hindsight, one might wonder if the real question should be not why liberalism seemed in such eclipse, but why it was so successful for so long. However, to adopt this as the basic question would be to fail to understand liberalism's enduring strength as mainstream American political thought. Worse, it would tend to discount its future. Liberalism's longevity is owed to its flexibility and adaptability, which in turn are grounded in its emphasis on procedure rather than substance.

Liberalism is so closely linked to modern capitalism that in practice it functions as the latter's political-legal arm. Liberalism prospers when capitalism prospers. While growth was easily achieved and before conflicting demands became problematic, liberalism effectively provided humane social services and some version of political opportunity for Americans of all classes and origins. It was the belief system and practical mechanism that implemented the American dream of material success, social mobility, and individual fulfillment. In many instances, it enabled individuals to realize those aspirations. In many others, it offered enough of a glimpse to be reassuring. For most people, liberalism became synonymous with American democracy, in sharp contrast to other political systems in existence. Liberalism simply meant opportunity with security—economic, social, and political. It solved the problems of its day and earned broad acceptance.

So we return to the original question. Why did this eminently practical and opportunistic governing belief system suddenly lose its support? What does this tell us about changing conditions and beliefs and about the future directions of American politics? As we have seen, much of liberalism's success depended on the United States' postwar dominance and the opportunity thus provided for sustained economic growth. Competitive advantages and the availability of resources and markets enabled the biggest American corporations and banks to expand rapidly. Their earnings, shared with workers in the form of increased wages and the taxes supporting new social services, were the essential pillars of affluence. This practical trickle-down distribution might not have occurred, of course, without continuing political pressure (through the liberal system) from ordinary people. Thus, some bases exist for the view that part of liberalism's problem today lies in excessive popular expectations.

However, it was not only the apparent success of the New Deal-Great Society that led to its eclipse. Its basic dual principle—protecting the individual while promoting business profitability—only postponed an inherent and inevitable conflict. Once the economic pie stops growing, conflict over its distribution and redistribution is bound to develop. The image of a zero-sum society is now familiar; one person's gain seems possible only if another loses.

The zero-sum principle seemed also to obtain in noneconomic fields. If an issue had to do with the respect and dignity accorded women or minorities, anything additional accorded to lower-status people seemed to be subtracted from those of higher status. Status seemed, in other words, to depend on there being somebody lower on the social ladder. Lower-middle-class white males were especially affected. The New Deal-Great Society government assumed responsibility for implementing civil rights that carried powerful status implications. Thereby it incurred risks that were only postponed by the general economic affluence. Inevitably, when that affluence diminished, much of the resentment would focus on the liberal government that was the apparent agent of all this change.

Thus, by the early 1970s, when inflation overtook growth and real incomes began to drop, all of these potential conflicts were waiting to explode. Only renewed growth, with reduced unemployment and permanent control of inflation, could effectively defer such an explosion. However, the nature of the American and world economies was changing rapidly, and growth was suddenly problematic. These changes raised compelling new questions for all political belief systems about both economic policy and the proper world role for the United States. Liberalism probably could not have extricated itself from the inertia of past problem definitions and remembered solutions even if it had had the appropriate new understanding and remedies in hand. In any event it did not.

As always happens in hard times, economic analysis and proposals started to dominate political thinking. Hard times raise questions in many minds about how well the whole social-economic system is working and for whom. They pose potentially powerful threats to social stability and cause policymakers to cast about for new solutions that have the promise of success. A deep recession—a politically costly cure for inflation—was the remedy eventually applied in 1981 to 1982. What remained unclear was what should be done about the more fundamental changes occurring in the American and world economies and how such policies might be incorporated into new or modified political belief systems.

The transformation underway has at least two dimensions. First, both *what* is produced in the world and *where* and *how* it is produced and sold are undergoing something of a revolution, a change comparable to the shift from agricultural to industrial economies in the nineteenth century. Instead of basic metals, heavy machinery, and labor-intensive durable goods, production is shifting toward lighter, high technology, and energy-efficient items. Computers and other information-managing systems are increasingly employed to control production processes, keep records, and manage distribution. Their capabilities are leading to a "knowledge society." Jobs in the service sectors are rising steadily, while jobs in heavy manufacturing are dropping even more sharply. The prospect of unemployability for many blue-collar workers in the older industries is high, and the prospect of widespread social dislocation is even higher.

The second dimension of the transformation stems from the rapid growth of integration and interdependence in the world economy. It is not only that most major corporations have become multinational in the scope of their operations. Components of various products move quickly from lowest-production-cost areas of the world to final-assembly locations and, as finished goods, to markets around the globe. Exports of American agricultural and manufactured goods and increasingly of services as well make up a vital share of all gross profit and generate a steadily growing proportion of all jobs. The ability of the United States to export its goods and services depends on the economic prosperity of other countries, their trade policies and success in finding markets for their own exports, world currency values and stability, and so forth. The same is true for all the countries that are our trading partners. Nations of the world never have been so mutually dependent.

Economic success in this new world economy, however, depends on the ability to effectively compete in the markets of the world. In this vital area, the United States suddenly found itself trailing other countries. Partly as a result of flows of American investment and the sale of technology abroad, foreign companies were able to exceed the productivity of American producers. For example, Americans learned in the late 1970s (with some shock) that the Japanese could produce cars that were better and priced lower than comparable American models. While Americans were losing ground in various areas, American per capita income dropped to tenth among the industrialized nations of the world. The country that had led the world in economic achievements during the postwar period appeared on the verge of being left behind.

Part of the reason for foreign companies' productive and competitive edge seemed to lie in their development of new forms of business-government cooperation. Investment, financing, and trade policies in Germany and Japan, for example, were closely coordinated by government agencies. Thus, new industries could be developed and markets captured quickly and purposefully. Given the vigorous government role in these successes, a major debate soon arose in the United States over whether the adoption of similar policies could return American companies to their former competitive position. The traditional American reluctance to accept deep government intervention in the economy stood in the way of such solutions, but the problem of declining competitiveness was widely acknowledged.

Another set of reasons for the eclipse of liberalism is more exclusively political. The liberal government of the 1960s, and particularly the Great Society of Lyndon Johnson, simply took on too many problems. The effort to solve so many problems led to a vast federal bureaucracy—a readily visible enemy about which practically everybody could find some reason to complain.

Most damaging of all, the same liberal government sought to do something about the status of American minority races. Efforts to help African-Americans, and disadvantaged people generally, led to an overwhelming reaction from lower- and middle-class whites that ultimately destroyed the electoral coalition that had for fifty years maintained liberalism in power. As the Democratic party sponsored civil rights legislation, affirmative action, busing to achieve school desegregation, and the war on poverty, it drew African-American and other minority support into its ranks. However, far greater numbers of whites abandoned the party for exactly the same reasons.

The changes that have provoked reactions are not limited to the substantial tangible gains of organized groups and movements. They include changes in the most basic cultural values that underlie the social order and give it meaning. For example, many people feel that our highly valued *concept* of the family is threatened by the availability of divorce and abortions, freer sexual relations, and franker acknowledgment and acceptance of homosexuality. One result has been a recent focus on social issues, with various groups seeking legislation to reverse many of these changes. Religious movements in particular have engaged in political activity to restore former standards. Equally strong and widespread is the feeling that somehow Americans today no longer appreciate the importance of work and have lost their sense of purpose and self-confidence under liberal government.

We must add to this catalogue of reactions the effects on the country of the Vietnam War. The war caused deep social divisions and marked many people for life. For the tens of thousands of men and women directly involved, the war and its aftermath at home were profoundly wrenching. Despite their many sacrifices and troubling experiences in Vietnam, they not only were not appreciated when they returned home but also often were ignored or even denigrated. Ronald Reagan used these frustrations very effectively in his presidential campaigns, and George Bush sought to do the same.

The Implications of Liberalism's Eclipse

The eclipse of liberalism was thus brought about in part by its own principles, in part by drastically changed world conditions, and in part by the consequences of its own successes. The political consequences of the eclipse of this mainstream-defining ideology, however, still reverberate throughout the American political and economic systems. At least temporarily, *liberal* became an epithet, a derogatory term used to smear an opponent. Any institution or policy that could be painted as liberal was in danger of attack. Major programs "to get government off our backs" abounded. Only candidates and proposals certifiably *not* liberal were welcome in the electoral arena.

A sharp drop in levels of popular confidence in political institutions and social leaders generally accompanied liberalism's eclipse. Surveys showed confidence levels to be at their lowest point since such studies began in the mid-1960s. A mood of antipolitics developed as many began to believe the critics. It appeared that all the good faith efforts of the 1960s failed or were counterproductive.

Finally, the eclipse of liberalism spawned a whole new range of contending and alternative ideologies, often defining themselves through their differences with liberalism. Some older liberals moved to the right as neoconservatives, mounting a biting attack on liberalism's alleged failures. Rising young leaders turned to technocratic, managerial, and cost-benefit criteria of action, distancing themselves with the label of neoliberalism. Both groups embraced capitalism's need for economic growth with an enthusiasm that would have embarrassed their liberal predecessors. An examination of the ideas of these heirs/critics and their love/hate relationship with liberalism is the subject of the next chapter. More distinctive challengers to the liberal mainstream are discussed later.

Before leaving liberalism, however, we want to add a caution. Liberalism served as the mainstream of American political thinking for nearly a century; it is far too soon to pronounce its death. Deeply embedded at the bedrock level of American political thinking, it clings to life. Continued celebration of the Constitution, as one example, amounts to reaffirmation of liberalism; scarcely an institution or value of American life does not somehow reaffirm liberal principles. It is much better to think of liberalism as temporarily eclipsed than dead.

Moreover, in the context of multiple new and polarized solutions offered for our current problems, the prospect always exists that agitation at the extremes will generate a desire for the moderate middle. Americans tend to carry the ever-present feeling that says, essentially, "A plague on both your houses." This desire for a moderate middle solution is the basis for our suggestion that liberalism might not be dead at all. Liberalism may be only awaiting an opportunity to locate itself on a middle ground between warring polar alternatives.

An example of such a middle solution is the collective product of the Stanford Research Institutes entitled *Seven Tomorrows: Toward a Voluntary History*. This work essentially condemns both extremes and offers a transcending synthesis, a "voluntary history." It is the product of knowing human beings who have a respect for diversity. All analyses and alternatives are cast in terms of avoiding every extreme—"Right or Left, optimistic or pessimistic, utopian or dystopian."[2] The principles that are to guide action are never clearly stated, except in contrast to what others seek. "With respect to energy and the environment, for example, we can improve upon the adversarial deadlock that now poses business against the environmentalists."[3] The result, according to the authors, is "seeing through the fallacy of total victory in a diverse and pluralistic world."[4] This sounds very much like liberalism.

It may be that the revived version of liberalism would have a qualitatively different character from anything that has gone under that label before. It would be ironic indeed if the eclipse of liberalism in the 1980s were only the prelude to the refurbishment of liberalism as the wave of the future. Given the needs of the nation, it probably would indicate a major new round of centralization and authoritarianism in the American political system.

ADDITIONAL READINGS

Blumberg, Paul. *Inequality in an Age of Decline*. New York: Oxford University Press, 1980.

Clecak, Peter. *Crooked Paths: Reflections on Socialism, Conservatism, and the Welfare State*. New York: Harper & Row, 1978.

Galbraith, John Kenneth. *Economics and the Public Purpose*. Boston: Houghton Mifflin, 1973.

Hacker, Andrew. *The End of the American Era*. New York: Atheneum, 1971.

Hart, Jeffrey. *The American Dissent: A Decade of Modern Conservatism*. New York: Doubleday, 1966.

Hartz, Louis. *The Liberal Tradition in America*. New York: Harcourt, Brace, & World, 1955.

Kaufman, Arnold. *The Radical Liberal*. New York: Atherton, 1968.

Lowi, Theodore J. *The End of Liberalism*. New York: Norton, 1979.

Roszak, Theodore. *The Making of a Counter Culture*. New York: Anchor Books, 1969.

Smith, Duane, and William Gerberding, eds. *The Radical Left: The Abuse of Discontent*. Boston: Houghton Mifflin, 1970.

Teodori, Massimo, ed. *The New Left: A Documentary History*. Indianapolis: Bobbs-Merrill, 1969.

CHAPTER 5

FIRST REACTIONS: NEOCONSERVATISM AND NEOLIBERALISM

Of all contemporary American ideologies, neoconservatism and neo-liberalism carry the most direct links with liberalism. Neoconservatism was essentially a revolt by senior liberals who felt betrayed by the changes of the 1960s. A major contributor to liberalism's eclipse, neoconservatism was elite-focused, supplying them with a sometimes bitter, but generally effective, critique. Essentially, neoconservatism provided much of the intellectual justification for the Reagan revolution in American politics.

Neoconservatism is relevant today chiefly as a historical phase in the ideological "right turn" of the 1980s, which occurred almost exclusively among elites. We examine its principles only briefly.

Most neoconservative thinkers work today in conservative or libertarian intellectual circles. There they focus on rooting out the last vestiges of liberalism from the universities. They are particularly active in the defense of Western high culture from the subversion of multiculturalism and "political correctness" (discussed in Chapters 6 and 9). Some neoconservatives, however, have allied with neoliberals who are engaged in the task of moving the Democratic party to the Right, out of the hands of the "new class" and other radicals.

On the other hand, neoliberalism is very much alive in the upper echelons of the Democratic party and its congressional and state leadership, and among social thinkers in the universities and the intellectual establishment. Neoliberals are the architects of a "new" liberalism that is much more responsive to business and more concerned for economic growth and the global competitiveness of the American economy. Neoliberalism premises strict limits to what can be accomplished by social policy. It stresses technocratic and managerial solutions rather than financial investments as the cure for social problems. Neoliberalism may be liberalism in a new guise, merely waiting out the days of liberalism's disgrace; nevertheless, it deserves full analysis here.

NEOCONSERVATISM'S LINKS TO THE PAST

Neoconservatism was a quite self-conscious movement of a small but highly visible number of intellectuals who were well grounded in the universities, the media, and the governing establishment. Many of these leaders were once active supporters of the New Deal; some even thought of themselves as socialists. Their rupture with liberalism and coalescence in the neoconservative movement was both a reaction against what they saw as the excesses of the 1960s and an insistence on carrying forward some vital aspects of the older liberalism to which they were committed.

Neoconservatives reacted against the radical demands and behavior of the New Left as well as the permissiveness and placating response of the liberals. They saw the civil rights and antiwar movements as representing excesses of democracy with far too little regard for authority. Moreover, they felt government was trying to do too many things in the way of social policies, simply creating an overload. Neoconservatives saw a new class of liberal social engineers who were attempting, through government, the impossible and undesirable task of changing the way people lived.

Neoconservatives were also carrying forward some basic principles that liberals in government seemed to be forgetting. They focused on both the traditional concern for individual freedom and the necessary vigilant anticommunism of the cold war. Freedom, it seemed, was being forced to give way before an egalitarian onslaught. It needed defenders before it was smothered by government programs and regulations. Most neoconservatives were marked in some way by the cold war and struggles against domestic Communist influence in the 1940s and 1950s. Liberals seemed to them to have forgotten all the lessons of that period. In particular, American foreign policy appeared to be lacking in firmness and political will in the aftermath of the Vietnam War. There was a real prospect that the carefully nurtured system for containing communism would crumble in the face of Soviet military strength and boldness, given this failure of American resolve.

Irving Kristol, perhaps the leading symbol of neoconservatism, summed up the movement's consensus as support for the welfare state but opposition to bureaucratic intrusion and paternalism; respect for the free economic market; support for traditional values and religion against the "counterculture" and its threats to order; opposition to egalitarianism in which "everyone ends up with equal shares of everything"; and insistence on a strong anticommunist foreign policy.[1] Using other terms, Midge Decter reached much the same characterization:

> I would call it an intellectual movement which combines a very bitter disillusionment with socialism and hyperactive liberalism with a high degree of American patriotism. Many of us are former liberals or socialists who think of themselves as people who are trying to restore the country to a kind of intellectual and spiritual health.[2]

The beginnings of neoconservatism date from 1965 to 1966, but the movement did not reach its peak of visibility and strength until the early 1970s. In 1965 Irving Kristol and Daniel Bell, both leading social commentators, founded one of neoconservatism's two leading journals, *The Public Interest*. The other is *Commentary*, the long-established journal of the American Jewish Committee. Under the editorship of Norman Podhoretz, it began to develop the neoconservative position in the late 1960s. Together, the two journals served as a platform from which a corps of regular contributors attacked the New Left and liberalism's apparent acquiescence to its demands. These regulars included many leading social scientists and literary or political figures, such as Edward Banfield, Midge Decter, Martin Diamond, Nathan Glazer, Sidney Hook, Seymour Lipset, Daniel Moynihan, Robert Nisbet, Aaron Wildavsky, and James Q. Wilson.

The development of neoconservatism was rapid, in part because of its adherents' ready access to the media, particularly for the purpose of attacks on the Left by people who seemed to have been former members of that very Left. Most of the energies of neoconservatism in these early years were invested in vigorous polemics against individual radicals, their claims and actions, and the public policies of liberal government in the late 1960s. The conservative press, particularly *The Wall Street Journal*, helped to make Irving Kristol and Nathan Glazer central figures in the new critique; the business community was generous in its praise and assistance. Established conservative think tanks gained new legitimacy from supporting the neoconservatives in a variety of ways. By the time of *The Public Interest's* bicentennial edition in 1976, neoconservatism had become well established as a major force on the American political spectrum.

NEOCONSERVATISM'S BASIC VALUES: THE SHIFT TO THE RIGHT BEGINS

The fact that neoconservatism emerged from liberalism should remind us that liberalism always had a pessimistic side, expressed most fully in the United States Constitution of 1787. Prominent here were concerns about the volatility of popular majorities and the felt need to create governing institutions by which self-interested factions would cancel out each other. Cooler and wiser heads then could evolve public policies more genuinely in the public interest, preserving the basic values and traditions of the society as times changed. In particular, liberalism, both by definition and in practice, stood for liberty and the protection of individuals' freedoms and property rights. For neoconservatives in the 1960s, this meant protection against the redistributing thrust from the Left and the confiscatory tendencies of government, both of which neoconservatives saw as immediate threats.

Neoconservatism incorporated more than a touch of organic conservatism. Its emphasis on the need for deference to authority, acceptance of traditional ways, and respect for moral, religious, and spiritual values is squarely in the organic conservative model. More than any other contemporary belief system, neoconservatism stressed the need for coherence between the animating values of the economic order and the underlying culture. It found this link in religious sources. Neoconservatives often used terms like *pragmatic, realistic*, and *practical*, but they did not mean opportunistic, goal-maximizing practices, as liberals might. Instead, they meant considering the status quo very seriously and respectfully, taking only such steps as those that *should* be taken to preserve and enhance the status quo.

One of the major issues on which neoconservatives took a stand against both radicals and liberals concerned the changing meanings of equality and freedom. Neoconservatives were alarmed at the implications of expanding the notion of equality; they were determined to defend earlier definitions of freedom. They saw equality of opportunity being pressed to absurd, equality-of-results lengths. This meant not only vast new (and unworkable) expansion of government, but also bureaucratic intrusions into all spheres of personal life. The result was an intolerable reduction of personal freedom.

Irving Kristol frequently argued the neoconservative position on the equality-freedom dichotomy. He insisted that liberals and radicals sought equality of results without any clear sense of what that would mean. Such vague yearnings resulted in policies that destroyed liberty—and liberty is both the essence of a free society and Kristol's highest value. He declared that the distribution of income achieved by capitalism is right because "it is better for society to be shaped by the interplay of people's free opinions and free preferences than by the enforcement of any one set of values by government.[3] For Kristol, the only alternatives to the distributions accomplished by capitalism inevitably involved intolerable coercion and sacrifice of liberty. Kristol denied that any philosophy that prefers equality has an "authentic attachment to liberty" and said:

> It follows that "social justice" may require a people, whose preferences are corrupt (in that they prefer liberty to equality), to be coerced into equality. It is precisely because they define "social justice" and "fairness" in terms of equality that so many liberal thinkers find it so difficult to detest left-wing (i.e., egalitarian) authoritarian or totalitarian regimes. And, similarly, it is precisely because they are true believers in justice-as-equality that they dislike a free society, with all its inevitable inequalities.[4]

Hardly any principle of domestic social policy drew as much bitter opposition or ridicule from neoconservatives as affirmative action. Nathan Glazer attacked the notion in 1975 in a book revealingly titled *Affirmative Discrimination: Ethnic Inequality and Public Policy*.[5] Midge

Decter led the attack on feminism and, particularly, on affirmative action, which she saw as "corrupting our society."

> Comparable worth is a vicious idea. . . . When female activists couldn't talk very well about equal pay for equal work, they invented comparable worth. The idea, if it gets established, is going to create a maelstrom in this society. It must not be allowed to happen.[6]

What both Glazer and Decter feared from affirmative action and other such policies was that they might lead to unreasonable expectations, government expansion, bureaucratic coercion, and an angry public reaction. They believed these all added up to the unraveling of the society, a process that was already underway.

The way to avoid coercion, of course, was through greater reliance on the economic free market. Neoconservatives acknowledged some imperfections in the market's operations but saw these as vastly preferable to the only alternative—bureaucratic coercion enforcing conformity to a single set of choices made by distant social engineers. Neoconservatives saw government as inherently unable to perform functions as well as the apparently uncoordinated activity of people responding to market incentives. Liberals in government—the "new class" that we take up in the next section of this chapter—were misguided in their offer to perform all these functions but even more in error when they encouraged people generally to expect so many things from government. In effect, liberals created expectations that no government could have even begun to fulfill. They thereby contributed to the crisis of authority that is the real American problem.

Neoconservatives firmly endorsed a limited, procedural concept of democracy. Even this sort of democracy can get out of hand, however. Any major involvement of people in public decision making carries serious dangers. The unreasonable expectations and increased participation encouraged by liberals in the 1960s led directly to popular pressures for a wide variety of changes and to a general attitude of disrespect for established ways. It was as if people were led to challenge or doubt all the traditional ways and to withhold respect for governing institutions and officials.

This theme of the excesses of democracy and the loss of authority was sounded by many neoconservatives. It was developed, for example, by Samuel Huntington, a political scientist, in his controversial essay in the bicentennial issue of *The Public Interest*.[7] Asserting that the problems of the 1960s stemmed primarily from too much popular participation and excessive expectations, Huntington called for greater power in government to enforce obedience and sacrifices where necessary. Robert Nisbet did much the same in *The Twilight of Authority*, a book whose title fully conveys its message.[8]

But neoconservatives believed that there was even more involved in the decline of authority and legitimacy in the leading institutions and standards of the society. Basic moral commitments and traditional practices were also undermined by this liberal pandering to majoritarian whims and special interest demands. Religion, the family, and social morality in general were falling before the rise of self-gratification and hedonistic short-term indulgence that liberalism encouraged. Michael Novak in particular argued strongly for a rebirth of religious and spiritual grounding for the basic institutions of the society, seeing this as the necessary foundation of faith in democratic capitalism.[9]

Perhaps the worst effect of the loss of moral fiber that neoconservatives saw in the United States was the failure to stand up for basic principles—particularly in international affairs. Neoconservatives saw the Soviet Union as an implacable enemy covertly building up its strength and waiting for the moment to attack vital American interests. Third World countries were hypocritically demanding assistance and playing self-interested, nationalistic games without regard for the stakes involved. Only firm assertion of the rightness of capitalist democracy and determined anticommunist vigilance would maintain freedom's shrinking domain around the world. An American isolationism or failure of will at this point in history would amount to consigning billions of people to the equivalent of slavery for the foreseeable future.

It seems clear that neoconservatives reverted to some older definitions of basic values and gave them a more consistently conservative character than was ever the case in traditional liberal thought. Social and economic inequality was a necessary accompaniment of freedom, which has paramount priority. The separation of social and economic life from political affairs was not only obvious but also necessary and desirable as a way of giving primacy to the private sector. Problems in the United States were more the result of people's personal failures, their excessive expectations, or the faulty ways that they sought social change than the result of structural flaws in the social, economic, or political systems. Neoconservatism may have originated in liberalism, but it more than made up for such early sins by the warmth of its current embrace with conservatism.

NEOCONSERVATISM'S PROBLEMS AND POSSIBILITIES: CONTROLLING THE "NEW CLASS"

The problems that neoconservatives saw as most important were not rooted in ecomomic conditions or social structures. Instead, they lay in the values and beliefs of leaders and followers in the American social system. In other words, with the exception of Soviet military strength and worldwide subversive activities, problems did not have objective content. They were quite real, but they took the form of willfulness or error in people's minds. The remedies that appealed to neoconservatives therefore were directed partly at the replacement or conversion of governing elites and partly at the restoration of certain habits and beliefs among the masses.

Problems

In the eyes of neoconservatives, the main problem of the failures of American leadership and the decline of the American civilization was the rise of a "new class" of middle-class professionals opposed to the basic values of the society that nurtured them. This new class started at an unprecedented level of affluence, encountered little in the way of character-building hardship to struggle against, and had easy access to higher education. They then directed their energies into the effort to enable everybody to enjoy the same opportunities, with little or no realization of how difficult that would be or why many people might not desire such ends. Most damaging of all, this class, whether in governmental positions or in private life, was egalitarian and antibusiness.

Once again, it was Irving Kristol who most vigorously mounted the attack. In his relentless critique of those who seek equality, he uncovered "an intelligentsia which so despises the ethos of bourgeois society, and which is so guilt-ridden at being implicated in the life of this society" that it despaired of American ways and had a fatal attraction for totalitarian regimes. He went on to say:

> We have a "New Class" of self-designated "intellectuals" who share much of this basic attitude . . . [and] pursue power in the name of equality. And then we have the ordinary people, working-class and lower-middle-class, basically loyal to the bourgeois order but confused and apprehensive at the lack of clear meaning in this order—a lack derived from the increasing bureaucratization (and accompanying impersonalization) of political and economic life. All of these discontents tend to express themselves in terms of "equality"—which is in itself a quintessentially bourgeois ideal and slogan.[10]

The false god of equality had combined with the rise of self-indulgence and the decline of religion to make for a basic cultural opposition to capitalist-liberal society. Some neoconservatives termed this "an adversary culture," and they located its basic source in the new class of antibusiness professionals. The exact composition and nature of this new class was not easy to pin down, in part because neoconservatives variously saw it as intellectuals, or intellectuals and professionals, or government workers, or all college-educated people. Peter Steinfels, the leading student of neoconservatism, says: "In neoconservative writings, references to the 'new class' make up in frequency and vehemence what they lack in precision."[11]

It is certainly clear that neoconservatism had identified a significant problem. It was partly people—the new class, whether defined and located specifically or broadly—but more particularly the beliefs that they held. The problem was located in the egalitarianism and antibusiness attitudes of this new class. Neoconservatives believed that it was there that the efforts for change should focus.

The second major problem that neoconservatives identified was located, by contrast, in mass publics, and particularly in their underlying culture. Essentially, the problem in recent years was that the dominant cultural principle had not been supportive of or even compatible with the others. The dominant principle generated by American cultural dynamics in the period from the 1960s to the present was one of indulgence and self-gratification. This was the "me decade." Although it was impossible for everyone's demands on the economy and society to be met, such demands had actually been encouraged by the new class, with its continuing emphasis on the right to equality. The decisive weakness of contemporary elites, in other words, had combined with the dominant inclination of masses of people in an incendiary mixture.

A society in which everybody seeks the maximum possible benefit for himself or herself without regard to others is not a pleasant or even governable society. Somehow, this underlying culture had to be controlled so that the appetites unleashed did not tear the society apart.

Possibilities

As we have seen, the reputation of neoconservatives was built largely on the style and acerbity of their critique of the New Left and the liberal effort to propitiate all their demands. If there had not been an apparent threat from the Left, neoconservatism might never have achieved its media visibility or its business support. Neoconservatives did not really propose a program for governing; they only outlined a critique of those who were doing so.

Nonetheless, an alternative program can be inferred from the criteria used against liberalism. Not surprisingly, it reflected fundamental neoconservative principles. First was the pervasive notion of limits to social possibility. Neoconservatives saw two leading possibilities. One was to depress public expectations, bringing about a return to realism in the people's public aspirations. The other was to replace or reconstruct the governing elite to install a new sense of the limits of government capabilities and a chastened vision of the importance of equality. This latter principle—equality—was really at the heart of the problem. Attempts to focus on and achieve equality are the death warrant of free society. Thus nothing was more important than controlling the thrust toward equality.

The other half of the neoconservative program was aimed at revitalizing the religious grounding of the capitalist order. Michael Novak led the way in trying to provide a new justification for capitalism that could harmonize the dominant principles of the three major sectors of social life. He began *The Spirit of Democratic Capitalism* with the premise that no system of political economy has so improved the quality of life and yet been so lacking in theological justification as democratic capitalism. What distinguished Novak's argument was the further premise that the combination of a capitalist market economy and political democracy was not a historical accident but rather a necessary relationship—one in which democracy depended on the existence of capitalism.

The problem, Novak admitted, was that "throughout the world, capitalism evokes hatred. . . . Even at home, within the United States, . . . the Achilles' heel of democratic capitalism is that for two centuries now it has appealed so little to the human spirit."[12] Mere acquisitiveness is not an uplifting principle of life. It has so many destructive consequences that most people turn away in revulsion when the moral basis of capitalism is seen to consist of little else. In fact, Novak claimed, there are genuinely uplifting moral values underlying capitalism. The ideals of democratic capitalism, he insisted, are the very bedrock ideals of Christianity itself. He concluded:

> Almighty God did not make creation coercive, but designed it as an arena of liberty. Within that arena, God has called for individuals and peoples to live according to His law and inspiration. Democratic capitalism has been designed to permit them, sinners all, to follow this free pattern. It creates a noncoercive society as an arena of liberty, within which individuals and people are called to realize, through democratic methods, the vocations to which they believe they are called.[13]

Novak added that God will judge whether people have in fact accomplished their tasks. By implication, democratic capitalism should be judged in terms of whether or not it has permitted them to do so.

This argument was neoconservatism's best effort to revive capitalism's underlying moral basis. It was not a program for new public policies. Rather it was a program for wholesale moral regeneration of millions of people. Its appeal to conservative intellectuals, and perhaps to theologians, seemed clear.

There is one area, however, where neoconservatives had a very concrete program for new public policy. This is the field of international relations, particularly relations with the Soviet Union. Neoconservatism stood for vigorous development of American military power and readiness to use it around the world to counter continuing Soviet expansionism. In terms of visibility, Jeane Kirkpatrick has been the outstanding neoconservative advocate of an interventionist posture for the United States, particularly in Latin America. Her position is widely shared among neoconservatives. Close relations with Israel are a cornerstone of Middle East policy. A generally hard line in any future arms limitation negotiations fits this perspective as well, as does continuing suspicion of the Soviet Union, regardless of apparent changes.

NEOCONSERVATISM'S IMPLICATIONS AND PROSPECTS

By and large, neoconservatives succeeded in impugning liberalism in the eyes of governing elites (always their primary audience) and in preparing the intellectual ground for the Reagan-Bush administrations' policies and personnel appointments. Having essentially won their chosen war, though at times by exaggerating their enemies and caricaturing their positions, individual neoconservatives have moved on, and they are now allied with conservatism, libertarianism, and even neoliberalism. We shall encounter their ideas again in those contexts.

NEOLIBERALISM'S LINKS TO THE PAST

The defining characteristic of neoliberalism is, in a term that neoliberals often use themselves, "pragmatic idealism," a tough-minded and non-ideological approach that recognizes fiscal and other limits while still seeking to promote social justice and equity. Sometimes defined as "compassionate realism," neoliberalism purports to readily help those in real need without attempting to be all things to all people.

Most importantly, neoliberalism recognizes the absolute necessity of economic growth. Because growth depends primarily on the expansion and profitability of the private sector, American entrepreneurs and risk takers are enthusiastically encouraged. In view of the rapidly changing world economy, however, government policies are crucial to private success. Thus, major new policies and even institutional changes become necessary to enable the U.S. economy to recover its leading role.

Neoliberals deny that they are merely liberals who have yielded to the supposed rightward movement of American political thinking. They vigorously insist that their program embodies new ideas synthesized with the humanitarian essence of liberalism. The result, they claim, is a realistic idealism that will be capable of inspiring and satisfying Americans to the end of the century and beyond. Restoration of American faith and hope is a central neoliberal goal. Indeed, it is seen as a necessity if the economic and social challenges of the day are to be successfully met.

Neoliberalism fell heir to the technocratic, managerial component of liberalism when the latter fragmented. While neoconservatism got most of liberalism's strong anticommunism and single-issue movements got much of its reform impulse, neoliberalism inherited liberalism's pragmatic determination to make government work efficiently and effectively. Neoliberals have real faith in the continued development of scientific, technological, and administrative capabilities. They are eager to apply such expertise to the task of making government work better. Working better, moreover, means more than efficiently fulfilling assigned tasks, which is important enough. It also means meeting the challenge of new conditions by furthering the cause of economic development in previously untried ways.

This is a significant and enduring strand in American thinking that links neoliberalism with the Kennedy and Franklin Roosevelt administrations, then reaches back to the Progressive era and through it to the first patron of modern capitalism, Alexander Hamilton. Leading neoliberals such as Robert Reich and Paul Tsongas cite John Kennedy as the model for much of their political orientation. They also view the New Deal's celebrated nonideological pragmatism as the appropriate way to solve today's problems. For example, Tsongas says, "I view my approach as compassionate realism . . . non-ideological, clear-eyed realism. My interest is in what works, not what should work, and then within the boundaries of what works my interest is in the application of liberal democratic values.[14]

Although he was never able to articulate his program in a positive manner, Michael Dukakis was a model of neoliberal thinking in 1988. In the early 1990s, as if in preparation for the next round of national elections, other neoliberals added new proposals. Robert Reich's *The Work of Nations: Preparing Ourselves for 21st Century Capitalism*[15] and a series of related position papers updated his views in a provocative manner. Ex-Senator Paul Tsongas, newly returned to politics, distributed his *A Call to Economic Arms: Forging a New American Mandate*[16] as a manifesto of his presidential campaign. Perhaps the most thoughtful effort to justify the neoliberal approach to public policymaking is Charles Anderson's *Pragmatic Liberalism.*[17] Tracing the roots of pragmatic liberalism back to the Progressive era and the American pragmatists, Anderson stresses the necessity of a sense of the public interest and purposeful government action to further it.

NEOLIBERALISM'S BASIC VALUES

Neoliberalism has made some significant adaptations of the mainstream American values. Particularly noticeable is the way that it has rather comfortably come to terms with the use of the national government. Neoliberalism proposes to transcend conflict between individuals and special interest groups, disdains adversarial processes generally, and seeks to rise above politics as usual in order to define and act on a shared public interest. While asserting respect for risk takers and the free economic market, neoliberals nevertheless propose a more legitimate allocative role for government than it has ever had. Generally, the government would act on behalf of agreements made by business, labor, and government. Small wonder that, at least in its early stages, neoliberalism was far more popular among former liberals and Democrats than among business executives. Let us see how modest changes in several basic values add up to neoliberalism.

The first important modification, significantly, occurs with respect to *individualism.* In "A Neoliberal's Manifesto," Charles Peters, after delivering a critique of liberalism, declares "the primary concerns of neoliberalism: community, democracy, and prosperity."[18] Although most of his argument addresses ways of accomplishing prosperity, he is very clear on the importance of community. There is no mention of individualism as such. Rather, he deplores a divided nation and, specifically, "the politics of selfishness that has divided this country for more than a decade."[19] In Peters's eyes, "The adversary approach to problems has come to dominate our national life, at a disastrous cost to all of us."[20]

The sense of a compelling need to find, articulate, and then implement the national interest seems relatively new in American politics. Furthermore, the idea of a national interest as a whole, larger than the sum of its component interests, is certainly new to the center of the spectrum. Both conservatives and radicals are confident that they can identify a national interest, but liberals traditionally have either denied that there was any such thing or viewed it solely as the net product of individual interests. Neoliberals are backing away from such views. They argue that such views left liberalism paralyzed, unable to act coherently on behalf of long-range social and economic needs.

How great a departure is involved in this assertion of primacy for the notion of national interest over self-serving individualism? The rejection of self-interest as a basis for action is a theme that runs through many neoliberals' writings. Lester Thurow, for example, derides "rugged individualism" and calls for "company loyalty" instead. Peters describes our pressing need for "a rebirth of patriotism, a rebirth of devotion to the interests of the national community, of the conviction that we're all in this together and that therefore fair play and justice for everyone is the vital concern for us all.[21] Some of this emphasis on national interest may be attributable to the context of economic crisis in which much of this work was written. However, this aspect of neoliberalism remains a significant departure from mainstream individualism of the past. It is most fully explored and justified in Anderson's *Pragmatic Liberalism.*

A second major adaptation in values concerns the notions of *freedom* and *property.* Economic growth is so vital to every other goal that entrepreneurs must be freed to use their property in more creative ways than has been the case. In short, there must be more freedom for property to produce wealth. Because changing world conditions make government assistance essential to the success of business, the needs of business begin to define the priorities of government. This ultimately leads to new mechanisms for achieving agreement between business, labor, and government, so that government may have a blueprint to carry out. However, we are getting ahead of our story.

Neoliberals want to encourage growth by freeing the risk takers, the old-fashioned American entrepreneurs. As Peters says:

> Economic growth is most important now. It is essential to almost everything else we want to achieve. Our hero is the risk-taking entrepreneur who creates new and better products. . . . We want to encourage the entrepreneur not with Reaganite policies that simply make the rich richer, but with laws specifically and precisely designed to help attract investors and customers. . . . We also favor freeing the entrepreneur from economic regulation that discourages desirable competition.[22]

Only economic growth will succeed in defusing the conflict that is captured in Thurow's metaphor of the zero-sum society.

These endorsements of growth suggest that neoliberalism has reversed the priorities assigned by liberalism to equality and freedom/property rights. Under liberalism, equality seemed to be expanding in meaning, challenging freedom for first place; here it is clearly relegated to a subordinate position. Freedom to produce new wealth is the highest priority, and all others follow. However, as all neoliberals would hasten to add, the freedom they endorse is not Reaganite unlimited freedom for the rich to do whatever they want. Instead, it is freedom channeled by broad public needs and goals, as expressed by the triumvirate of business, labor, and government.

The third modification concerns *equality* and *justice*. Where do they fit in the neoliberal rank order of values? It seems clear that equality is being returned, more or less, to the older definition of equality of opportunity. Social justice, too, is being equated with equality of opportunity. Together they receive reduced priority because they have to be adapted to a rank order shaped by the expansion of freedom and property mandated by the overwhelming need for growth. So redefined, equality and justice are genuine neoliberal goals. Often, however, endorsement of these values is qualified carefully by concern for economic growth, as in the following lines from Tsongas:

> The more we want to solve the great human injustices in our society, the more we are going to need a full throttle economic engine. One cannot exist without the other . . . Pro-business, some would call it. And so it is. Aggressively so. But commonwealth is what it is as well.[23]

Neoliberalism at first seems to offer less change in regard to the fourth value of *democracy* than in regard to the other values discussed. Peters ranked democracy as one of neoliberalism's three primary concerns, but the notion is undefined and its requirements unexamined. There are similar endorsements from almost every other neoliberal as well as an equivalent lack of analysis of what democracy means or what (if any) obligations it entails. The conclusion seems warranted that by *democracy* they intend traditional liberal democracy.

However, when we discuss the neoliberal program for political revitalization, we shall see that one implication of the new arrangements for mobilizing cooperation behind decisive government action is a reduction in democratic participation. Thus it may be that neoliberalism actually involves a contraction in the public decision-making role from that traditionally offered by liberal democracy. We must defer this controversial issue until we take up the neoliberal proposals for change in political structures and practices.

With respect to the concept of human nature, neoliberals clearly draw back from the more reformist liberals' sense that people are or could be cooperative, good, and rational. Images of excessive selfishness requiring change or control abound in neoliberal writings. Speaking with specific reference to rivalry with the former Soviet Union, but clearly intending his point to have general application, Tsongas expresses a characteristic neoliberal assumption:

> Man's instinct for survival is paramount. In many respects it is the ultimate reality. . . . Man views man as aggressive, and that aggressiveness is in evidence in every walk of life. Sports are the most obvious example, but our entire free enterprise system is based on aggressiveness. . . . To a degree we all inherit a basic aggressiveness, and political philosophy must take this into account.[24]

Individually, these refinements in the basic values are relatively modest. However, when taken together and when applied in neoliberal proposals for solving today's problems, they begin to add up to a substantial new role for government in serving the needs of the private economy. This latter feature gives neoliberalism its distinct character as a body of beliefs.

NEOLIBERALISM'S PROBLEMS AND POSSIBILITIES

Two documents from the early 1990s can serve to illustrate the neoliberal analysis of problems and their proposed solutions. Both see the American economy sliding toward second-rate status, with growing prospects for a steadily declining standard of living and commensurately increasing social problems. Both call for a more active government responding to the public interest rather than individual self-interest.

The first is the work of Robert Reich, a Harvard political economist, adviser to Democratic candidates, and prolific writer. In *The Work of Nations* and newspaper articles derived from it, Reich argues that "vestigial thinking" hampers our understanding of the American economic problem. This is an inclusive term pertaining to mid-century images of a mostly independent national economy producing a variety of products with a highly differentiated labor force, and the then-known array of government methods for promoting national prosperity.[25]

Reich argues that capital is now so mobile that there is only one global economy; savings and investment will flow to wherever they can secure the best return, and goods and services will be produced at the lowest-cost site for delivery anywhere in the world. The scope of what a government can and should do to promote well-being of its people is thus quite limited but for that reason extremely important.

The United States is best understood, according to Reich, as a regional segment of the global economy, with a labor force made up of "symbol analysts, routine producers, and in-person servers." The first category (technicians, managers, and so forth) are well enough educated for the present and relatively well off in world terms today. The other two categories (assembly line workers and retail or service workers) are not well trained and will continue to fall further and further behind their counterparts elsewhere in the world who will be better trained and/or work for lower wages.

Under these circumstances, Reich calls for massive government-sponsored investment in education and training, in the health of the younger generation, and in the transportation and communications systems of the country. These are the only elements of the new global economy that are really *national* in character, and thus they are within the reach of social action. They are essential because they are absolutely vital to competitiveness in that new economy. These investments are to be financed through restoring a progressive income tax, cutting the military budget, and capping or taxing Social Security benefits.

The second work is somewhat in contrast to the first. Paul Tsongas' *A Call to Economic Arms* is more aggressively nationalistic and perhaps burdened by some "vestigial thinking." Much of the analysis of the reasons for American noncompetitiveness in the global economy is the same, however. Tsongas says:

> There is no reason why the United States should not be the pre-eminent economic power on earth. No reason whatsoever. We have the land, the resources, and the people. What we lack is the leadership. Our political leadership has chosen to ignore difficult economic realities. It has, instead, decided to finance short-term avoidance by placing the nation under crushing and unsustainable debt. As a result, America is facing great economic peril. We are daily witnessing this ever-mounting national debt, the inexorable sale of America to foreign interests, and the steady deterioration of our capacity to compete in the global marketplace.[26]

In addition to the economy, Tsongas identifies other areas for public attention: education, the environment, energy, foreign policy, and the revival of community spirit and purpose in American culture. He calls for a new American mandate to enable the national government to purposefully set about accomplishing all these goals.

While these two thinkers offer modestly contrasting programs, they share with all neoliberals the conviction that more purposeful government, acting on behalf of a newly developed public interest, is mandatory. As neoliberals move from analysis of problems toward programs to solve them, the world seems to be characterized by a general drift and decline that clearly calls for new kinds of government action. Neoliberals are almost as probusiness as the Reagan-Bush administrations, but from an entirely different perspective. They deny that a combination of laissez-faire reliance on the free market and favoritism for the rich few will benefit the many whose interests depend on renewed economic growth.

Neoliberals maintain that only a well-designed and comprehensive program of government incentives, assistance, and upgrading of both physical infrastructure and human resources will generate a period of sustained and widespread prosperity. No single business or industry or even the entire business community has the perspective or capacity to forgo immediate advantages and act in the long-range interest of the whole economy. Besides, much of what business needs, such as trade agreements and favorable fiscal policies, almost by definition can be provided only by government. The free market is simply inadequate as a device to serve the needs of sustained growth. The sooner that enlightened businesspeople come to terms with this new reality, the better.

Neoliberals do not first clarify their values and then march systematically to solutions. Perhaps more than the adherents of other belief systems, they find their values in the patterns of solutions they work out for problems and *then* celebrate them. In the following paragraphs, we survey three major, widely shared components of that program. We then return to the question of neoliberalism's vision for the future.

Industrial Policy   Neoliberalism is distinguished by its comprehensive approach to economic renewal. In the context of neoliberalism's image of decline and transformation in the U.S. economy, government has multiple policy obligations. First, it must set up a system of incentives and financial assistance to enable the shift of capital from older, declining industries to the areas of future opportunity, principally in high technology production and applications. This help could be in the form of national development banks or loan guarantee programs, retraining or relocation assistance for workers, and various forms of aid to communities affected by the massive shifts of capital and jobs.

Next, government should restrict imports and promote exports so that declining industries gain temporary protection and new producers can enter potential markets promptly. Declining industries should be helped only for the period it takes to modernize and return to competitiveness or to shift capital and workers to new uses in an orderly manner. National government assistance should come with strings attached. Recipient companies might be required to make specific improvements in facilities or practices, or the government might insist that workers or public representatives be given seats on the board of directors.

Greater energy independence is another important part of neoliberal industrial policy. It requires sustained emphasis on conservation, greater efficiency in all energy use, and development of alternative energy sources. Such changes could be accomplished in part through taxation and other incentive policies. Although the greatest emphasis is on developing renewable energy sources to the fullest possible extent, nuclear energy is not ruled out as one of the necessary sources.

Neoliberals also champion a major and sustained program to rebuild the infrastructure of the American economy. It is estimated that U.S. highways, bridges, terminals, water and sewer systems, and the like, will require hundreds of billions of dollars in repair and improvements over the next decade. If funds could be made available, this effort also would stimulate the economy. Neoliberals also would provide widespread training and retraining of workers as a form of infrastructure development in human capital.

Neoliberals propose a variety of new institutions for negotiating agreements among business, labor, and government and for planning the implementation of these programs. Some, like investment banker Felix Rohatyn (architect of the financial "rescue" of New York City in the mid-1970s), believe that a large new development bank run by leading bankers should do the job. Others prefer economic advisory councils of various kinds that, in most cases, report to the Congress. The first question is what kind of national economic planning should be undertaken. The second, equally important question is whether planning should occur in an open, political process or in a process protected from politics and managed by insiders and experts.

Education for Excellence and Competitiveness　Neoliberals focus particularly on education as the means to restore American leadership in various fields. In this emphasis, they are hardly unique, but it serves well as the primary outlet for their commitment to equality of opportunity and fits their sense that merit-based standards need to be revived. Neoliberals see a need for a major federal role, both in funding and in encouraging particular types of research and experimentation. With regard to education, their basic position again is that only a national perspective, in which all our needs are identified and ranked and resources allocated efficiently to meet them, can be adequate to solving the acute problems that exist.

The major goals to be served by this educational renaissance are the restoration of American competitiveness in business and leadership in science and technology. The national interest is the first beneficiary; individuals' opportunities are secondary. In 1983 two prestigious national commissions, though appointed by the Reagan administration, issued reports consonant with these neoliberal goals. Both made a major point of education's relevance to the ability of American producers to compete in the world marketplace.

Restoring Political Vitality and Government Capacity   Neoliberals are committed to finding a way to rise above the individual self-seeking, special interest powers, and adversary process of American politics. They seek a more decisive government with full capacity to act in the general public interest, but they also want a way to link the democratic expression of public preferences with that new government capacity. Indeed, neoliberals can sound almost conservative when they talk about the need for decisive government action despite probable opposition from various sides. Lester Thurow offers an example.

> Our society has reached a point where it must start to make explicit equity decisions if it is to advance. . . . We have to be able to decide when society should take actions to raise the income of some group and when it should not take such actions. It we cannot learn to make, impose, and defend equity decisions, we are not going to solve any of our economic problems.[27]

Political pressures constitute a major problem for government's capacity to make reasoned decisions in the public interest. Neoliberals have not resolved the question of whether to try to find ways to achieve agreement in an open, political process or to simply insulate government decision makers against politics and try to legitimate their decisions in some other way.

NEOLIBERALISM'S IMPLICATIONS AND PROSPECTS

Neoliberalism is distinguished by the fact that it proposes to extend the Hamiltonian use of government further than has ever been contemplated. This would amount to a major reversal of the dominant free market principle of American political thinking. No doubt that principle would continue to be honored in rhetoric for some time, but it would have been fundamentally changed in meaning.

If neoliberalism were successful in gaining the willing involvement of business, labor, and government—and in constructing mechanisms that would permit agreements to be reached and implemented—it would create a government capability unprecedented in American experience. With this new government role would come a managerial and technocratic role for experts that would exceed even that of the early New Deal or the most engineering-oriented days of the Great Society. Data gathering and interpretation, technical analyses, policy recommendations and comprehensive oversight all would be vital to effective central direction of this sort.

If the neoliberal framework were in place, many people from both the Left and Right probably would be concerned about the emergence of a corporatist system. The term *corporatist* usually is applied to those political-economic systems in which all major interests are brought together in some way so that government can act decisively. This is ostensibly done for the good of the whole, but in practice it has always been for the benefit of the few most powerful individuals or corporations.

Discussion of the prospect of corporatism usually calls up images of business leadership or at least eagerness on the part of business to be first among equals in a newly centralized system. This is certainly not the case in the United States today. Neoliberalism has a major selling job ahead, as its proposed business constituency seems at best tentative and skeptical and often openly opposed. Neoliberalism has had success with the most "progressive" larger corporations and banks, particularly those heavily involved in international markets, trade, and investments. However, the basic business response to neoliberal programs has been one of skepticism and clear preference for Reaganite "free market" policies, that is, reductions in taxes and regulations and general withdrawal of government from intervention in the economy.

Organized labor, on the other hand, has been a grudging supporter of neoliberal industrial policy—even if it has resented being the target of frequent neoliberal criticism. In the context of current pressures for givebacks and concessions, together with declining membership, labor has been hard put to find a new policy it could advocate. Given this lack of alternatives and the fact that labor's semiautomatic influence within liberalism is no longer meaningful, industrial policy apparently has seemed the least damaging option.

Neoliberals are increasingly clear in their understanding of what is at stake. They are searching for ways to communicate the urgent need for an instrument of adaptation. Lester Thurow, for example, has stressed his belief that broad changes are needed, even though he immediately adds that he does not expect others necessarily to agree.

> The time has come . . . to admit that the pursuit of equity and equal economic opportunity demands a fundamental restructuring of the economy. Everyone who wants to work should have a chance to work. But there is no way to achieve that situation by tinkering marginally with current economic policies. The only solution is to create a socialized sector of the economy designed to give work opportunities to everyone who wants them but cannot find them elsewhere.[28]

Robert Reich bluntly states the long-term nature of the neoliberal perspective and program: "We're building new frameworks. Administrations come and go. The frameworks can remain for generations."[29]

Neoliberals count on the capacity of this new program to mobilize support from a large number of people who recognize the need to think freshly about the country's broad range of unprecedented problems. It is not just economic revitalization that they seek, but social and political revitalization as well. As Charles Peters notes, that will require willingness to take risks—the risks that necessarily accompany opportunity.

> Risk is indeed the essence of the movement—the risk of the person who has the different idea in industry or in government. . . . Risk-taking is important not only in career terms but in the way one looks at the world and the possibilities it presents. If you see only a narrow range of choices, if you are a prisoner of conventional, respectable thinking, you are unlikely to find new ways out of our problems.[30]

Despite its respectable origins, neoliberalism seems at this point to be caught in much the same way that reform liberalism always was. It offers a plausible and in essence not very threatening route to social and economic improvement. However, when it comes to actual implementation, its program seems too radical for more than a small portion of it to be realized. Most difficult of all is mobilizing a constituency around a program designed to save capitalism when the capitalists themselves are demonstrably unenthusiastic. Only prolonged economic crisis, with more drastic solutions being urged from both the Left and Right, can really provide the context within which neoliberalism can gain strength enough to be a decisive force. If such developments occurred, however, neoliberalism could succeed to liberalism's center role on the American spectrum.

ADDITIONAL READINGS

Anderson, Charles W. *Pragmatic Liberalism*. Chicago: University of Chicago Press, 1990.

D'Souza, Dinesh. *Illiberal Education: The Politics of Race and Sex on Campus*. New York: The Free Press, 1991.

Etzioni, Amitai. *An Immodest Agenda: Rebuilding America before the 21st Century*. New York: McGraw-Hill, 1983.

Glazer, Nathan. *Affirmative Discrimination: Ethnic Inequality and Public Policy*. New York: Basic Books, 1975.

Hart, Gary. *A New Democracy: A Democratic Vision for the 1980s and Beyond*. New York: Quill, 1983.

Kristol, Irving. *Two Cheers for Capitalism*. New York: Basic Books, 1978.

Novak, Michael. *The Spirit of Democratic Capitalism*. New York: Simon & Schuster, 1982.

Peters, Charles. "A Neoliberal's Manifesto." *Washington Monthly*, May 1983.

Peters, Charles, and Phillip Kiesling, eds. *A New Road for America: The Neoliberal Movement*. New York: Madison Books, 1985.

Reich, Robert B. *The Work of Nations: Preparing Ourselves for 21st Century Capitalism*. New York: Alfred A. Knopf, 1991.

Reich, Robert B., and Ira Magaziner. *Minding America's Business: The Decline and Rise of the American Economy*. New York: Harcourt Brace Jovanovich, 1982.

Steinfels, Peter. *The Neoconservatives: The Men Who are Changing America's Politics*. New York: Simon & Schuster, 1979.

Thurow, Lester. *The Zero-Sum Society*. New York: Basic Books, 1980.

Tsongas, Paul. *The Road from Here: Liberalism and Realities in the 1980s*. New York: Alfred A. Knopf, 1981.

———. *A Call to Economic Arms: Forging a New American Mandate*. Boston: Foley, Hoag and Eliot, 1991.

PART III

CHALLENGES FROM THE LEFT

CHAPTER 6

REFORM LIBERALISM: RACE, GENDER, ECONOMICS, AND CULTURAL DIVERSITY

Middle-class reformers have always sought to expand and achieve equality in American life. In the 1960s black ministers led a multiracial coalition in an epic struggle for civil rights. In the late 1960s and early 1970s, a vigorous feminist movement arose to press for full citizenship for women. By the mid-1970s, it seemed clear to many reformers that the goals of racial and gender equality required a related struggle for economic rights and opportunities. In the 1980s and 1990s, the search for equality was expanded to include the goal of gaining acceptance for all the diverse cultures represented in the United States. Though focused in the nation's colleges and universities, this goal also applied more generally to workplaces, government, and cultural life. Efforts to achieve the goal generated a vigorous reaction from conservatives.

What these ideologies and movements share is the long-established tradition of reform liberalism, reaching back at least to the Progressive era of the early twentieth century. They all seek more of what they value—equality, dignity, quality of life—but within the givens and limits and procedures of the existing social and economic systems. For decades these ideologies and movements set the reform agenda for liberalism, often maximizing their leverage through vigorous use of the law and litigation. With the decline of liberalism and the capture of the courts by conservatives, however, their characteristic strategy of lobbying and litigation has become less effective.

These movements are primarily grounded in the middle class but may sometimes seek to reach out and offer leadership to working-class people. They are almost entirely oriented toward reform (change within existing structures and procedures), but occasionally they give rise to subgroups that seek reconstructive change (change that involves fundamentally different economic or social structures or cultural ways of thinking). Adherents seek change almost exclusively within their single area of concentration, but from time to time they see their concerns as overlapping with other reform groups, thus requiring some degree of integration.

As we explore the distinctive origins, values, and perspectives of each major ideology/movement, we try to identify the moments when the defining lines of race, gender, class, exclusively reform focus, and single-issue concentration are breached, or crossed, in some way. This identification is important because the impact of the reform ideologies depends very much on the extent to which they can integrate with each other, deepen into a consolidated critique and program, and emerge as a united force in politics.

EQUALITY

Racial Equality

Perhaps the oldest of these movements to achieve equality is in the area of race. Although much of the early antislavery agitation fell far short of advocating equality of the races, it was grounded in an important moral position. Whites were charged with responsibility for their relationships with other human beings, in this case black people. The same paternal sort of responsibility was involved in white relations with the indigenous population, native Americans. Despite the racist mythologies that arose to justify treating one group as property and the other as savages, this moral dimension combined with the commitment to equality as articulated in the Declaration of Independence to sustain a nagging opposition to the dominant practices of white America.

In the early decades of the nineteenth century, the movement's primary focus was, naturally, slavery. Slave insurrections were the basic manifestation of black resistance until free and escaped blacks took up the abolitionist campaign along with white ministers. The abolitionists provoked Southern reaction, expanded their ranks with Northern white support, and eventually helped trigger the Civil War. Much of this white support melted away soon after the war's close. Reconstruction, and thus federal government support for the welfare of blacks, effectively ended with a political party bargain in 1877 that conceded the presidency to the Republicans in exchange for the withdrawal of troops from the South.

For the next decades, blacks, with a scattering of white allies, were left to their own devices. Their circumstances in both the North and South were such that basic questions of life and survival dominated their concerns, rather than more advanced or subtle concepts of equality with whites. Out of their often desperate day-to-day struggles soon emerged the beginnings of an enduring dichotomy within the movement for racial equality. Some black leaders sought integration into white society as an eventual goal but economic and educational advancement for all blacks as a first priority. They were willing to wait until they had built a base of self-help experience and economic strength before laying claim to full equality. Other black leaders insisted that blacks could never become fully equal unless they demanded all their rights as American citizens from the start, even if that meant confrontation. They denied that this meant that only a few especially capable blacks would rise while the others were left behind.

This dichotomy reflected a basic disagreement involving both ends and means. The ends ranged from integration into white society as individuals and on essentially white terms to cultural pluralism, separatism, and nationalism—that is, an arm's length relationship between strong, self-sustaining black communities and white America. The means ranged from docile acceptance of white domination while blacks acquired education and economic strength to outright conflict to attain acceptance from whites as full citizens. The disagreements between Booker T. Washington and W. E. B. DuBois fit squarely here.

Washington believed that blacks had to improve their own economic and social status, individually and collectively, and needed white support to do so. He was willing to trade away immediate claims for citizenship rights in order to build black strength and believed that on the basis of such strength integration and equality ultimately would be possible. DuBois thought that no black achievements were safe unless they were protected politically by the right to vote and other means of exercising power; blacks therefore had to insist on all their rights immediately. He sought integration on terms of complete equality in which blacks as a group enjoyed fully equal status. Some black leaders, such as Marcus Garvey, believed that their only future lay in abandoning all efforts to enter white American society. They believed blacks needed to seek a national existence apart from the United States.

As Jim Crow laws and segregationist practices reached resurgent heights in the early twentieth century, DuBois, other militant blacks, and a number of white supporters formed the National Association for the Advancement of Colored People (NAACP). In those times, the goal of ending segregation was radical enough to be viewed as subversive. Nevertheless, the NAACP stood at the forefront of reform-oriented liberals in demanding for blacks the realization of the long-established liberal value of equality.

Following World War II, the movement gathered momentum, spurred in part by support from white liberals, the trade union movement, and the example of newly independent Third World countries. The NAACP artfully conducted a legal campaign challenging Jim Crow laws and segregation practices. Slowly segregation in public schools and then in all other public places fell before the Supreme Court ax. In an unprecedented display of courage in the face of multiple forms of intimidation, individual blacks soon began to press for the civil rights that had been denied them for centuries.

Perhaps the most inspiring reform leader of this era was the integrationist Reverend Martin Luther King, Jr. King not only organized and led a variety of bold and successful nonviolent campaigns among blacks in the

South but also developed a broad base of support among middle-class northern whites. His themes included racial equality and harmony, first put forth in the famous speech "I Have a Dream," which was delivered at a massive biracial rally in 1963, and the necessity of civil disobedience to unjust laws. The latter theme was summed up in his equally famous "Letter from Birmingham City Jail," written while King was awaiting trial for such disobedience, in which he declared:

> One has not only a legal but a moral responsibility to obey just laws. Conversely, one has a moral responsibility to disobey unjust laws. . . . A just law is a man-made code that squares with the moral law or the law of God. An unjust law is a code that is out of harmony with the moral law. . . . All segregation statutes are unjust because segregation distorts the soul and damages the personality. . . . Actually, we who engage in nonviolent direct action are not the creators of tension. We bring it out in the open where it can be dealt with.[1]

Despite the dangers King endured, culminating in his assassination in 1968, and the militancy he and his followers displayed, King's approach was challenged by other African-Americans for being too moderate. Black power advocates and such other leaders as Malcolm X charged that King's ultimate goal of integration into white society could only occur on white terms, which would keep blacks permanently in a second-class status. Malcolm X was a vigorous and effective speaker who stood for black assertiveness and immediate access to jobs, education, and full citizenship "by any means necessary." This was widely understood as condoning the use of violence where necessary, a view encouraged by Malcolm X's frequent references to "the ballot or the bullet." Malcolm X, the first of the great black leaders to be assassinated, was killed in 1965 in New York City.

The momentum of the civil rights movement carried over into the 1970s, but the tide began to turn as white reaction developed and conservatives came to power. Affirmative action efforts were blunted, and resistance to quotas in employment, housing, and education stiffened. Nevertheless, more and more African-Americans were elected to public office in the 1980s, including several big-city mayors, and a significant number of black professionals became visible in the middle class. The Reverend Jesse Jackson led his Rainbow coalition of blacks and whites in impressive campaigns for the Democratic presidential nomination in both 1984 and 1988. However, the income, occupation, education, health, and status of blacks as a group remained stalled at a level substantially below that of whites, and there appeared to be a distinct resurgence of racism in the early 1990s. Both African-American and other leaders began to question whether the average black was in fact better off than before the civil rights movement began.

In this context, black leaders again faced the dilemma of seeking white support without yielding to the kind of white premises and practices that would perpetuate dependency. Angela Davis, speaking in 1986 to the white women's movement, called for a genuinely multiracial membership and program that would reach out to black women.

> We must begin to create a revolutionary, multiracial women's movement that seriously addresses the main issues affecting poor and working class women. . . . An issue of special concern to Afro-American women is unemployment. . . . Black women scholars and professionals cannot afford to ignore the straits of our sisters who are acquainted with the immediacy of oppression in a way that many of us are not.[2]

Other African-Americans turned to the militancy of Malcolm X for inspiration, which led to a rebirth of popularity of his speeches from the 1960s. However, in the mainstream of black thought in this discouraging time appeared to be a renewal of the moral claim for white support so forcefully put forth by Martin Luther King. The historian Manning Marable, for example, stressed the still-dominating experience of slavery as a source of that moral claim.

> Is the democratic vision an illusion for AfroAmericans, or a dream deferred? . . . the faith of a people in bondage remains the moral guide for their descendants. The organic history of black Americans is a pattern of suffering and transcendence, of sacrifice and hope for the future. . . . The moral imperatives of the slave community still find their way into the discourse and programs of a Jesse Jackson.[3]

That such moral claims are effectively addressed only to "the agonized conscience of the liberal white middle class . . ." led Cornel West to be skeptical of gaining racial equality through populist majorities in the United States. His discouragement was expressed this way in 1986:

> It is important to note that the two most important public acts associated with black progress—the Emancipation Proclamation (1863) and the Brown vs. Board of Education case (1954)—were far removed from the collective will of the American people. In fact, Congress would not have passed either if consulted, and both would have lost in a national referendum.[4]

Despite the reverses of the 1980s and the feeling that momentum toward progress had about run out, there can be no doubt that the efforts of the 1960s and 1970s had a dramatic effect on the United States. Major new legislation was put on the books, and the legal rights of all citizens were greatly expanded. Not only AfricanAmericans, but also native Americans, Hispanics, Asian Americans, and other racial and ethnic minorities had been politicized and brought much closer to the mainstream of American life. The reality of full equality for all minorities remained elusive, of course, and gave both bitterness and new energy to the demand for racial equality in the 1990s.

Gender Equality

Because the movement for equality between the sexes in the United States always has been linked with that for equality between the races, it was not surprising that a new feminist movement burst upon the scene in the late 1960s. Feminists had made themselves individually heard in the eighteenth century and had been active in the abolitionist movement of the early nineteenth century. However, their most visible beginning lay in the Seneca Falls Convention of 1848 and its Declaration of Sentiments drafted by the convention organizers, particularly Elizabeth Cady Stanton. One of the prominent voices on the floor of that convention and the source of the decisive argument for the declaration's passage was the black abolitionist Frederick Douglass.

What feminists of that period sought should sound familiar. Their aims included voting equality, which took seven decades to achieve; legal equality, which is still unfulfilled; and genuine cultural-social equality, which lies even beyond that. These dimensions of equality have proved very difficult to wrest from patriarchal American society. Even blacks, long closely associated with feminists in the campaign to make equality a fact in the United States, have on occasion proved inconstant. The Equal Rights Association, established jointly by black abolitionists and white feminists before the Civil War, for example, essentially fell apart after the war over the issue of whether to grant black men the vote before granting it to women of all races.

For this reason, along with deep-seated white male resistance and denigration, feminists were forced to go it alone. So they did, pressing ever more vigorously for acceptance of a notion of equality that would allow women to vote. Suffrage became the exclusive focus of the women's movement for several decades. Ironically, it was achieved only when white male voters felt more threatened by the disruptive prospects of increasing (male) immigrant votes than those of women. Even then, leading anarchist-feminists like Emma Goldman were telling women that true emancipation would require far more than the right to vote and own property.

It took the multiple stirrings of minority movements for racial equality and white movements for social justice to reawaken the unfulfilled aspirations of women. The new movement, born in the 1960s, had both middle-class and radical origins and continues to have both moderate (though far-reaching) and radical goals. Middle-class women began with Betty Friedan's *The Feminine Mystique*. Friedan articulated the unexpressed sense of frustration and lack of "personhood" that many women felt in the midst of apparent affluence. A more radical critique was generated by women who were participants in the early civil rights and antiwar movements. Their critique grew in part out of their experiences in these movements. Though running the same risks as men, they were being patronized or exploited in intolerable ways by their "comrades."

The more radical women argued that men were acting out patriarchal dominance in ways that denied basic human dignity. This dominance was particularly galling when many such men announced they were in the process of building a new and better social order. For the liberal moderates in the 1970s, feminism meant equal pay for equal work, equal responsibility for child rearing and home maintenance, and full equality in career and life opportunities (necessitating, for example, legal access to divorce, abortion, and child support). These were significant demands to impose on the American social structure, as the strength of the soon-generated reaction testifies.

The actual gains of the women's movement since the late 1960s, though perceived to be significant, have been relatively modest. The Equal Rights Amendment never passed, and it remains on the table. Though the 1973 decision *Roe v. Wade* guaranteed access to safe, legal abortions, antichoice forces never quit trying to reverse or undermine it. Soon the federal protection of *Roe* will be gone, and the necessity to fight for a woman's right to choose will be back.

Though women entered the work force in record numbers, gains in higher-paying, traditionally male occupations were slight. Women make approximately seventy cents to each dollar earned by a male, in spite of equal opportunity laws and the institution of comparable worth in several states. Similarly, in the political arena, women constitute far from half of the elected officials of this nation. In 1990 women accounted for only 17 percent of those elected to state legislatures and 5 percent of those in Congress. Presently only two women serve in the United States Senate.

On the other hand, the public perceives great strides achieved by women—perhaps too many too soon. Not surprisingly, reaction has come from outside of the women's movement.

> Legal scholars have railed against the "equality trap." Sociologists have claimed that "feminist-inspired" legislative reforms have stripped women of special "protections." Economists have argued that well-paid working women have created a "less stable American family." And demographers . . . have legitimated the prevailing wisdom with so-called neutral data on sex ratios and fertility trends; they say they actually have the numbers to prove that equality doesn't mix with marriage and motherhood.[5]

There were contrasting studies to show that child care either damaged or improved child development. The theory that female-headed households resulted in dysfunctional (black) males resurfaced. Feminism was held responsible for the destruction of the family, and the destruction of the family was responsible for poverty, teenage pregnancy, crime, the decline in public education—practically all the social ills of the 1990s.

More troubling is the reaction that has come from within the women's movement. The feminism of twenty years ago was about "equality of opportunity in jobs and education, to our own political voice, to our right to safe access to abortion, and for child care."[6] However, as women took advantage of opportunities and moved into the work force, they encountered a second set of problems: how to have a career *and* a family?

In her 1981 book, *The Second Stage*, Betty Friedan again gave voice to the difficulties women (especially middle-class women) were having.

> It becomes clear that the great momentum of the women's movement for equality will be stopped, or somehow transformed, by collision or convergence with basic questions of survival in the 1980s."[7]

Women are working two jobs. The gains made in the outside world did not remove their responsibilities for home and family. Concepts such as "having it all," "the mommy track," "Superwoman," became common parlance as women struggled to take their place in the working world while retaining "their place" in the home world. The public/private split was impossible for them to maintain.

Feminist response to the problems of the second stage falls along a moderate to more radical spectrum. The moderate feminists see the backlash not to the gains, but to the *prospect* of gains. "The antifeminist backlash has been set off not by women's achievement of full equality but by the increased possibility that they might win it."[8] For these feminists, the agenda of twenty years ago is still top priority, that is, passage of the Equal Rights Amendment, passage of the National Freedom of Choice Act (seen as necessary due to the imminent reversal of *Roe v. Wade*), pay equity, child care, and equality of opportunity for all women for all jobs. The argument is that the problems women presently face will be vastly helped by accomplishment of the original goals. Continued pursuit of the basic agenda of the first stage is the solution, not the problem.

Feminists who fall somewhere between moderate and radical on the spectrum argue that experience has shown that achievement of basic rights and equality of opportunity are not sufficient. Two complementary strands compose this argument. The first is that the structure of the workplace and the home must be altered to fit the new reality. In the workplace, family-leave policies, flexible hours or job sharing practices, on-site child care, and other policies are necessary to make equal opportunity a reality. Similarly, men must learn to share not only the child rearing and housework but also the *responsibility* for child rearing and housework. In other words, this brand of feminism has moved from the "personal is political," to the "personal and productive is political."

The second strand is a complementary argument that would bring women's values, nurturing and caring, into both the workplace and the political arena. These feminists do not just want what men have or to behave as men have behaved.

> We did not move for equality only to get a few jobs that only men had before. We did not move to equality to exchange our old frustrations as housewives for the strokes and the heart attacks that are making the men die too young. We moved for a personhood for woman and an equal voice in our society, but if it was worth fighting for, we have to be true to our own basic values as women; the values of nurturing and of life, to which we subscribe.[9]

These feminists argue that women must be active, enact and win public and private policies that restructure the workplace and the family, enter and play the game on their own terms, but leave the basic rules intact.

The more radical feminists of this era have moved to a basic cultural level. They have taken the restructuring argument a giant step further. It is not enough to add nurturing women or more women's issues to the basic agenda—the entire agenda must be reconstructed. Carolyn Heilbrun's definition of feminism illustrates the argument:

> A feminist, as I use the word, questions the gender arrangements in society and culture (all societies and cultures) and works to change them; the desired transformation gives more power to women *while simultaneously challenging both the forms and the legitimacy of power as it is now established.* (Emphasis added)[10]

Works such as *Women's Ways of Knowing: The Development of Self, Voice, and Mind*[11] and *In a Different Voice: Psychological Theory and Women's Development*[12] argue that women *are* different creatures, but not biologically. Rather, they are cognitively different, which results in a different way of approaching the world and solving its problems. For example, "the responsibility orientation [tending to be females] is more central to those whose conceptions of self are rooted in a sense of connection and relatedness to others."[13] This results in a problem-solving style that tries to maintain personal relationships, create win-win situations, and generally lower the level of adversariness.

For these feminists, the basic problem lies in a culture dominated by the male way of approaching the world. Feminists must challenge not only the structure of the workplace and the family but also the very definitions and assumptions underlying these institutions. It cannot be done by simply adding feminist values to existing structures or getting more feminists into positions of power. The very structures and the nature of power itself must be changed—it requires a cultural transformation.

Obviously, these three response categories of feminists have similarly contrasting views of the next step. The more moderate feminists, those who believe the immediate problem continues to be the institution of the original goals, fight in the political arena. There are public-policy goals that can be met, for example, passage of the National Reproductive Freedom Act. It takes electing more feminists, and educating, lobbying, and pressuring the present elected officials.

Then there are the feminists who have given up on the traditional approach. In the forefront of this point of view is the National Organization of Women (NOW). Its argument is that the standard political parties and politicians have amply proved that they are unable to respond to feminist's concerns. The U.S. Senate Judiciary Committee hearings on the confirmation of Clarence Thomas to the United States Supreme Court was a galvanizing event for this position. As Patricia Ireland, NOW Executive

Vice President, said in her keynote speech to the 1991 national NOW conference in New York City:

> This movement will challenge incumbents who have abandoned the dream of equality and the hope of a decent quality of life for future generations on the planet and will challenge the present unresponsive two party system.[14]

Ellie Smeal, former president of NOW and founder of the Fund for the Feminist Majority, describes her vision of a new party as

> not just a new party, but one dedicated to equality for women, and an expanded bill of rights for the twenty-first century, including freedom from discrimination based on sex, race, sexual orientation or preference, religion, age, health condition or disability; the right to safe, legal, and accessible abortion and birth control; the right to adequate food, housing, health care, and education; to clean air and water; to a clean environment free of toxic waste; and the right to be free from violence.[15]

More moderate feminists find the NOW position untenable. As expressed by Marianne Means:

> A third party represents a political sideshow, something going on outside the main tent in which the real action is taking place. Those who join it leave behind whatever influence they may have exerted in the main arena.[16]

And:

> The folly of a third party might be excused if it had the slightest prospect of succeeding. . . . But women are not a political monolith, any more than men are. They are individuals who make up their minds individually.[17]

This disagreement illustrates a fundamental difference between these two strands of moderates—those who believe women are individuals with simply different policy/issue positions and those who believe women/feminists represent a different voice.

Finally, of course, the radical feminists argue that a third party would only be relevant if it attacked the entire structure of power and had transforming capabilities. They are more concerned with transcending the "polarization between women and women and between women and men to achieve the new human wholeness that is the promise of feminism."[18] "[T]he rights orientation is more common to those who define themselves in terms of separation and autonomy,"[19] that is, tend to be men. Whether in a third party, in one of the two existing parties, in an organization, or living and working day-to-day, the feminist responsibility is to continue to fight to transform the basic rules of the game, in whichever game she participates. For the radical feminist it is important not only to take part in the public domain but also to contribute to the redefinition of what it is to be public and to wield power.

Economic Equality

One of the most enduring of middle-class reform traditions is that of seeking greater economic equality. Embedded in notions of social justice and Christian equity, it took its modern form in reaction to the sharpening of inequality that occurred with capitalist industrialization. For some, it was simply the moral obligation to help the poor survive. For others, it implied limits on the actions of giant corporations, or guarantees of jobs or income for all. Most advocates of racial and gender equality also recognized the necessity of making jobs, income, and opportunities equally available to all. Some academics went on to urge reconstruction of the economy in the direction of public ownership and control (that is, democratic socialism).

In all of these instances, inequality in distribution of wealth and income—often along racial and gender lines—is recognized as a primary fact. Most reformers see economic inequality as an inevitable by-product of an economic system that is basically good (or, perhaps, merely tolerable or even undesirable but unchangeable). Such people devote themselves to seeking a more equitable distribution under the given circumstances of the present economy.

In the case of the academic democratic socialists, however, there is explicit understanding that the problem of inequality is linked to the existence of distinct social classes in which the upper, or ruling, class dominates the lower and working classes; fundamental change in the structure of the economy and social order is therefore required. The concept of class as a (or the) major source of division among people can also be used tactically, as we shall see, as a means of trying to unite people whose initial grounds for political action are based on race or gender.

The great bulk of advocates of greater economic equality are middle-class reform liberals (ministers, lawyers, academics, journalists) whose arguments often involve an assertion of rights to certain levels of income or to a job. Many issue a call for an economic bill of rights. A leading example is the 1986 National Conference of Catholic Bishops pastoral letter on Catholic social teaching and the U.S. economy entitled "Economic Justice for All." The bishops declare in their section on principal themes that all people have a right to a job and that society has a special obligation to the poor. They also say:

> We judge any economic system by what it does for and to people and by how it permits all to participate in it. The economy should serve people, and not the other way around. . . . When people are without a chance to earn a living, and must go hungry and homeless, they are being denied basic rights. Society must ensure that these rights are protected. In this way, we will ensure that the minimum conditions of economic justice are met for all our sisters and brothers.[20]

Similarly, the former law school dean Paul Savoy, writing in *The Nation* in 1991, called for adding to the Constitution such affirmative rights as (1) rights to adequate nutrition, clothing, housing, health care, and other social services needed for basic human dignity; (2) rights of families to special protection and assistance; (3) the right of individuals to an adequate education; (4) rights to a job, if necessary in the public sector, with equal pay for equal work; (5) rights to a broad array of social welfare services; and (6) rights to a healthy environment.[21] Savoy's call was accompanied by detailed suggestions on how such a new bill of rights might be drafted and enacted by a popular movement devoted to a new vision of American society.

Full employment is at the center of this movement for greater economic equality, and creation of an enforceable right to a job often lies behind the goal of an economic bill of rights. Academic advocates of greater economic equality also endorse full employment and other economic rights and go on to justify them as the extension of democracy from political life to economic and social life. One example, from a book by three well-known democratic socialist economists, is shown in Table 6.1.

The commitment to economic rights as the extension of democracy is a principle of long-standing, as this 1966 statement by the prominent essayist and critic Irving Howe makes clear:

> To preserve democracy as a political mode without extending it into every crevice of social and economic life is to allow it to become increasingly sterile, formal, ceremonial. To nationalize an economy without enlarging democratic freedoms is to create a new kind of social exploitation. Radicals and liberals may properly and fraternally disagree about many things; but upon this single axiom concerning the value of democracy, this conviction wrung from the tragedy of our age, politics must rest.[22]

Most of these middle-class reformers assume that democracy is in full flower in American politics and needs only to be extended to the workplace and throughout the society through the creation and enforcement of new legal rights. This is a language that is understandable and appealing to many Americans and so may offer greater hope for success. However, the concept of class is much less familiar, and many Americans are uncomfortable or fearful when it is applied to the United States. Many democratic socialists, therefore, avoid explicit reference to class or the word *socialism*, preferring instead such euphemisms as *economic democracy*.

To build a political movement capable of challenging dominant orthodoxies and ruling elites, however, some broad uniting umbrella must be found to bring together people who have been mobilized by single issues (peace, the environment, nuclear energy) or special distinctions (race, gender). One approach is clearly the all-encompassing concept of social class. Some reformers have sought to substitute class and the general notion of (shared) economic deprivation for the otherwise divisive and fragmenting appeals of race or gender or special issues. Others use a second approach and simply call for a coalition of all groups with a reform agenda under the banner of a new (third) political party.

Table 6.1   A Typical Economic Bill of Rights

I. **Right to economic security and equity**

   1. A decent job
   2. Solidarity wages, comparable pay, and equal employment opportunity
   3. Public child care and community service centers
   4. A shorter standard work week and flexible work hours
   5. Flexible price controls

II. **Right to a democratic workplace**

   6. Public commitment to democratic trade unions
   7. Workers' right to know and to decide
   8. Democratic production incentives
   9. Promotion of community enterprises

III. **Right to chart our economic future**

   10. Planning to meet human needs
   11. Democratizing investment
   12. Democratic control of money
   13. Promoting community life
   14. Environmental democracy
   15. Democratizing foreign trade

IV. **Right to a better way of life**

   16. Reduced military spending
   17. Conservation and safe energy
   18. Good food
   19. A national health policy
   20. Lifetime learning and cultural opportunities
   21. Payment for home child care in single-parent households
   22. Community corrections and reduced crime control spending
   23. Community needs information and reduced advertising expenditures
   24. Equitable taxation and public allocation of resources

SOURCE: Samuel Bowles, David M. Gordon, and Thomas E. Weisskopf, *Beyond the Waste Land: A Democratic Alternative to Economic Decline* (New York: Anchor, 1983), p. 294.

An example of the former is the academic socialist Ann Ferguson, whose most recent work is entitled *Sexual Democracy: Women, Oppression, and Revolution*. She explicitly seeks to use class (and even to expand upon it) as a means of uniting feminists and antiracists in a coherent analysis and program. She says in her conclusion:

> Feminists and leftists with a class and race consciousness must realize that challenging the present social order involves both effective coalition strategies for uniting women and men across race and class boundaries and an explicitly socialist-feminist agenda for reconstructing the welfare state. . . . Only if and when a full democratic socialist economy is achieved . . . could we expect to institutionalize an antisexist and antiracist state. . . . Feminists and progressives must find ways to make political and friendship bonds across gender, racial, and economic-class lines to unite in the long, complex struggle for such a socialist, feminist, and antiracist program.[23]

A perhaps equally ambitious, if less abstract, attempt to bring about an alliance among reformers is that of the third-party advocates. The call for a third party came in the early 1990s from diverse reform sources, ranging from the National Organization of Women to academics and activists to the publisher of *The Progressive*, a Left-liberal journal. The latter, Matthew Rothschild, issued a call in 1991 for a unifying vehicle on the Left that may serve as an illustration of all of these. Echoing the sentiments of many reform activists, he says:

> The left in America is splintered into a thousand fragments: environmentalists, anti-interventionists, gay and lesbian rights activists, feminists, pro-choice defenders, insurgent labor unionists, consumer activists, civil libertarians, human rights advocates, social reformers, anti-racist workers, Native American rights activists, and disability rights activists. We're all doing good important work, but we're disconnected and atomized. This not only contributes to loneliness and burnout, it also adds to our general ineffectiveness. We are far less than the sum of our parts.[24]

Rothschild sees the Democratic party as a trap, as do most other serious reformers on the Left. Where they disagree is over the issue of how best to unify the Left—in the relative isolation of a third party, which offers purity and defeat, or through some other educational and organizational vehicle.

Regardless of the vehicle chosen, this wide spectrum of reformers is asking precisely the right question, and one that we shall return to again in our final chapter: is it possible for reform advocates, including radicals, populists, and reform liberals, to find some way of uniting their forces to make an impact politically? If so, they might reconstruct both the ideological spectrum and the practical directions of American politics. If not, the status quo or its conservative successor seem likely to endure in power.

CULTURAL DIVERSITY

In the late 1980s and early 1990s, the cause of race and gender equality began to develop a more global perspective and take on a new form— *cultural diversity*, or *multiculturalism*. These terms imply greater awareness of, respect for, and ability to communicate with the other cultures of the world, members of which greatly outnumber Americans. Some of them are represented in the United States by minorities such as Hispanics, African Americans, Asian and Pacific Islanders, and native Americans (often known collectively as Third World People or people of color). Better ability to understand and communicate with other cultures of the world was a principle that drew ready support from the international side of the business community, as well as from those who saw the crisis of global ecology as a compelling issue.

Promoting awareness of and ability to cope with cultural diversity made at least abstract sense in the light of the fact that a rapidly growing proportion of all Americans are people of color and the apparent imperative that the United States adapt to a competitive global economy involving many other cultures. When purposefully applied in the American educational system, this effort quickly sparked a major ideological and political controversy. Why and how it did so are briefly examined in this section. The major significance of the cultural-diversity movement, however, may lie in the way it served to revive and refocus the dying neoconservative ideology. (This development is reserved for Chapter 8.)

In the United States the educational system is never far from the center of politics. It is, after all, the principal means by which the traditions, culture, and beliefs of the society are transmitted to rising generations. For employers it is the source of a future skilled work force; for individuals it is the chief route to social mobility. The K-12 system has the broadest impact and costs the most, but higher education, with its prestige and visibility, is the fulcrum of change and the fountainhead of future K-12 personnel and practices.

The educational system is also preeminently a middle-class institution in its social function and makeup, and in its do-gooder professional ethos. Because of its social makeup of mostly service-oriented teachers and other middle-class professionals, it has always been a willing change agent for the society and at the forefront of efforts toward social improvement. Ever since *Brown v. Board of Education of Topeka* (the 1954 Supreme Court decision ending legal segregation), the educational system has been (controversially) on the cutting edge of the movement for racial equality. Gender equality as well as ecological and environmental awareness naturally followed as they were embraced by many middle-class professionals.

For all these reasons, the educational system operates in a context of continuing criticism. The criticism of the early 1980s was summarized in widely acclaimed books such as Allan Bloom's *The Closing of the American Mind*[25] and E. D. Hirsch's *Cultural Literacy*,[26] and in the public speeches and actions of the then Secretary of Education William Bennett. Together, they argued that the educational system had lost touch with fundamental values and principles and that the traditions of Western civilization were simply not being adequately inculcated in the youth of America.

Viewed analytically, the issues surrounding education in America—and particularly the crucial component of higher education—can be seen in two categories. The first category has to do with access—who is admitted to colleges and universities, what they find there in the way of people like themselves (faculty, staff, and students), and the conditions that help them to feel at home and able to learn. The second category has to do with what will be learned—a combination of what is taught in the official curriculum and what is communicated and received by students through the structure and practice of colleges and universities.

Both sets of issues were addressed vigorously by the reform agenda of university educators in a sustained program cumulating in the 1980s and 1990s. Admission practices were changed to recruit minority students aggressively, sometimes favoring them in admission standards and financial aid. Faculty hiring and retention efforts shifted toward affirmative action for women and minorities, sometimes at the cost of standards as they had been understood in the older white male EuroAmerican terms. Some universities sought to create conditions that would enable a critical mass of minority students and faculty to function comfortably on their campuses.

A related thrust was the movement to institute multicultural literacy in the curriculum. The substance, concepts, and sources of the curricula of most courses had to be changed to reflect diverse cultural perspectives. Western culture could no longer dominate, and lesser-known (to most Americans) authors and perspectives had to be presented on nearly equal terms. On some campuses this meant requiring ethnic-studies courses or using course materials that challenged dominant EuroAmerican interpretations of history and/or truth itself.

Academics who came together under the banner of multicultural literacy sought to put women and minorities back into history, in part so that today's female and minority students could see people like themselves and learn of their contributions, and in part to tell the story in a less biased or celebratory fashion. Although not done at the cost of abandoning Western self-knowledge, these changes did have the effect of making Western culture less exclusively the source of all civilization. In reaction to Bloom's and Hirsch's critique, the authors of a 1988 manifesto declared such views outdated in today's world:

> Both writers seem to think that most of what constitutes contemporary American and world culture was immaculately conceived by a few men in Greece, around 900 B.C., came to its full expression in Europe a few centuries later, and began to decline around the middle of the nineteenth century.[27]

What is at stake in the eyes of supporters of the multicultural movement is an image of how the United States could come to know itself better, including its own biophysical environment, and then to develop a higher quality of dignity and mutual respect among all citizens. The same 1988 manifesto states their purposes comprehensively:

> Americans need to have a better grasp of the European heritage and a clearer understanding of American history and culture, to know its depths and soul. Americans need to broaden their awareness and understanding of the cultures of the rest of the world. Other histories and cultures reveal ancestry and knowledge that has bearing on who we are and where we are going. By understanding more about our immediate locale, the native soil we stand on and the other living things that share our world, we expand our imaginations and expand our culture.[28]

Changes of this magnitude in institutions of such importance could not fail to provoke dramatic reactions. A remarkable outpouring in the 1990s of books, articles, and speeches charged that the universities had been captured by radicals of the 1960s, who were now the tenured professoriate. Moreover, it was argued that pressures from militant women and minority students had caused university administrators to enforce discriminatory standards in admissions, hiring, and retention, as well as to institute absurd curricular changes that trivialized the great traditions of Western civilization. Worst of all, it was said, these faculty, students, and administrators combined to deny free speech to all who dissented.

The term used to summarize all these lamentable changes was *political correctness* (frequently, just *PC*), meaning a slavish adherence to a single doctrine of mindless multicultural egalitarianism. This reaction is explored in detail later, but the following example may serve as representative:

> Ostensibly, the aim of PC is to protect minorities and enforce awareness of their dignity and human worth. In practice, it destroys free speech, intellectual standards, and the ethical-moral canons on which western democracy (as yet there is no other kind) is based.[29]

The attack on the new approach to history reached a crescendo in 1991 when a Smithsonian Museum exhibit in Washington, D. C., entitled "The West as America," presented some revisionist interpretations of how the United States had acted (and understood itself) during the years of western expansion. Not only neoconservative authors and magazines but also several U.S. senators, joined in attacking the "political correctness" of the commentary accompanying familiar paintings. This led some spokespersons for the cultural-diversity movement to point out the cultural and ideological dominance that were at stake in the conflict.

> "Political correctness" ranks with the swine flu epidemic and comet Kohoutek as molehills transformed into mountains by a gullible media. . . . In most assaults on "political correctness," the bogeyman is "multiculturalism"—the movement to expand subjects like history and literature to include the experiences of previously neglected groups. Critics of "The West as America," however, are after larger game—nothing less than an entire interpretation of the American past. What they want is the kind of relentlessly celebratory account of American development so common in the 1950s. . . . Today, it seems, the New World Order requires a West free of exploitation, racism, and other inconvenient realities of American life.[30]

Clearly, the process of education (and particularly higher education) will remain an arena for ideological and political conflict. How we understand our history and our culture(s) is integral to who we think we are and what we want to be. Such questions are highly charged politically, even (or perhaps particularly) at times when our formal politics do not seem able to focus on choices of future directions. Educational institutions and practices not only offer a special opportunity for middle-class reform efforts but also serve to mobilize the reaction of others—both conservatives and the less activist lower classes.

THE BASIC VALUES: REFORM LIBERALISM

These four movements (for racial equality, gender equality, economic equality, and cultural diversity) were often uneasy allies and, occasionally, competitors for the leadership role on the reform side of liberalism. They have been set on their own by that belief system's decline. Indeed, it can be argued that their very aggressiveness is in part to blame for the strains on liberalism and the reaction that led to its fragmentation. In any event, these movements now have no joint home; each is obliged to find its own way as a special interest.

At the level of basic values and beliefs, the movements still have much in common. It is precisely because of what they share and what they are developing in the way of changes that they remain potentially powerful reform vehicles on the American political spectrum. None can achieve more than part of its goals by itself. To fulfill their specific goals and their larger potential, they must reach a fuller integration than ever occurred within the liberal framework. What we shall see in this section is that the *potential* clearly exists for a coherent new package of 1990s-style reform values and beliefs. Realization of such potential, of course, is an entirely different matter.

As might be expected of movements long on the cutting edge of liberal reform, the definitions of the basic values that underlie the programmatic movements tend to the left of the U.S. spectrum. Instead of individualistic solutions, for example, each of the four more or less naturally turns to collective responsibility. The use of government or other collective means to achieve goals comes much more readily to these movements than to most of the other belief systems. This may be inherent in the public nature of the goods they seek, but it is nevertheless distinctive. Their adherents also all stress solidarity among the members of their sharply defined constituencies. They have a stronger sense of community and mutual obligations than do most of the belief systems. Their sense of what it means to be an individual includes less personal responsibility or isolation and is more an acknowledgment of interdependence among people.

Those in all four movements grant importance to property rights but rank certain other rights ahead of property. In particular, they give first place to the intangible dimensions of their highest values. These highest values all involve *conditions* or *qualities* rather than merely tangible elements. Status, dignity, respect, peace, clean air and water, natural beauty, and the reduction of hazardous risks to various kinds to life and health— all these values involve at least some aspects that are unmeasurable, especially in monetary terms. They can only be sensed or felt and are certainly not reducible to cost-benefit calculations.

Few people from any of these movements make the connection between the rules of the political-legal arena and the social and economic conditions that lie behind them. They do not see democracy as limited or denied by virtue of inequalities of wealth or power in the private world. They trust that their goals are all available through the political world alone. In other words, in this respect these movements are truly *liberal* belief systems.

The movements are making their most original contributions with respect to the values of equality and freedom. Here they are pressing forcefully toward new definitions with far-reaching implications.

We noted earlier that the movements for racial and gender equality have given the principle of equality its dynamism in the last three decades. They began by accepting liberalism's belief in equality of opportunity at face value. They merely sought to make that notion of equality real by obtaining full citizenship rights for minorities and women, mainly through litigation. For a while, obtaining the right to vote and equal access to jobs were wholly engaging tasks. The movements met with and had to overcome layers of resistance built from centuries of unconcern and semiconscious unwillingness to yield white male prerogatives.

The attempt to make equality of opportunity real soon raised new questions. Clearly, advocates of racial and gender equality could not be satisfied with merely formal definitions of the principle. They would have had to close their eyes to the social and economic facts. As a group, minorities and women were less educated or trained for the jobs that carried the higher salaries, security, and status. However, not just a lack of skills stood in the way. In many cases long-established practices had perpetuated patterns based on past experience (or discrimination). Seniority rules, for example, favored those who already possessed particular skills or qualifications. Apprenticeship opportunities often were allocated to the sons of craftsmen who had long been established in a given trade. More generally, national patterns of assigning certain jobs almost exclusively to one race or sex were rooted deeply in American cultural traditions and proved hard to alter by purely legal means. Indeed, they were hard to alter by any means. People, including the very minorities and women whose interests were at stake, had to come to *think* differently from before. This is precisely what put these movements at the cutting edge of change in the general understanding of equality.

In short, the liberal principle of equality of opportunity simply was not adequate to the kinds of changes these movements sought. The supplementary notion of affirmative action was tried for a while. It meant that special efforts had to be made to recruit minorities and women for particular jobs. When equally capable people were found, minorities or women should be given precedence in hiring or admission. Affirmative action was seen as a means of compensating for past patterns of discrimination. It didn't work well for two basic reasons. The first was that there were far too few minorities and women in the appropriate educational and skill categories to fill the jobs that were available. The social, cultural, and economic facts of life in the United States were so entrenched that the society simply could not quickly produce a whole new mix of people with the requisite backgrounds and aspirations. The second reason was equally powerful. Most white males as well as some minorities and women resisted affirmative action either openly or subtly. The notion seemed to deny individual merit and personal achievement as the bases for advancement, running counter to long-established values. Many argued it would lower the quality of performance overall. It was also resisted as another instance of government-promulgated social engineering. Even with the supplementary effects of affirmative action, equality of opportunity as a basic principle would require decades to generate real equality in jobs alone, and jobs were only one of several important parts of the notion of equality that these movements sought.

What racial and gender equality required and what these movements had to press for, consciously or not, was something that would reach the deepest social, economic, and particularly cultural levels where the roots of inequality lay. The movements were forced, in other words, beyond equality of opportunity and toward something like equality of condition. In the American context, however, the latter was much too drastic a step to be taken all at once. Understandably, the movements' attempts were reluctant and tentative. In the 1990s, such aspirations are still far from complete or even conscious, and many adherents to these movements' beliefs probably would deny them. However, there is no other place for them to go. Either they confront the underlying reasons for inequality, or they content themselves with a *very* long timetable for achieving the equality they genuinely seek.

An analogous process seems to be underway in the understanding of freedom, this time with the economic right and equality movements in the forefront. They are not advocates of freedom in the traditional liberal sense of freedom from government restraints on the use of property. Instead, they identify other threats to the individual—threats that would destroy the life or quality of life of that individual as well as succeeding generations. They seek a freedom from fear and destruction; they seek a freedom to hope, to look forward to continued human life on the planet. There is more than touch of genuine conservatism in this changed definition: for almost the first time, explicit consideration is being given to the needs and conditions of life for generations yet unborn. Sacrifices are to be made by people today in order that future needs may be better served.

This sort of freedom can be thought of as a vast expansion of the idea of individual rights. It makes them collective and adds new dimensions to "life, liberty, and the pursuit of happiness." It relocates the major threats to individual development and fulfillment opportunities. The danger to freedom now comes from rigid and technocratic corporate and government policies that endanger the earth, land, and sky—and people.

This new definition of freedom also involves fundamental change at the cultural level. It requires Americans to think differently about basic personal priorities and social purposes. Individually, people might have to restructure their personal values. Affluence might have to give way to survival, perhaps including vast new transfer programs to other nations. As a society, the United States would have to become less technological, much less profit oriented, and less militaristic. Merely to state such imperatives may make the prospect of change seem highly unlikely. It is. However, this is the *direction* in which the movements' beliefs and goals lead.

Underlying such changes is a more optimistic view of human nature. People can be more collectively oriented, willing to sacrifice their immediate wants for the sake of their children and future benefits that they might not realize themselves. This kind of change is similar to what the movements for racial and gender equality are also asking of Americans. All four movements think about the character of society in longer-range terms than has been usual in the American experience. This change in orientation is quite fundamental and not easily accomplished. Yet, all four of these programmatic movements seem to point in this same general direction.

PROBLEMS AND PROSPECTS: THE QUESTION OF INTEGRATION

Each of the four movements carries with it the basic dilemma of reform liberalism. On the one hand, they see their respective problem area as *the* problem that the nation must somehow resolve in order to make good on its basic values and goals. In their early stages, they tend to hold to the view that all that is really required to solve the problem is for people of good will to reach an adequate understanding, add to their numbers, and work together to bring the matter to the attention of both the public and policymakers. Then the currently wrong or mistaken policies can be replaced by more appropriate versions. Many advocates never go beyond this sort of analysis.

As movements progress, however, some people recognize that in fact a number of policymakers are not just mistaken about the correct policy. Some officials are strongly committed, with the support of many constituents, to carrying out the wrong policies. This perception generally leads to an attempt to work hard to replace such policymakers at the next election. Less often, these people see that the wrong policies endure or recur despite changes in officials. This realization can lead to efforts to reform particular government institutions.

Each movement has worked hard and achieved significant results. Nevertheless, the problems they set out to solve seem barely ameliorated. At the same time, each set of beliefs has begun to inch farther left on the American spectrum. Even this slight movement has left them feeling just a bit exposed and perhaps vulnerable to the uncomfortable charge of being extremist. This is particularly true with respect to the values of equality and freedom, where change is greatest and increasingly difficult to conceal. Each movement is caught in the same powerful bind: inadequate results but excessive reputation.

The dilemma posed is essentially that of the conflict between a *liberal* analysis and preferred approach to solution and a *radical* goal that can only be achieved through a more radical analysis and solution. Each movement would prefer to see its problem as isolated, separate, compartmentalized, *and* as capable of being solved without fundamental challenge to or change in basic American values, economic structures, or social and cultural traditions and practices.

The perception of a major problem, however important and personally consuming, as part of a more general set of problems facing the social order—and at the same time requiring change in the basic values, structures, and cultural patterns of the society—is truly staggering. Those who arrive at this perception are in danger of simply becoming paralyzed by it. The easiest and most natural response they can make, therefore, is to deny their own insight, go about their business, and keep on trying to resolve things without threatening any important societal underpinnings.

However, problems do not seem to get solved this way. So the pressure to move toward deeper analysis and more fundamental solutions continues to build. All the time, of course, new generations of recruits to any given movement insist on giving the established reform methods a full try. They resist extremism until all other remedies have been proved clearly insufficient. The movement is caught between being mainstream enough to draw new supporters and convincing even its long-term adherents that mainstream remedies really will not work. Each policy change actually accomplished provides ammunition to those who want to give the established liberal procedures every possible opportunity to deliver before they will even consider more drastic alternatives.

What if all these problems really *are* connected, perhaps all products of the same basic causes? The deeper analysis from the radical Left argues that what really prevents these movements from achieving their ends are some intimately interconnected factors that lie at the most basic level of American values and economic and social structures. In short, the problem is a capitalist economy, complicated by racism, patriarchy, and other supporting values.

The radical description of the capitalist system sounds terribly crude, particularly to reform liberals. They have heard it many times before and each time have resisted the conclusions that the radical arguments urge upon them. If they had not, they would no longer be reform liberal advocates of movement goals. Reform liberals are in constant dialogue with radicals to their left and mainstream liberals to their right. Theirs is a middle position that *they* have come to treasure, just as liberals do in relation to the broader spectrum. It has the merit of being (usually) safe and yet more satisfying than the liberal avoidance of commitment.

A major factor distinguishing reform liberals and radicals, and also serving to preserve the former's position despite its frustrating dilemma, is the boundary between procedural and substantive democracy. We have stressed that liberals, and all the programmatic movements with them, are totally committed to the procedural version. This means that they look almost exclusively at the political-legal arena when they think about democratic rights or the enforceable scope of equality. They accept the notion of a wall of separation between the political world, where equality is a properly enforceable right, and the social-economic world, where inequality reigns without consequences for democracy. It does not matter that this amounts to a logical contradiction; what does matter is that it is a basic tenet of liberal faith and endures as such.

This acceptance of the wall of separation as right and proper is a major bulwark of reform liberalism. As long as it stands, faith in the capacity of the liberal-procedural system is a necessary ingredient—or else the programmatic movements have no basis for hope that they will someday succeed. The alternative, of course, is to breach the wall and begin to see social, economic, and cultural factors as coherently integrated with the (no longer separate) political world and as controlling outcomes within it. Once this happens, new explanations for the lack of success of any of the programmatic movements become possible. All of a sudden, there are no more mysteries about why those movements are constantly frustrated.

As already suggested, such an explanation and the remedies it would suggest might prove paralyzing—more paralyzing, perhaps, than the reform liberal dilemma was frustrating. Many Americans shrink from an explanation that implies the necessity or desirability of decisive action to effect change. To commit oneself as fully as is required to accomplish such decisive action can threaten one's career, social relations, and eventually one's personal identity and entire life adjustment. This is more than most middle-class people bargain for when they set out to help solve what they believe to be a minor problem troubling their otherwise satisfactory social order.

ADDITIONAL READINGS

Allen, Robert L. *Black Awakening in Capitalist America*. New York: Doubleday, 1969.

Belenky, Mary Field, et al. *Women's Ways of Knowing: The Development of Self, Voice, and Mind*. New York: Basic Books, 1986.

Bond, Julian. *A Time to Speak, a Time to Act*. New York: Simon and Schuster, 1972.

Davis, Angela. *Women, Culture, and Politics*. New York: Vintage Books, 1990.

Deloria, Vine, Jr. *We Talk, You Listen: New Tribes, New Turf*. New York: Macmillan, 1970.

Eisenstein, Zillah, ed. *Capitalist Patriarchy and the Case for Socialist Feminism*. New York: Monthly Review Press, 1979.

Evans, Sara. *Personal Politics: The Roots of Woman's Liberation in the Civil Rights Movement and the New Left.* New York: Alfred A. Knopf, 1979.

Friedan, Betty. *The Feminine Mystique.* New York: Norton, 1963.

_____. *The Second Stage.* New York: Dell Publishing, 1981.

Gilligan, Carol. *In a Different Voice: Psychological Theory and Women's Development.* Cambridge, Mass.: Harvard University Press, 1982.

Hewlett, Sylvia Ann. *A Lesser Life: The Myth of Women's Liberation in America.* New York: William Morrow, 1986.

King, Martin Luther, Jr. *Why We Can't Wait.* New York: New American Library, 1964.

Marable, Manning. *How Capitalism Underdeveloped Black America.* Boston: South End Press, 1983.

Mitchell, Juliet. *Woman's Estate.* New York: Vintage Books, 1970.

Rendon, Armando. *Chicano Manifesto.* New York: Macmillan, 1971.

CHAPTER 7

WORKING-CLASS REFORM: PROGRESSIVE POPULISM, LABOR, AND THE RAINBOW

Populism refers to the effort by ordinary citizens to restore power and opportunity to themselves by confronting the wealth and power of big government, big business, and big labor. The label comes from the 1890s movement, which challenged the banking industry, the big corporations, and both major political parties through a program that would have claimed popular control of the economy and restored economic opportunity for individuals. This historical version of populism also involved, as minor elements, the reassertion of rural communities' traditional values, such as strict religion, nativism, patriarchal family structures, and often racism.

Progressive populists of the 1990s particularly emphasize the more equitable distribution of wealth, income, *and* political power. They believe that democracy requires full acceptance of minorities, women, and other disadvantaged groups; only a community-grounded, bottom-up process of decision making is capable of reempowering ordinary citizens. *Conservative* populists (analyzed in Chapter 8) are more concerned with social issues, that is, abortion, prayer in public schools, crime, and changed relations between the races and genders. They are often opposed to the social changes of the last decades and assign a lower priority than the progressive populists to the bottom-up kind of democracy.

Jesse Jackson and the Rainbow coalition were the principal national electoral vehicle for asserting the progressive populist position in the 1980s. Other prominent figures who describe themselves as progressive (or "democratic") populists include Senators Tom Harkin and Barbara Mikulski, former Texas Secretary of Agriculture Jim Hightower, and writer-activists such as Harry Boyte, Studs Terkel, Kevin Phillips, and Gar Alperovitz. Today's progressive populism also encompasses the reform efforts of many grass roots community organizations, local labor unions, minorities' and women's groups, and individual activists. Rank and file labor struggles (strikes, job preservation, boycotts) and local issues often serve as a catalyst for community-based coalitions of disparate groups.

New in the 1990s, and giving a sharp edge to this revived progressive populism, is the dramatic upward redistribution of wealth and income

111

accomplished during the Reagan years. Senator Harkin saw this clearly in 1985.

> The populist movement is built on the premise that freedom and democratic institutions depend on the widest possible dissemination of wealth and power. But we've come to the point where too few people have too much money and too much power—we haven't seen this kind of imbalance since the late 1800s.[1]

Five years later, the celebrated Republican strategist and self-described conservative populist Kevin Phillips published his fourth major book entitled *The Politics of Rich and Poor: Wealth and the American Electorate in the Reagan Aftermath.*[2] In it he documents and deplores this upward redistribution. Reversing a career's commitments, Phillips declares his expectation and his hopes for a surge of progressive populism that could activate the Democratic party and redirect the course of American public policy.

LINKS TO THE PAST

Today's progressive populism is the principal heir of the social democracy tradition in the United States. This tradition reaches back to prerevolutionary days and forward through Thomas Paine and Thomas Jefferson to the women's rights and abolitionist efforts of the early nineteenth century, the trade union struggles of the 1880s, and the agrarian populism of the 1890s. Populism has always been the mass base for the most radical change seekers of any period in American history. Other ideologies, such as anarchism, socialism, or the more recent economic democracy, have had highly visible advocates and made dramatic appeals for working-class support. However, the great bulk of Americans on the Left have remained populist in their attitudes and actions.

In the twentieth century, particularly in the 1930s, Populists combined with labor organizers, a few Progressives, and some Socialists to keep alive a genuinely American radical-democratic tradition. While it continued in muted form through World War II, populism was nearly crushed by a combination of conservative and liberal attacks during the cold war aftermath. In the 1960s, however, the tradition was reborn, first as the (mostly student) New Left, focused on civil rights and opposition to the Vietnam War, and then as a claim for economic opportunity and citizen empowerment.

Because the New Left lacked economic analysis or a program and because the times were relatively good for most people, it never reached much beyond its initial student constituency. However, many individuals who were politicized by the civil rights, antiwar, feminist, and student movements of the 1960s soon began to seek a deeper explanation for the poverty, discrimination, militarism, and corporate dominance that they saw in effect. They began to focus on the structure and unequal distribution patterns of the American economy and on the lack of real political power in the hands of ordinary citizens.

One of the first expressions of the move toward economic analysis and prescription came in the early 1970s. Jack Newfield and Jeff Greenfield published *A Populist Manifesto: The Making of a New Majority*, declaring their purposes in this way:

> This manifesto is . . . an effort to return to American politics the economic passions jettisoned a generation ago. Its fundamental argument is wholly unoriginal: some institutions and people have too much money and power, most people have too little, and the first priority of politics must be to redress the balance. For the past two decades, most of conservative politics has been based on fear—fear of Communists, fear of blacks, fear of crime. We believe the only antidote to fear the only thing deeper than fear, is self-interest. Thus, the political appeal of the program we suggest in this manifesto is based not on moralistic or humanitarian grounds, but on pure self-interest.[3]

The twin pillars of progressive populism are (1) economic redistribution and opportunity, meaning jobs, adequate income, and access to essential services (education, health care, housing) for all; and (2) democratic empowerment of ordinary citizens, so that they can control the forces, particularly the immediate local ones, that affect their everyday lives. When the economy is relatively prosperous and most people have the services they need, as seemed to be the case in the late 1960s, populism tends to give priority to the second of these pillars. When times are hard, however, economic redistribution regains first place in populist rhetoric and organizing strategy.

For these reasons, the rebirth of populism was accompanied in the late 1960s and early 1970s by post-New Left writings that used the appeal of democracy and sought its extension to the economy. These writers called for both economic democracy and democratic socialism, terms that were not always carefully distinguished.

The term *economic democracy* came into general use with the California campaign of Tom Hayden for the U.S. Senate. His "campaign for economic democracy" remained a loose alliance of local organizations devoted to the general cause and not any single candidate.[4]

Hayden was a founding member of the New Left who helped write its famous Port Huron Statement in 1962. His own career illustrates one of the tracks by which people came to be economic democrats. His 1980 book, *The American Future: New Visions beyond Old Frontiers*, is one of the major documents of the movement. It sets forth a complete agenda of needed policy changes and a design for democratizing the society. Another somewhat deeper and more programmatic book that helped give the movement its name is Martin Carnoy and Derek Shearer's *Economic Democracy: The Challenge of the 1980s*.[5] The authors are both California based, one an economist and the other an urban planner, respectively. Both are deeply involved in local and state politics as economic democrats.

Many other reform movements of the late 1960s and early 1970s served as sources for what became the economic democracy movement. Recruits came from the environmental, ecology, antinuclear, antimilitary, consumer and public interest, minority, and feminist movements. Many of them had considerable experience in these Left-liberal political activities, developing valuable political skills—along with considerable frustration. A few came from movements as diverse as the alternative technology, "steady state," or "human scale" movements that opposed continued economic growth and consumption.

What moved them toward economic democracy was the shared sense that the problems they sought to solve were rooted in the nature of the corporate economy. Whether they focused on sheer size and power of the largest corporations, or on the dominant role of money in financing campaigns, or on the sense that inequalities of wealth and power are part of the basic nature of the U.S. economic system, the trail led back to the private economy. In any event, economic democrats came to believe that their original goals could not be achieved unless the existing power of big corporations was curbed. Democratizing changes were required, they believed, in the private economy. To accomplish that, they needed allies from other like-minded movements; coalition under the economic democracy umbrella made sense.

Economic democrats came also from another major source—the left wing of the labor movement with its commitment to full employment. The goal of providing a job for every person able and willing to work has been part of organized labor's aspirations ever since the New Deal. However, it too has proved to be an elusive goal. It is apparently too radical for labor's liberal supporters as it consistently gets traded away when organized labor makes its accommodation with the dominant elements in the Democratic party.

In the present declining state of the trade union movement, however, most of the established leadership has joined the neoliberal call for a new industrial policy. Within the industrial policy approach, job development is a secondary priority and the notion of *full* employment is totally absent. This has freed the remaining fragment of labor leadership and a number of Left-leaning supporters among economists and others to develop a comprehensive new program for full employment.[6]

The democratic socialist component entered contemporary populism primarily through the efforts of academics who sought to rework the socialist tradition into a new American synthesis of economic, cultural, and political strands. (For the history of American socialism and its Marxist connections, please refer to the Glossary.) The most traditional example is the cluster of economists and others around *Monthly Review*. Started during the cold war, *Monthly Review* is an explicitly Marxist journal that has made an important place for itself on the American Left. More icono-clastic are the chiefly academic economists and others associated with the Union for Radical Political Economy and the mostly ex-New Left activists associated with the periodical *Socialist Review*.

Some democratic socialists no longer even refer to Karl Marx. His concepts and methods have been fully melded with the principles developed by the many American democratic socialist thinkers. Moreover, those who make their adaptations of Marxian ideas explicit often take great pains to distinguish their beliefs from those of contemporary Marxists and today's socialist countries. In part they do so because in the United States a fair hearing for explicitly socialist beliefs is almost impossible unless advocates disassociate themselves from what Americans see as foreign ideas and repressive systems.

Democratic socialism is distinguishable from economic democracy even though some socialists may use the latter term to avoid the problems just noted. Democratic socialism is a holistic and integrated body of beliefs in which all facets of a society are seen as coherent and mutually supporting. The problems that generate change-seeking movements—feminist, minority, ecology, antiwar—are one and the same. They form an interrelated package that can be addressed effectively only as a unit.

Democratic socialists acknowledge no threshold whatsoever between economics and politics. They do recognize, however, that part of their task is to help others break down the wall of separation that their society has erected—but that's not all. To reconstruct the economic and political system, one must also reconstruct the cultural base and personal identities that are produced within that society. Herbert Gintis clearly expresses this interpenetration of politics and all other aspects of social life.

> Individuals are themselves produced by the political practices they engage in. Just as work produces not only goods, but also transformed people with transformed capacities and social relations, so politics produces people as well as decisions. . . . Thus our first task will be to characterize politics in such a way that it becomes clear that it is not restricted to one sphere of social life, but is present at all sites of social activity—the state, the family, the economy, education, the scientific and cultural communities, the media, and the like.[7]

Both economic democracy and democratic socialism helped to provide the new populist movement with a deeper economic analysis and a greater appreciation of the potential scope of democracy. What really renewed the economic focus, energy, and mass organizing potential of today's populism were the harsh economic and social conditions imposed on poor, minority, and working-class people during the 1980s by the deliberate actions of the Reagan administration.

First came the policy changes of 1981. The Republican president and Democratic Congress combined to drastically cut taxes for the rich and spending for the poor, setting in motion a historically unprecedented upward redistribution of wealth and income. The harshest recession since the Great Depression of the 1930s soon followed, from which many poor and working-class people have never recovered. Labor unions were particular targets of combined corporate and governmental attack, but services to the needy, such as housing and health care, were also sharply reduced.

A wide variety of local labor, community, minority, and women's groups vigorously reacted. Studs Terkel termed all this grass roots activity "a movement awaiting coalescence." A more optimistic Jeremy Brecher argued that the coalescence was already underway. He saw it as

> the first fruits of a new social alliance which is unheralded at the national level—and virtually unreported in the national media—because it is being built at the grassroots. Over the past few years, once insular movements have been reaching out to cooperate at the local level. They have created literally hundreds of coalitions and alliances, large and small, formal and informal . . . coalitions to support strikes, run movement activists for public office, resist plant closings, secure working women's rights.[8]

Brecher further emphasized the catalytic and central part played by local labor unions. Instead of hard hats countering peace demonstrators and ethnics abandoning blue-collar loyalties in reaction to radicals, he stressed labor's role in emerging grass roots coalitions involving

> women's, African-American, Latino, Asian-American, gay, lesbian, environmental, farm, senior, students, handicapped, peace, human rights, anti-intervention, citizen action, consumer, and other movements.[9]

BASIC VALUES

Progressive populism today is straining to establish a concept of democracy that encompasses its twin pillars of economic redistribution and opportunity, and empowerment of ordinary citizens. It focuses, therefore, on the principles of equality and participation in a revived local community. To adequately express these values and goals and to set the movement apart from conservative populism is a conceptual, linguistic, and *political* necessity. The populist activist Mike Miller captures both pillars very neatly:

> A powerful new movement to reclaim democracy is emerging today in America. It is built on the basic values of liberty, justice, equality, and community. It also claims the traditional values of family, religion, neighborhood, work, and national pride. It needs a richer language to distinguish itself from dominant cultural themes of material success, "me-first" and America first, private (corporate) enterprise as the guarantor of economic progress. Whether democratic populism can provide that language is the challenge facing its proponents.[10]

Populism is also distinguished in the eyes of its adherents by the attachment that ordinary citizens feel toward equality and empowerment. For some, this intensity alone distinguishes populists from ideological liberals and conservatives. The Texas populist Jim Hightower put it this way in a speech entitled "Kick-Ass Populism," which was given to the National Press Club:

> My point is that the great center of American politics is not square dab in the middle of the spectrum, equal distance [sic] from conservatism and liberalism. Rather, the true center is in populism. [sic] Which is rooted in the realization that too few people control all the money and power, leaving very little for the rest of us. And they use that money and power to gain more for themselves. Populism is propelled politically by the simmering desire of the mass of people to upend that arrangement. Now this is hardly a centrist position, if by centrist you mean moderate. But it is at the center of most people's political being, and it is a very hot center indeed.[11]

Hightower argues that the bulk of Americans are egalitarians whose interests are not represented by either major political party. Americans are "folks who have a deep belief in old-time, little-d democratic ideals of fairness, of egalitarianism, of tolerance and pluralism."[12] He insists that these traditional American values, which are intensely held, put populists (and the majority of Americans) on the left of the political spectrum. In characteristic fashion, he quotes a farmer friend and then elaborates:

> "Hell, Hightower, there's nothing in the middle of the road but yellow stripes and dead armadillos. We want you out there fighting for us—getting out there on our side of things." And that's not just a few people who feel like that, it's not just labor, it's not just poor folks, it's not just minority, environmentalists, Volvo-driving liberals; I contend it is the American majority, including the dirt farmer and the hard-scrabble rancher, including the main street business person, the entrepreneur, the nurses and the keypunchers, the waitresses and the clerks.[13]

Today's progressive populism also emphasizes solidarity and harmony among different groups—race, gender, labor, and community. In part this is essential to building a sustainable, viable coalition among groups formed out of separate cultures or interests. It also reflects a conscious intent to create a better, more democratic society, not just to seek special interests within the existing system. In this regard progressive populism provides some practically oriented working-class support for the reform liberal goal of developing cross-cultural respect and understanding through education.

These populist commitments are often subsumed within a general emphasis on redefining and fulfilling democracy for all Americans. For two primary reasons, democracy should be extended to all areas of social and economic life.

The first is to convert the illusory equality of citizens in the political world into a reality. Until there is greater equality in the economic and social worlds, the accumulation of wealth, status, and power in a few hands will continue to shape the outcomes in politics. At the very least, great inequalities of wealth and power deny the goals of democracy. In some cases they make the great principle of democracy into a mere sham. Discrimination on racial and sexual lines, although having independent sources, is also encouraged by economic factors.

The second reason is that only if democratic practices are extended throughout all areas of social life—the family and the workplace, for example—can people really develop the sense of personal worth and solidarity with others that permits a full life as a human being. People need to feel that they are in control of their lives and not the mere pawns of others. Their capabilities need to be exercised to become real. Moreover, the results of cooperative action to solve problems, such as organizing work to achieve both efficiency and quality of product, lead ultimately to a better life for all.

The basic means of accomplishing this democratization is participatory decentralization. People *must* be able to take part in making the decisions that affect their lives. Translated, this means that important decisions must be made where people can actually be present to take part. Both initial choices and continuing implementation must be subject to the preferences of those affected. Particularly crucial to the new democracy are democratization of the workplace, employee ownership plans, and, most important, social control over capital investment.

Some on the Left think of this change in terms of the formation of a new social contract. A social contract is, of course, a fiction. It is an image of an underlying agreement among people with respect to organization of their social order and the distribution of rights and responsibilities. Trying to characterize its nature forces people to pay attention to the first principles, purposes, and priorities of their system. One major work expresses the need for a new social contract as follows:

> We believe that a New Social Contract in America must reaffirm and energize the fundamental dynamic of our history: democracy . . . [Some people] think that the way out of the current crisis is to leave decisions to a few—the "experts" in our complex industrial economy. But increased expertise and corporate bureaucratization for the sake of higher private profits is precisely what has made post-World War II America head down the road to crisis. . . . America must now find ways . . . through *greater*, not less, democratic participation.[14]

Populists also endorse individualism in the sense of individual rights, extending it from the political-legal world to the economic world. Nearly all talk in terms of the right to a job, economic rights in general, or an economic bill of rights. Many of those who start from a commitment to full employment promptly translate that goal into an individual right to a job. An example is Representative John Conyers's draft legislation, the Recovery and Full Employment Act, the first declared purpose of which is "the establishment of an enforceable right to earn a living."[15]

The idea of rights extends well beyond the right to a job at wages adequate to sustain a moderate standard of living. It includes various dimensions of economic and social security, such as rights to education, housing, health care, environmental quality, and adequate retirement income. In part, this is intended to establish a floor of social and economic guarantees, a kind of minimum level of conditions for all that will make equality of opportunity more genuine. It is also part of the populist notion of freedom, which requires assurance of certain levels of social and economic conditions (or security) so that people will be free to develop themselves in directions of their choice.

The manner in which the extension of individual rights to the economy intersects with a version of freedom is well illustrated in excerpts from two quite different sources. The first is the call for a new social contract in which "government does not restrict liberty; it expands it and makes it a reality."[16] The second is from a leading alliance of organizations called the Full Employment Action Council. After asserting the right to a job as part of human freedom, the alliance goes on to describe "the essence of the freedom we desire."

> The national government cannot emphasize certain kinds of freedom and forget others. Free markets reward those who have market power, but they do not improve opportunities for those who have little wealth or income. . . . Freedom is indivisible. We cannot emphasize only those forms of freedom that benefit mainly the powerful.[17]

Populists also modify the traditional view of individualism with their concern for fostering and developing community life and the capacity of communities to control their own futures. A variety of communities is envisioned in which each community has the ability to affect what happens to it. In part, this is also the way that democracy is to be extended.

> Greater democracy means that those with jobs will have much more to say about the way those jobs are organized; those who live in communities will have more to say about what happens to those communities—even whether a plant can simply up and leave after thirty years.[18]

Let us try to summarize briefly what progressive populism is doing with and to traditional American values. It seems clear that it has expanded the notion of individualism in significant ways. Self-orientation has been supplanted by notions of community and of shared risks and opportunities. An even greater expansion, though one that might be thought to preserve the isolated-individual focus, is occurring in the extension of individual rights to the economy. At some point in the expansion of rights, a fundamental change in the nature of the society itself will be involved.

At the same time, property rights have just as clearly been downgraded, and nonowners given a major voice in deciding how property should be used. Equality has been expanded beyond equality of opportunity into the realm of equality of condition. Similarly, freedom has been redefined to fit with this new version of equality and to mean space or security to try to realize basic human aspirations. Contracts, law, and established procedures generally play a much lesser role than they did under more liberal reform beliefs. Indeed, they are often seen as part of the way that dominant corporations deflect reform efforts. However, populists are not unwilling to use litigation or initiative and referendum tactics to harass corporations and banks and their political agents.

What is involved here is an expansion of the notions of equality and freedom even beyond those that were being generated by reform liberal movements. This expansion puts an equivalent pressure on the other basic values in a coherent democracy-promoting direction. The version of democracy sought is a fresh, new substantive variety. Procedural democracy has been examined and found wanting on two counts: its incomplete nature in the political world (race, sex, and other discrimination) and its complete absence in the economic world.

Democratic socialists, in particular, believe that political democracy in the United States is corrupt and degraded—a sham. Inequalities of wealth and power, inherent in capitalism, make for domination of politics and people by corporations and the wealthy. To extend *this* sort of democracy is to foster illusions. In effect, these theorists start with the limitations and defects of political democracy today, searching for causes and solutions in order to maximize the democratic qualities of life for all citizens. It does not take long before their inquiry identifies capitalist social relationships as well as its inequalities, the profit motive, and unlimited corporate power at the seat of the problem.

For example, in an excellent little book with the disarming title *On Democracy*, the political theorist authors flatly declare:

> For its realization, democracy requires the abolition of capitalism. Again, this is not because of the materially unsatisfying character of life under capitalism, but because of its structural denial of freedom. To choose democracy is to choose against that denial.[19]

That is putting the matter rather bluntly, but the same message has been spelled out at greater length by several other students of democracy in the United States.[20]

Democratic socialists have no sense of separation between politics and economics, much less of a wall between the two. However, they recognize that to most Americans, *democracy* is a term that applies only to politics.

The first task, therefore, is to show that political democracy is incomplete without at least some measure of popular control over the uses of private wealth and power. They want to illuminate the fact of conflict between democracy (revered) and capitalism (questionable) in American life. If the wall of separation can be breached, many goals become possible. Changes in value definitions are only one of the possibilities. Changes in established conceptual assumptions, such as that of an inevitable conflict between equality and efficiency, are another. The economist Herbert Gintis declares the strategy as follows:

> We shall initially apply our conception to capitalist production, arguing that democratic production is not only more conducive to worker satisfaction and growth, but is also efficient and provides superior production. This is in direct contrast to traditional economic theory, which holds that through the logic of profit maximization, capitalist production is maximally efficient and worker satisfaction cannot be improved without lowering efficiency, wages, and product quality. We will then apply our conception of democracy to the organization of the family.[21]

In other words, democracy is not only paramount as a value, but it is also to be generalized to every aspect of social life, particularly economic activities. The payoffs from institutionalizing democracy include popular control and personal development, familiar enough aspirations if always incompletely realized. They also include improvement in every function—in the efficiency of the economy and the quality of its products, for example. This is a new, deeper, and more pervasive claim for democracy, well beyond the goals sought by multiplying rights or participatory mechanisms.

The notion of community is a vital one for progressive populists, both as a priority in its own right and as the arena for individual participation and development. In a major recent work entitled *The Deindustrialization of America: Plant Closings, Community Abandonment, and the Dismantling of Basic Industry*,[22] the economists Barry Bluestone and Bennett Harrison focus on a concern for American communities. For example, the title of the first chapter is "Capital vs. Community." Communities are described as social as well as geographic entities; they are, in fact, the basic unit of social life, and, as such, they are entitled to protection and enhancement in every possible way. The authors go on to propose new powers for communities over corporations and their investment decisions. They also advocate a comprehensive community-based democratic planning system.

PROBLEMS AND POSSIBILITIES

The populist understanding of problems in the United States and its strategy for change are well summarized by activist Mike Miller as follows:

Democratic populism points us in several important directions: (1) Wealth and power are concentrated in the hands of too few people, particularly those at the helm of major business and governmental institutions. (2) The capacity of average people to define their own problems and to come up with solutions to them should be understood as central to a vision of a democratic future in America, as well as to an understanding of its revolutionary past. (3) If we are to successfully challenge concentrated wealth and power, we need to begin by building and strengthening autonomous organizations and institutions that are deeply rooted in the experiences and values of people in local communities.[23]

Populists do not underestimate the difficulties they face. One major obstacle is the isolation and decline of organized labor in the United States. After the 1980s, labor was at its lowest point in membership and political weight since the 1920s; only 17 percent of the labor force remained in unions. New contracts were more likely to involve concessions or "give backs" than improvements in wages or working conditions. The natural divisions and tensions between genders and among races, classes, and localities fragment the working class and pose a second obstacle. Third, populists tend to turn nationalist and protectionist, blaming other countries and/or their workers for the troubles of Americans.

Paradoxically, the decline of organized labor freed some rank and file elements in local unions from control by their distant international leadership. Using this opportunity, they could build local alliances with community and other groups to support strikes and put pressure on employers through boycotts, buy outs, and job-preservation campaigns. With labor and economic issues at the center, diverse organizations work together (somewhat) more easily. Some populist leaders have begun to stress the shared needs of workers and disadvantaged people worldwide. Senator Barbara Mikulski, for example, included these lines at the close of a major speech to populists and trade union organizers:

In order to be leaders, we have to be leaders not only in our neighborhood, but in the world. One of the ways we fulfill ourselves is global linkage here and around the world. So when we organize trade unions in Detroit, let's link ourselves up with those trade unions struggling to survive in Poland. When we're organizing the mine workers in West Virginia, be sure to keep in mind the exploited farm workers in South Africa. As we struggle with the issues of immigration about who gets into our country, let's remember around the world another issue, the emigration of those who would like to get out, like Soviet Jews. As we work for battered women here in America, let's remember the battered women everywhere. When we take on the bullies in this country, let's make sure we don't support the bullies in other countries.[24]

When populists look at the economy, they see a flawed American capitalism, dominated by giant, often multinational corporations. These corporations represent aggregations of assets so vast and so global that they operate without effective control by any government. Thus, corporations can transfer their productive facilities anywhere in the world, avoiding higher-wage areas and effectively depressing all wage levels. They can close up still profitable plants to invest in whatever offers the highest returns, regardless of the impact on workers. They can pollute, discriminate, and use scarce resources with impunity.

Of most significance today is the fact that these corporations have violated their tacit contract with workers and consumers to share a fair proportion of their earnings in the form of wages and taxes. Instead, the corporations have almost unanimously sought to roll back wages, crush the unions, and slash both social programs and the taxes that support them. For working people this has meant a steady decline in real wages; joblessness and the threat of joblessness; and sharply reduced government support, financial and otherwise.

These cutbacks hit hardest at the very people who make up the populist constituency. Minorities and women are the most likely to be affected by reductions in government social-assistance programs. Environmentalists are aggrieved by loosened environmental protections, lower air and water pollution standards, and the like. Antiwar advocates are shocked by the scope of the military buildup. This last is particularly provocative.

To all on the Left, one of the most damaging commitments of the American government—and one that enjoys widespread support from American business—is its vast investment in military expenditures. Hundreds of billions of dollars are taken out of the U.S. economy and simply wasted. Many more jobs could be produced and far more useful facilities built or products developed if the same sums were invested in other areas or simply left in the hands of consumers to spend as they wished. Populists uniformly contend that military spending is wasteful as well as dangerous in its effects on the global arms race. Some go beyond this to say that American capitalism has come to depend so heavily on this massive injection of public funds that some equivalent prop, such as a vast public works program, will be necessary to accomplish a transition away from heavy military expenditures.

What this military investment really shows, in the eyes of many populists, is the complete irrationality of modern capitalism. New weapons of mutual destruction are produced in numbers far exceeding what could ever be used. Not only does this great expansion in military spending occur at a time when most of the world's people, including substantial numbers of Americans, are barely subsisting, but it actually is used as a reason to further reduce expenditures on social programs that enable poor people to have some chance to improve their life situations. In this way, as well as through the unprecedented national budget deficits resulting from these policies, the costs of the current military buildup are passed to future generations.

The irrationality of modern capitalism only begins with the massive waste of military spending. Many products are so shoddy or dangerous that buyers can be found only through vast advertising campaigns that serve no useful purpose except that of making a profit. Meanwhile, real needs go unmet because higher profits can be made elsewhere. Public, social goods, such as the air, land, and water, are polluted or seized for private profit, destroyed, and then dumped on the public for reclamation. Systematic waste becomes a defining characteristic of modern capitalism.

This warped set of priorities is specially damaging at a time when so many real needs are felt by so many people. Moreover, in order to defend and maintain these priorities, money and influence are widely deployed in the political world, corrupting the media, political campaigns, and the representative process. The result is an increasingly crass and ignoble public life. Mainstream economists are essentially apologists for those remedies that are congenial to the owners and managers who created this set of priorities in the first place. Martin Carnoy, Derek Shearer, and Russell Rumberger state the case, suggesting the different way in which economic democrats would try to solve the problems.

> We believe that economists and other governmental policy makers cannot improve the situation primarily because . . . they accept a set of ideological assumptions about the "naturalness" and "perfectibility" of capitalism as an economic order. . . . [But] we think it is crucial to political-economic discussion to accept openly the fact that assumptions about ownership and power are part and parcel of the economic problem. Rather than discussing the best methods for "fine tuning" the economy, we want to shift the debate to strategies for changing the structure of the economy so that it better serves the interests and needs of all Americans. . . . Neoclassical economics represents a point of view, a political position, a set of assumptions about the way the world should be and about human behavior. We will present an alternative view based on an alternative set of assumptions.[25]

The future looks even less promising than the present. Populists believe that the economy's structural problems are such that recoveries will be only temporary periods preceding the return of inflation. Furthermore, recoveries are highly segmented: they reward upper-middle-class people but have little constructive impact on ordinary workers, minorities, women, or those who are steadily dropping out of the middle class.

Possibilities

Populists historically have emphasized their critique of the current distribution of wealth and power rather than set forth specific alternative proposals. This has begun to change, however, as populism has grown and incorporated former economic democrats and democratic socialists. In a major essay entitled "Toward a Tough-Minded Populism," Gar Alperovitz warns that a simple antigovernment position might prevent populism from dealing effectively with the monumental problem of managing the economy to maximize growth, fairness of distribution, and environmental protection. He argues that the only way to enable real participation in the necessary economic planning is to restructure government itself.

> A serious populism—one that cares about both progressive and humane values and participation—had better begin to develop a truly regional long-term vision. . . . I am suggesting that the only answer . . . is a long-term vision of how, specifically and concretely, this great nation might begin to be restructured into semiautonomous regional units capable of managing, under democratic control, the separate regional economies.[26]

Alperovitz explicitly calls for a class-based program that would promote black-white unity and help to achieve the political breakthrough needed to implement the fundamental changes that economic conditions require.

This challenge calls into question many proposals that have been made on the Left in the last years for economic change of various kinds, usually focused on the national government. The latter remain the dominant elements of the populist program. The essence of the populist program is the extension of individual (personal) rights to include economic and social rights. This means restoration of the social wage or social safety net, full employment, social control over investment, and extensive democratic planning. Nearly every major publication on the Left includes some form of an economic bill of rights such as that earlier described.

The steps in the process of economic reconstruction also have been agreed upon. (Democratizing political steps are assumed to come first, so that this redistribution of wealth and power will be possible.) First is the rebuilding of the various national government protections instituted since the New Deal against the dangers of life under capitalism. These include all the forms of assistance to the poor that were so sharply cut back during the early years of the Reagan administration.

An expanded version of the social wage would reorder the taxing and spending priorities of the national government. A truly progressive tax system would be needed to replace the inequitable and regressive system now in effect. In particular, the taxes on the rich and the corporations eliminated in 1981 would have to be restored. Spending for military purposes should be drastically cut back, both to reduce the dangers of the arms race and to make funds available for social needs.

The next task would be to begin to redirect private investment toward social concerns instead of maximizing profits at the expense of workers and communities. The principal means to this end is plant-closing legislation. This would require corporations to give notice of their intent to close or move plants from one community to another. In some versions, corporations would have to provide moving or retraining allowances to workers, community compensation, or opportunities for the community or workers to buy the plant and operate it themselves.

Once these basic protections were secured, restructuring of the economy could begin. Growth is essential to provide for full employment, but it must be growth without the recurring threats of inflation or unemployment and without destruction of the environment. This combination of priorities means that planning and a major role for the national government in controlling the rate and character of growth are imperative. Full employment implies a necessary major role for government, in opposition to the still dominant free market principle. The Full Employment Action Council points up the deficiencies of the current economy.

> While the market can be a marvel at promoting short-run efficiency, it cannot solve larger problems. Markets by themselves cannot protect the environment, secure the health and safety of workers, eliminate discrimination, promote equal opportunities and adequate income levels for households, foster long-run basic research and innovation, and ensure national security.[27]

Broad democratic participation in an elaborate new planning system, from the lowest levels of local jurisdictions to the heights of national decision making, would be required. New institutions for planning probably would have to be created at the local level, perhaps with the incentive of federal funding. Either new or newly democratized national institutions would be required to synthesize and implement the local recommendations. An example would be a newly democratized Federal Reserve Board in which representatives of workers and consumers would break the bankers' monopoly, giving the public genuine control over the value and availability of money and credit.

Populists are well aware that it is far easier to design economic programs than to achieve and hold the political power necessary to implement them. Indeed, there is some impatience with those who do not see economic renewal and social change as irretrievably linked to political change. The basic point is well stated by Alan Wolfe, a political scientist:

> Americans who live with an economy that must throw people out of work in order to control inflation should not be surprised that they have a political system that must disenfranchise its citizens in order to choose its leaders. Much talk is heard in the 1980s of the need for a program of economic revitalization. Yet, as was true also in the 1940s, economic direction must come from the political system, and American politics is stagnant. America needs a program of political revitalization before its economy will begin to work again.[28]

Another important dimension of political revitalization is the formation of a new and class-based realignment of voters in electoral politics. Former nonvoters and regular voters alike, particularly women and minorities, must unite in a broad new coalition that sees economic and other national policies in terms of the *class* biases that they involve.

Finally, the new ways of thinking and acting in politics must eventually focus on the reconstruction of political institutions. These must be made more democratic and more effective in serving public rather than special interests. Many argue that such reconstruction has now become more possible because of the very severity of our economic problems and the danger involved in the mainstream remedies. Alan Wolfe summarizes the situation well:

> Political revitalization—a path out of America's impasse—is possible, *if* it is based on three propositions. First, the American people must take whatever steps are necessary to guarantee their security: against inflation and unemployment at home and against the possibility of nuclear war and an uncontrolled arms race abroad. Second, Americans must create for themselves a public authority that will help them achieve this security, which requires both a strong government at home capable of planning and intervening in the public interest and a strong international authority capable of countering the self-interest of nation states. Third, the majority of the American people must recognize that they have in common a class position and that they must be as willing to use government to support that position as business, in the past, has been willing to use government to support its position.[29]

In other words, a self-conscious and class-based movement must hold together and act coherently to implement its will through the national government for a sustained period of time. Only in such a manner can the Left come to power and achieve its program.

Populists acknowledge that the working class has never shown this solidarity and capability in American history, but they deny vigorously that this means that no such movement is possible. Michael Harrington, one of the most prolific of democratic socialist writers, has argued consistently that "there is a massive objective basis for class politics in America today which *could* be actualized by political movements and economic events."[30]

IMPLICATIONS AND PROSPECTS

Progressive populism appears to have made some early progress, inspired in part by the economic hardships affecting its primary constituency throughout the 1980s and early 1990s. Much of this success took the form of local coalitions focused on specific local issues. Before populism can become an organized force in American politics, however, two major obstacles must be overcome. One is the continuing suspicion on the part of minorities and women—and of some populists themselves—that populism's localism and community grounding will again embrace racism and sexism. The second is the necessity of finding an adequate political vehicle to carry the populist cause forward. This might be electoral politics or some alternative. If the vehicle is electoral, it could be issue-based action, a third party, the Democratic party, or a party within the party such as the Rainbow coalition.

Populists are well aware that the possibility of fragmenting their fragile coalitions is ever present. In 1985 two insightful observers pointed out this danger.

> The association of localism, traditionalism, and populism with a dark side of racism and demagogy is historical reality. Appreciation of the deep wellsprings of democratic decency and common sense in Americans should not obscure the continuing traditions and threat of racism, anti-intellectualism, and chauvinism that are deeply embedded in the political culture in general and in that of ethnic blue-collar Americans in particular. To say local and populist is not necessarily to say democratic, open, unbiased.[31]

Both women and African-Americans associated with progressive populism echo this warning. While Jesse Jackson and his thoroughly populist message were warmly received by white farmers and workers, the possibility of harking back to earlier values and prejudiced attitudes remains. The duality in populism and the difficulty of adequately incorporating women's perspectives are well discussed in an essay by Elizabeth Kamarck Minnich entitled "Toward a Feminist Populism."

> A populism that speaks not just of "the people" but of "the peoples" of this land, that affirms diversity, can and has included women on its list. But women are not one more issue, one more cause, one more subject. . . . There is no issue that is not a "women's issue," and those who simply add us to their agenda as if we were one more item cannot be trusted. And, of course, when populism reverts to its bigotry in the name of "old American values," women as well as minority men are in serious danger.[32]

These concerns have drawn a candid response from Senator Harkin. He readily acknowledged the danger that people's fears and insecurity can lead to demagogic or intolerant behavior, but he responds, simply, that leaders need to trust people to make sound judgments when they have all the facts and time to reflect on them.

> Public opinion is a knee-jerk reaction to something that doesn't sound right. Public will is something deeper, it has to do with people's understanding, their deepest motivations, their value system, what their goals are, what they feel is important for their family and their community and their society. You have to discern that, dig that out. That to me is what populism is. It's going after that public will, digging, finding out what's under that skin. I see populism, and the kinds of things we're doing on a grassroots level, as giving people the information and data they need to make an informed decision.[33]

In a similar vein, Harry Boyte acknowledges the need for a serious struggle to assure that progressive populists continue to understand local communities as cooperative support systems and to prevent them from becoming oppressive or from demanding conformity. He asserts the need for a culture of democracy that is capable of making communities into liberating and developmental opportunities for all people.

Throughout the 1980s the only national political vehicle for progressive populism was the Rainbow coalition. However, many felt the Rainbow was too much the personal instrument of its leader, Jesse Jackson. More fundamentally, some populists see no use for electoral politics; others limit themselves to seeking specific goals through the initiative process. Probably the majority feel the need for a presence in national politics. For them, the choice appeared to narrow to participating in a third party (the route of the original Populists in 1892 and 1896) or seeking to expand their influence within the national Democratic party.

Third parties have an uphill climb against the rules and traditions of the American electoral system. Therefore, many populists feel such a choice would be self isolating and perhaps even self-destructive. In the 1980s, many devoted their efforts to forming strong, local, progressive coalitions that would either endorse acceptable candidates or enter candidates of their own in Democratic primaries.

The emphasis on base building and on the Democratic party is visible in the career and speeches of Jim Hightower. In 1986 he unexpectedly took himself out of the race for a Senate seat in Texas on the grounds that the organizational base had not been adequately built. He emphasized that his candidacy, even if victorious, would only be a transitory phenomenon. It would be better in the long run to build a lasting coalition around a set of issues and a continuing program.

Hightower continued to assert the need for Democrats to respond to

> the majority of Americans down at the 7-11 picking up a Budweiser and a Slim Jim and wondering if there's anybody in America who's going to stand up on their side . . . those are the people the Democrats must begin to speak to.[34]

He regularly talks of the importance for Democrats of remembering their base,

> the people who are the true Democratic Party, including the blacks and Mexican Americans in our culture, including the women. . . . The mass of people who are in the middle class, the lower middle class, and the lower economic classes in our society—that's the vast majority. We cannot abandon that base. . . . [35]

Probably most populists agree with Hightower—some kind of presence in the Democratic party is the most effective means of furthering their cause. The issue, however, can never be finally put to rest. Too many activists have been frustrated for too long in trying to move the Democratic party in progressive directions.

ADDITIONAL READINGS

Bluestone, Barry, and Bennett Harrison. *The Deindustrialization of America: Plant Closings, Community Abandonment, and the Dismantling of Basic Industry*. New York: Basic Books, 1982.

Bowles, Samuel, David M. Gordon, and Thomas E. Weiskopf. *Beyond the Waste Land: A Democratic Alternative to Economic Decline*. New York: Anchor, 1983.

Boyte, Harry. *The Backyard Revolution: Understanding the New Citizen Movement*. Philadelphia: Temple University Press, 1980.

Boyte, Harry, and Frank Reissman, eds. *The New Populism: The Politics of Empowerment*. Philadelphia: Temple University Press, 1986.

Brecher, Jeremy, and Tim Costello, eds. *Building Bridges: The Emerging Grassroots Coalition of Labor and Community*. New York: Monthly Review Press, 1990.

Carnoy, Martin, and Derek Shearer. *Economic Democracy: The Challenge of the 1980s*. White Plains, N.Y.: M. E. Sharpe, 1980.

Carnoy, Martin, Derek Shearer, and Russell Rumberger. *A New Social Contract: The Economy and Government after Reagan*. New York: Harper & Row, 1983.

Cohen, Joshua, and Joel Rogers. *On Democracy: Toward a Transformation of American Society*. Baltimore: Penguin, 1983.

Green, Mark. *Winning Back America*. New York: Bantam, 1982.

Hayden, Tom. *The American Future: New Visions beyond Old Frontiers*. Boston: South End Press, 1980.

Herreshoff, David. *The Origins of American Marxism: From the Transcendentalists to DeLeon*. New York: Pathfinder, 1973.

Lekachman, Robert. *Greed Is Not Enough: Reaganomics*. New York: Pantheon, 1982.

Piven, Frances, and Richard Cloward. *The New Class War*. New York: Pantheon, 1982.

PART IV

CHALLENGES FROM THE RIGHT

CHAPTER 8

POPULIST CONSERVATISM AND THE CHRISTIAN RIGHT

Two overlapping ideologies also emerge from a lower-middle- and working-class base—the conservative side of populism and the Christian Right, or New Right. They are readily distinguishable by their focus on social issues such as prayer, abortion, and traditional gender roles; by their religious fervor, drawn from the evangelical, fundamentalist, and charismatic groups of several denominations; and by the strength and permanence of their anticommunism. They share concern for the social issues, religious values, and anticommunism with the neoconservatives (see Chapter 5) and organic conservatives (see Chapter 9). However, their class origins, fundamentalism, and militant methods make regular working coalitions difficult to achieve or maintain.

When they do address economic matters, populist conservatives and the Christian Right often take laissez-faire and antitaxation positions. Their most likely link in this respect is with the business community, which has no higher priorities and few other concerns. Sometimes on economic issues they sound like libertarians (see Chapter 9), but the strength of the commitment to government action on the social issues makes more than momentary agreement impossible.

These two overlapping ideologies, distinctively, have already crystallized into an almost exclusively white national movement. They made significant achievements in the 1980 and subsequent elections, with resulting appointments to the U.S. Supreme Court. Full control of religious television and a vast funding system stand behind them.

Prominent figures in this movement include presidential aspirant Pat Robertson and his Christian Broadcasting Network, columnist Pat Buchanan, author Phyllis Schlafly, political organizers Paul Weyrich and Richard Viguerie, and Barbara LaHaye of Concerned Women of America. As we shall see, a large number of religious, pro-life, stop-ERA, antigun control, and other political groups provide a wide-ranging infrastructure of communication and support.

The notion of populist conservatism is an important insight for understanding the New Right. To be radical, majoritarian, lower-middle class, and conservative at the same time is completely unprecedented in modern American politics, and yet the combination is a logical one. When liberals are in control, there is no reason to accept the status quo. There is also no way to change it except by majority action, hence the conjunction of radicalism with conservatism. Paul Weyrich makes the point as follows:

> We are radicals who want to change the existing power structure. We are not conservatives in the sense that conservatism means accepting the status quo. We cannot accept the status quo. . . . We have to take a turn in the other direction. The New Right does not want to conserve, we want to change—we *are* the forces of change. And if people are sick and tired of things in this country, then they had best look to conservative leadership for that change.[1]

The way to change things is through mass political action. Thus, populist conservative is the way to understand all these characteristics in an incisive manner.

LINKS TO THE PAST

Three main strands converged to make up this ideology and movement. Chronologically, the first emerged in the late 1950s and early 1960s from the Christian television evangelists, particularly Pat Robertson's Christian news-and-comment programs. The image of the television evangelists suffered some in the 1980s from scandals and internal conflicts, but the scope and strength of this system was only marginally affected.

Pat Robertson's Christian Broadcasting Network, untouched by others' problems, has been perhaps the most effective. The "700 Club," hosted by Robertson, developed into a combined fund-raising and news-and-comment program on the order of CBS's "60 Minutes." It features guest appearances of world figures, particularly from the Reagan administration, and consistent editorializing from a New Right perspective. A multimillion-dollar business, it has spun off a university and served as the mobilizing base for Robertson's presidential effort in 1988. Through the 1970s and 1980s, the Christian television programs together raised tens of millions of dollars and mobilized hundreds of thousands of people for New Right purposes.

The second contingent came from the young conservatives, many of them Catholics. They had been politicized by Senator Joseph McCarthy's antiestablishment anticommunism, inspired by William F. Buckley's *National Review*, and drawn into action by Senator Barry Goldwater's campaigns for the Republican nomination and the presidency in 1964. Their work began to build a mass base within the Republican party for militant conservative policies. With the help of southerners and northern ethnics, that base would eventually take control of the party from the liberal, internationalist, East Coast Republican establishment.

The Goldwater campaign is widely recognized today as the start of America's "right turn" in politics. The significance of broad populist

support for Joe McCarthy's anti-Communist attacks on the liberal establishment should also be acknowledged. For several years, the senator
enjoyed high approval ratings from a broad spectrum of Americans, particularly Catholics and working-class people. Pat Buchanan sums up Mc-
Carthy's meaning:

> To the Americans who sustained Joe McCarthy for four years, he was saying
> that the governing American establishment, our political elite, was no longer fit
> to determine the destiny of the United States; it had disqualified itself by
> having poured down a sewer everything for which twelve million Americans
> had fought and bled and died . . . and by having delivered up half the world to
> Joseph Stalin.[2]

Buchanan correctly interprets this phase in U.S. history as bitter, class-
based resentment against the loss of "half the world" to advancing communism. It was the beginning of the end of liberalism's authority to
govern. McCarthy lost support, Buchanan argues, only because he took on
the popularly respected U.S. Army. Today, after almost four decades,
McCarthy remains an evil figure only because the liberal press has been
determined to make him such. Buchanan sees the present-day United
States as "bitterly divided against itself" over fundamental value questions presaged in the McCarthy controversy:

> The Senate censure of Joseph McCarthy, as a political struggle, had much in
> common with the impeachment of Richard Nixon. The passions were identical;
> the coalitions for and against both men were roughly the same; and both men
> were despised antagonists of Establishment liberalism and the American
> Left. . . . Joe's lasting contribution was to have ripped the bandages off the
> underlying wound in America's body politic: Them or us.[3]

The third and decisive component was built in the mid-1970s from the
available base of angry populist conservatives of Middle America. Combined with some religious elements, they were purposefully and politically
mobilized by the organizers of the New Right. The immediate trigger was
President Ford's appointment of Nelson Rockefeller (the embodiment of
wealthy, liberal Republicanism) as vice president.[4] The appointment of
Rockefeller was the final provocation in a long series of moderate Republican accommodations with big government and free-spending liberalism evident even in the Nixon administration. A group of young
conservative activists, experienced in Republican politics, resolved to put
principles before party. It was time to organize the constituency they were
sure was available for a consistently conservative program. At the center
of this new group of activists were four men.

Paul Weyrich, with the financial support of the wealthy Joseph Coors,
already had been instrumental in starting or reshaping several conservative organizations. For example, he had helped revitalize the Heritage
Foundation, a think tank that publishes policy-oriented work by conser-

vative scholars. He had made the American Legislative Exchange Council, originally a clearinghouse for information for state legislators, into the principal means of providing these legislators with the conservative viewpoint on issues. In 1974, again with help from Coors, he started the Committee for the Survival of a Free Congress (CSFC). This organization raises funds and supports conservative candidates for Congress, providing extensive training in the techniques of campaigning as well as financial help.

Howard Phillips founded the Conservative Caucus (CC) in 1975 as a way to mobilize constituents in as many congressional districts as possible to keep conservative pressure on elected representatives and senators. By 1980 the Conservative Caucus had hundreds of thousands of contributors, a budget upward of $3 million, and organizations in 250 districts. It had spun off a research foundation, sponsored several newsletters reporting on legislators' actions, and developed a speakers' bureau and a number of other services for conservative candidates and officeholders.

John (Terry) Dolan helped to start and became the chairman of the National Conservative Political Action Committee (NCPAC) in 1975. NCPAC collects campaign funds and channels them to conservative candidates and causes. Taking advantage of the opportunities available to political action committees (PACs) under current laws, NCPAC runs advertising campaigns aimed at defeating liberal elected officials who are on the wrong side of issues such as abortion and the Panama Canal treaties. It was particularly successful in targeting and helping to defeat liberal senators in 1978 and 1980. Dolan also served as chairman of the Washington Legal Foundation, which sponsors litigation for conservative purposes, and Conservatives Against Liberal Legislation (CALL), a lobbying group.

Richard Viguerie is the publisher of *Conservative Digest*, a monthly journal reporting on all New Right activities through original articles and reprints of important speeches or statements. He is also the head of the Richard A. Viguerie Company (RAVCO), a sophisticated and totally computerized direct-mail operation that handles the fund-raising and communications system for all the other conservative organizations. Viguerie is widely credited with having mobilized money and people behind the New Right organizations with an effectiveness previously unknown in American politics.

With these four men and their organizations at the center, the New Right was launched. In his words, Viguerie perceived that they shared the following characteristics:

1. A developing technical ability—in direct mail, in mass media, in practical politics.
2. A willingness to work together for the common good.
3. A commitment to put philosophy before political party.
4. An optimism and a conviction that we had the ability to win and to lead America.[5]

The label *New Right* was first applied by the sympathetic, then-conservative columnist Kevin Phillips in 1975 in the course of an assessment emphasizing the social conservatism of the groups. Phillips made the point that the New Right represented a significant departure in American politics. They stressed cultural and social issues instead of the almost exclusively economic issues of the Old Right. He argued that if the New Right was able to make a firm link with that Old Right, the combination of issues would be very powerful.[6] In an important book, the devotedly conservative William A. Rusher, publisher of *National Review*, made a similar argument. Social conservatives, many of whom were former Democrats, should seek alliance with the economic conservatives of the Republican party, if necessary through a "new majority party."[7]

The New Right has moved in that direction throughout its brief existence. Its first task, however, was to mobilize a significant constituency of social conservatives; making itself felt in Congress and in presidential politics would follow. In addition to the key groups discussed, several other groups have played important secondary roles in this mobilization process. Richard Viguerie's widely distributed *The New Right: We're Ready to Lead* offers a comprehensive list of the more important ones as the following:[8]

> Citizens Committee for the Right to Keep and Bear Arms (and the associated Second Amendment Foundation)
> Coalition for Peace through Strength
> National Right to Work Committee
> Heritage Foundation (and the associated publication *Policy Review*)
> Washington Legal Foundation
> American Legislative Exchange Council
> Committee for Responsible Youth Politics
> Conservative Victory Fund
> Life Amendment Political Action Committee
> American Life Lobby
> National Pro-Life Political Action Committee
> Public Service Research Council
> Conservatives against Liberal Legislation
> National Tax Limitation Committee
> Stop ERA
> American Security Council
> Council on Inter-American Security

The New Right gained its first victory in 1977 with a well-coordinated campaign to stop changes in the election laws. From the summer of 1977 to the spring of 1978, it took the leadership that the Republican party was unwilling to exercise in opposition to the Panama Canal treaties. That campaign nearly succeeded and added 400,000 new names to the New Right mailing lists. Another result was that eight senators who voted for ratification were defeated in the November 1978 elections. Five others did not seek reelection, in part because of New Right opposition.

Perhaps more important in the long run, in 1977 and 1978 the New Right began to build a "profamily" coalition. Antiabortion groups; the stop-ERA campaign; and organizations opposing pornography, gay rights, and childrens' services were all started or extensively supported by New Right activists. At about this same time, the tax revolt, symbolized by the success of Proposition 13 in California, began to spread, also with heavy support from New Right money and campaign personnel.

Finally, in 1979 the decision was made to try to incorporate the "religious right" within the network of organizations and direct mail communication that is the heart and soul of the New Right. Several groups were founded for this purpose. First came the Los Angeles-based Christian Voice, which brings a New Right perspective on legislative voting records to the attention of tens of thousands of ministers and many more lay members. The next group founded was the Moral Majority, under Jerry Falwell. The Reverend Falwell was already well known for his "Old Time Gospel Hour," which reaches as many as 50 million people a week. The Moral Majority was credited with defeating several liberal senators in 1980. It also probably provided Ronald Reagan with a significant portion of his winning electoral margin. The third group, also begun in 1979, was the Religious Roundtable. It brings thousands of ministers together four or more times a year to hear a variety of New Right speakers.

By 1980 the organizational structure of the New Right had reached out to its full range of social and religious issues. It had prepared the way for a right-wing conservative triumph of major proportions. In its own eyes, it required only a consolidation period to become as permanent a governing majority as the American political system has ever known. The potential of the New Right is well summarized by Kevin Phillips.

I submit that the New Right combines three powerful trend patterns that recur in American history and politics. First, to some measure it is an extension of the Wallace movement, and as such represents a current expression of the ongoing populism of the white lower middle classes, principally in the South and West. All the right symbols are present: antimetropolitanism, antielitism, cultural fundamentalism. Second, the New Right is closely allied with the sometimes potent right-to-life or antiabortion movement, the current version, perhaps, of the great one-issue moral crusades of the American past—the pre-Civil War abolitionists and the early-twentieth-century prohibitionists. And this one-issue element, in turn, folds into the third phenomenon—the possible fourth occurrence of the religious revivals or "Great Awakenings" that have swept across the land since the middle of the eighteenth century. If so, the *religious* wing of the New Right may be the *political* wing of a major national "awakening."[9]

BASIC VALUES

The values of the Christian Right are not just distinct versions of the traditional American values. Instead, values and assumptions grounded in the Bible take precedence over, or serve to give entirely new definitions to, the standard values. American politics thus becomes a battle of ends and not means, a battle for the triumph of the Lord; there can be neither compromise nor accommodation with opponents. For these reasons, the Christian Right is a driving force in the long-term reconstruction of the American political spectrum, and its values cannot be analyzed in our usual format.

The basic assumption by the Christian Right is that the origins of the United States were God given. Phyllis Schlafly writes:

> The Declaration of Independence is the official and unequivocal recognition by the American people of their belief and faith in God. It is a religious document from its first sentence to its last. . . . The nation created by the great Declaration is God's country. The rights it defines are God-given. The actions of its signers are God-inspired.[10]

Pat Robertson says that the Constitution is

> the finest instrument of self-government ever struck by human hands. It wasn't just human hands. It was a divine instrument. And that instrument assumes throughout all of its pages the existence of God, the existence of the Bible, the existence of spiritual principles. And these men attempted, under God, to form a nation that was governed and ruled by eternal principles . . . They were looking at the Holy Bible.

Pat Buchanan has put the source of governing values—and thus the nature of the battle yet to be fought—in these terms:

> The Old and New Testaments are not only infallible guides to personal salvation; they contain the prescriptions for just laws and the good society—for building a city set upon a hill. . . . Religion is at the root of morality; and morality is the basis of law. . . . The only option the traditionalist and the conservative have, then, is never to cease struggling—until we have re-created a government and an America that conforms, as closely as possible, to our image of the Good Society, if you will, a Godly country.[12]

What this means for the future of American politics, according to Buchanan, is conflict of the most fundamental kind.

> We no longer share the same religious faith, the same code of morality, the same public philosophy. It is not simply about the role and responsibility of government that we disagree; today, our ideas of freedom and virtue and patriotism collide. . . . Our political and social quarrels now partake of the savagery of religious wars because, at bottom, they are religious wars. The most divisive issues in American politics are now about our warring concepts of right and wrong, of good and evil. . . . We have become "two nations."[13]

The values dominating the Christian Right, and the redefinition to be applied to the standard American values if necessary, flow from a literal understanding of Biblical texts. Fundamentalists (of any denomination) believe in the direct and literal application of the Bible to contemporary affairs, particularly moral questions. Born-again Christians (of any denomination) have had a religious experience in which they have accepted Christ as their personal savior and now seek to follow his teachings rigorously. Evangelicals (again, of any denomination) are Christians who aggressively seek to convert others to their faith and its behavioral requirements.

A public profession of faith in God and strict adherence to his teachings are preached as part of following God's word. A stringent moral code must be instituted, particularly with respect to restoring the traditional patriarchal family (and its child-rearing practices) and severely punishing crimes of all kinds (including the death penalty).

Some members of the Christian Right take literally the prediction in the Book of Revelation of a final battle preceding Christ's second coming and establishment of his kingdom. They differ over how soon this will happen and how much Christians will have to endure before it does. This belief, however, lends urgency and authority to the Christian mission to take over and Christianize secular social institutions. A professional observer notes, "the concept that Christians are Biblically mandated to 'occupy' all secular institutions has become the central unifying ideology for the Christian Right."[14] One leader articulates this commitment as follows:

> The Bible says we are to . . . rule. If you don't rule and I don't rule, the atheists and the humanists and the agnostics are going to rule. We should be the head of our school board. We should be the head of our nation. We should be the Senators and the Congressmen. We should be the editors of our newspapers. We should be taking over every area of life.[15]

Two great obstacles stand in the way of restoring the United States to godliness. Both are summary statements of everything the Christian Right most opposes and must destroy. The first is secular humanism, and the second is communism.

Secular humanists believe that human rationality, and particularly developing scientific knowledge, can solve problems and guide humankind to a more rational and satisfying life. The Christian Right sees secular humanism as denying the existence of God and replacing him with a human-centered world in which humankind is left alone without God's guidance. Secular humanism is seen as particularly pernicious when it comes to dominate in the schools of the land. Secular humanism's domination is most readily visible in textbooks, where God is rarely mentioned and his creation of the world is ignored or disparaged.

Only a short step further and secular humanism becomes a kind of shadowy movement seeking control of the country and the world. Tim LaHaye, author of *The Battle for the Mind* and a major leader of the Christian Right, sets forth the problem:

Simply defined, humanism is man's attempt to solve his problems independently of God. Since moral conditions have become worse and worse in direct proportion to humanism's influence, which has moved our country from a biblically based society to an amoral "democratic" society during the past forty years, one would think that humanists would realize the futility of their position. To the contrary, they treacherously refuse to face the reality of their failures, blaming them instead on traditional religion or ignorance or capitalism or religious superstitions.[16]

LaHaye goes on to identify the ACLU, the NAACP, and NOW as leading organizations in the humanist conspiracy. In a manner typical of other Christian Right spokespersons, Phyllis Schlafly extends the scope of the humanist program:

Humanism works for the establishment of a "secular society," a "socialized economic order," world government, military disarmament, and population control by government.[17]

In this respect, secular humanism seeks essentially the same goals as communism.

Communism, the second obstacle to restoring godliness in the United States, is the greatest threat of all. Not only is it a belief system in complete opposition to everything the Christian Right stands for, but it is a powerful military presence mortally threatening the United States. Communism seizes every opportunity and uses any means to advance ruthlessly across the world. It can only be countered by an equally far-flung and ruthless countermovement. Quite literally, communism embodies evil; the Soviet Union is Satan. The president of the Religious Roundtable frames the conflict as between good and evil:

I believe there are really two philosophies at warfare, contending for the minds and the allegiances of men. One of them, on the Left, represents the Soviet Union and says there is no God. Minor premise: man is good. . . . On the other hand, the philosophy that I adhered to was that of Western Civilization, headed up by the United States of America. It operated on the philosophy that there is a God. Minor premise: man is imperfect.[18]

The "minor premise" contrast in this statement includes an important point. The Christian Right knows that human beings are imperfect, fallen, and in need of God's light to guide them. Not much can be done for them *except* to provide such guidance. The communists—and their domestic cousins, the secular humanists—believe human beings are inherently good. They only behave badly because of their surrounding environment, which can be improved through human rationality.

What do these compelling values and assumptions imply for the Christian Right's interpretation of standard American political values? Clearly the individual is central to the temporal world, but human nature is inherently irrational and self-interested. Individuals need God's guidance.

They must, if necessary, be required to live in accordance with his commandments. Freedom can mean only freedom to do as one should, in keeping with God's teachings. Equality is an illusion, particularly when used to justify government action that impinges upon God's rules.

Government is the proper agent to assure proper behavior. At the least, it must facilitate other organizations' efforts to do so; that is, it must support the work of the churches and religious organizations. Democracy, however, presents a problem. It has served as a screen for secular humanist policies and practices. Only a God-guided democracy is appropriate. When majorities act contrary to God's will, they must be opposed.

Combining these Christian values and assumptions with the necessary redefinitions of standard American values results in a quite conservative posture. The ideology and movement encompass many people. The goals are sought through electoral politics in which majorities determine the outcome. Hence the term *populist conservative* is quite appropriate.

PROBLEMS AND POSSIBILITIES

The New Right sees itself as representative of a neglected middle class that is under extreme pressure from a combination of other sectors of the population—the rich, the militant minorities and poor, and the new class of government bureaucrats and allied professionals. This last group uses the power of government to make the powerless, hard-working middle pay the costs of the gains demanded by the poor and minorities and supinely granted by the controlling rich. It is as if the three groups worked together to make Middle Americans pay. Furthermore, none of them have any respect for *either* Middle Americans *or* their traditional values.

In New Right thinking, a new elite came into power in the 1930s. Steadily multiplying itself, it has dominated the executive branch and the judiciary ever since. This elite is cosmopolitan, amoral, self-indulgent, and materialistic. It acknowledges no limits and is contemptuous of families, work, self-sacrifice, community, and the moral and social order. According to the New Right:

> Its ideology . . . is liberalism—a set of ideas and values that ostensibly upholds equality, liberty, and the brotherhood of man but which is amazingly congruent with and adaptable to the political, economic, and social interests (the structural interests) of the groups that espouse it. . . . Liberalism flourishes almost entirely because it reflects the material and psychological interests of a privileged, power-holding, and power-seeking sector of American society.[19]

It is not just the dismissal and denigration of families and communities that the New Right resents about the new class of federal bureaucrats and professionals managing the government. What also triggers bitter and active resistance is the *attitude* with which that new class goes about its work. Here is how the matter is perceived by another New Right leader:

Nothing has contributed more to white populist disillusionment than the breathtaking hypocrisy and condescending arrogance shown by the establishment over the race issue. . . . While the wealthy remained immune (because they could afford to send their children to private schools), populist Americans have been expected to welcome the social and racial experimentation which bodes only disaster for themselves and their communities.[20]

In the eyes of the Christian Right, big government in the hands of the liberal establishment and, secondarily, feminism are leading manifestations of secular humanism. Together, they are responsible for diverting the United States from its early path of Christian virtue. Free and available abortions, legally protected pornography, ready divorce, and the prohibitions on prayer and other religious observances in public schools forced integration through busing, affirmative action, permissiveness and homosexuality, the welfare state's creation of dependency, rapidly rising crime, widespread drug and alcohol usage—these are only some of the effects of their continued dominance.

The same governing establishment utterly failed to appropriately understand and respond to the overwhelming menace of communism, represented in its most expansionist and dangerous military form by the Soviet Union. Trade agreements, economic assistance, arms-control agreements, and even the containment policy of the cold war period are misguided accommodations with Soviet tyranny. The ruling liberal establishment (the State Department, the media, the liberal foundations and foreign policy associations), even under conservative presidents, systematically underestimated the Soviet threat and its utter dishonesty and contempt for treaty obligations.

To combat secular humanism and communism, the twin perils to the survival of a moral America, all the Christian Right resources must be fully mobilized. An appropriate strategy must address both the domestic and foreign aspects of the threat.

Pat Buchanan proposes solutions to many of the domestic problems with a set of ten amendments to the U.S. Constitution (shown here in condensed form as Table 8.1).

With respect to those amendments, Buchanan declares:

All of the above are populist amendments, designed to broaden the scope of human rights and restore the power of the people to shape their own society and destiny. They would diminish the power of unelected judges and enhance that of elected officials. . . . Conservatives have nothing to fear from a constitutional convention and much to gain by focusing national debate on the issues that divide the Republic. A call for a constitutional convention would reveal which of the two parties is populist, and which elitist, which trusts and which fears the people.[21]

Buchanan's goal is a constitutional convention that would restore presidential authority and moral principles. He argues that it is absurd to fear

Table 8.1 Ten Proposed Constitutional Amendments

1. For purposes of this Constitution, the unborn child shall be considered a "person" whose right to life shall not be abrogated without due process of law.

2. Nothing in this Constitution prohibits the states from imposing capital punishment upon conviction for heinous crimes or for habitual criminal offenders.

3. English is the official language of the United States, and Congress may legislate to this end.

4. All federal judges and justices of the Supreme Court shall be subject to reconfirmation by the Congress every eight years.

5. Decisions of the Supreme Court may be set aside by a two-thirds vote of both houses of Congress, with the approval of the president.

6. The Twenty-Second Amendment to the Constitution (restricting presidents to two full terms) is hereby repealed.

7. The president shall propose and Congress shall adopt, for each fiscal year, a budget balanced between projected revenues and expenditures.

8. Nothing in this Constitution prohibits the free and voluntary expression of religious faith or religious instruction and association within the public institutions or public schools of the United States.

9. Discrimination on the basis of race, either in favor of or against any citizen, is prohibited by this Constitution, as is the use of racial criteria in the involuntary assignment of children to public schools.

10. Coterminous with each presidential election, the American people may, through popular initiative and referendum, invalidate or make laws for the United States.

SOURCE: Condensed from Patrick J. Buchanan, *Right from the Beginning*, (Washington, D.C.: Regnery Gateway, 1990), p. 356.

what a convention might propose because the people always have the power to reject any proposal. In the meantime, the specific amendments in Table 8.1 would serve to focus national debate and election-year issues.

Other issues not covered in the amendments continue to be major foci of Christian Right efforts. For example, after the successful defeat of the Equal Rights Amendment, Concerned Women of America shifted its efforts toward blocking equal pay for women in the labor force ("comparable worth.") Phyllis Schlafly turns the argument against itself in a populist manner:

> The comparable worth advocates are trying to freeze the wages of blue-collar men while forcing employers to raise the wages of some white and pink-collar women above market rates . . . it is always an elaborate scheme to devalue the blue-collar man.[22]

Control of Labor Unions

Working through the National Right to Work Committee, the New Right has taken aim at the power of the labor bosses and their unions. Campaigns are overtly focused on the unrepresentativeness and raw power of labor leaders. However, in practice their result is often to weaken severely trade unions in general. One major tactic has been to promote passage of right-to-work laws (statutes prohibiting collective bargaining agreements from requiring that all employees join the recognized union at a particular site). Such laws have been enacted in several states. They effectively undercut union financial support and membership strength, making organization much more difficult. At the national level, the New Right has succeeded in cutting back union-supporting legislation.

Paul Weyrich explains these motivations by linking big labor with big business. He says:

> Most of our fathers belonged to unions. We are anti-big business. The problem is that big unions turned into part of the problem. The New Right does not believe that unions per se are evil, as did the economic purist conservatives of the 1930s; we do not want to abolish unions. We merely recognize that today's big union leadership is unrepresentative of union membership, and, worse, uncaring of membership's concerns. We see that the big union bosses abuse members' hard-earned contributions.[23]

The New Right also has been strongly opposed to the formation of unions of public employees. The grounds are twofold: it is inappropriate for such workers to be unionized, and unionization here adds to the total cost of government.

Race and Crime

Crime has been another major focus of New Right energies. Racial antagonisms and fear often lie unacknowledged in the background of New Right discussions about the problem of crime in the United States. Those on the New Right have endorsed any number of stricter punishments, including capital punishment, for various forms of crime. Much of their activity has taken the form of attacks on courts and judges for showing such great regard for the rights of accused defendants that convictions become very difficult and for imposing excessively light sentences when convictions *are* obtained.

Racial antagonism is closer to the surface in such issues as school busing for purposes of integration. The New Right has regularly supported antibusing groups and promoted legislation to prohibit busing. However, they argue that such activity is not racially motivated but based on their belief in the principle of neighborhood schools.

Opposition to the proposed constitutional amendment to give the District of Columbia the same voting rights in Congress as states enjoy again reveals this combination of racial and other concerns. It is the link with other issues that makes the D.C. amendment seem so threatening to New Right aims and generates such vigorous opposition. As an editorial in *Conservative Digest* advised:

> If you want to add to the United States Senate two more sure votes against a strong national defense, against effective internal security measures, against tax cuts, for gun control, for publicly financed abortions, for homosexual

privileges, for ERA, for Big Labor, and above all, for big government, then support the proposed constitutional amendment to give the District of Columbia full voting privileges.[24]

Gun Control

The issue of registering, controlling, or outlawing certain kinds of guns is surely among the most explosive in American politics today. The National Rifle Association, though a very effective opponent of gun control, has maintained at least some distance from the New Right, but several similar organizations are closely linked with it. The Firearms Lobby of America and the American Legislative Exchange Council, for example, have carried much of the responsibility for opposition to the D.C. amendment as well as gun-control legislation.

More narrowly focused on gun control alone are the Citizens Committee for the Right to Keep and Bear Arms and Gun Owners of America, both with state affiliates or tax-deductible legal and educational foundations. All of these groups oppose all forms of gun control. They argue that guns represent the last line of defense of individual rights and freedoms. Hundreds of thousands of Americans stand with them on these questions.

The primary battlegrounds of the struggle against secular humanism, however, are the schools and the right to abortion. As Buchanan says:

> There is no more important battle shaping up in America than for the hearts and minds of the next generation. Whether that generation will be traditionalist and Christian, or agnostic and atheist, whether its code of morality and ethics will be based on Judeo-Christian beliefs or in the secular nostrums of the moment, will be largely determined by America's public schools.[25]

The Christian Right advocates breaking the state's monopoly over schooling by providing tax support to parochial and private schools. One consistent proposal is a voucher system allowing parental choice and thus competition among schools. In addition, disciplinary powers should be restored to school authorities and religious observances reinstituted. Most of all, textbooks must be purged of humanist teachings, and Christian morality restored.

The Christian Right sees a woman's right to choose abortion as an act of murder, legitimized out of self-indulgent self-interest on the part of women influenced by the feminist movement. Schlafly links feminism's (alleged) willing violation of divine laws to humanism:

> Just as humanism is based on atheism and the notion that man is at the center of the universe, Feminism puts woman at the center of the universe. They chose the word "liberation" because they mean liberation from home, husband, family, and children.[26]

The most visible of the Christian Right's antiabortion activities are the direct-action efforts of Operation Rescue, founded in 1988 by the Reverend Randy Terry. They engage in blockage of entrances and other acts of civil disobedience at a number of abortion clinics and selected sites throughout the country.

The global confrontation with communism has led elements within the Christian Right to form a number of international organizations. They each follow different strategies in the various arenas around the world. Because their origins and goals differ so sharply, many will no doubt continue their efforts despite what might appear as the demise of communism. Deep suspicion of the wiles of Soviet communism, the possibility of revival and/or suicidal military attack by die-hard Communists in the Soviet Union, a reenergized Communist China—such beliefs can provide a rationale for Christian Right activities for at least another decade. Pat Buchanan, for example, declares:

> True peace requires the de-Leninization of the Soviet Union, the replacement of Lenin's party in Moscow by a regime, military or civilian, responsive not to the Leninist ideology of endless war, but to the legitimate aspirations of the captive peoples within the Soviet Union. . . . Indeed, both the Russian and the American people share the same enemy, the Communist party of the Soviet Union.[27]

By implication, the same analysis applies to Cuba, North Korea, the People's Republic of China, and perhaps other countries as well.

The first organizations were formed to counter the ultra liberal National Council of Churches and its counterpart, the World Council of Churches. First came the American Council of Christian Churches and then the International Council of Christian Churches. These led to Dr. Fred Schwarz's Christian Anti-Communism Crusade, which has been particularly active in Third World countries such as the Philippines.

In the 1980s the attack on the National Council of Churches and the World Council of Churches was stepped up by the formation of the Institute on Religion and Democracy (IRD). The institute also campaigned against links between churches or individual ministers and the U.S. peace movement. Working through the National Association of Evangelicals (NAE), a group representing more than 50,000 churches, the IRD helped to develop a counterweight to the peace and arms-control efforts of the mainline church organizations. The World Without War Council emerged from the Peace, Freedom, and Security Studies program of NAE. It focused on ways to undercut organizations seeking peace and nonintervention in Latin America.

In addition to efforts to strengthen anticommunism at home and abroad, the Christian Right has asserted a special interest in promoting the cause of Israeli strength and independence. Despite some anti-Semitism in the past, the Christian Right has come to support Israel for two reasons: its important military significance for U.S. interests in the Middle

East, and its special religious significance as the site of Jesus' life and the place where Biblical prophecies will be fulfilled. A kind of Christian Zionism has developed to promote support for Israel; the Israelis have reciprocated with regular participation in such organizations as the National Religious Broadcasters.

Finally, the Christian Right stands for "an aggressive new nationalism."[28] Foreign aid should be extended unilaterally if at all; aid to corrupt or unfriendly governments should be terminated; the United Nations should be evicted from American soil; and, if possible, the big U.S. banks should be left to collect their own debts. American military power must be maintained at a high state of readiness, and economic policy should pursue trade advantages and concessions wherever needed.

IMPLICATIONS AND PROSPECTS

In spite of its successes, there is a problem in the future for the populist conservative-Christian Right ideology and movement. Can it continue to work in coalition with the mainstream of American conservatism in the Republican party? This mainstream is made up of the organic conservatives and libertarians, sometimes referred to as the Old Right. (Their incomplete synthesis is analyzed in the next chapter.) The problem for the New Right, however, should already be clear. Populist conservatism has only its anticommunism in common with the others. It does not support either big business *or* a laissez-faire government. It stands instead for decisive government action to reinstitute Christian morality. Moreover, populist conservatism emerges from a lower- and lower-middle-class base and is militantly antielitist.

ADDITIONAL READINGS

Buchanan, Patrick J. *Right from the Beginning*. Washington, D.C.: Regnery Gateway, 1990.

Crawford, Alan. *Thunder on the Right: The "New Right" and the Politics of Resentment*. New York: Pantheon, 1980.

Diamond, Sara. *Spiritual Warfare: The Politics of the Christian Right*. Boston: South End Press, 1989.

Hunter, William A. "The New Right: A Growing Force in State Politics." Washington, D.C.: Conference on Alternative State and Local Politics, 1980.

Klatch, Rebecca E. *Women of the New Right*. Philadelphia: Temple University Press, 1987.

Noonan, Peggy. *What I Saw at the Revolution: A Political Life in the Reagan Era*. New York: Random House, 1990.

Phillips, Kevin P. *Post-Conservative America: People, Politics, and Ideology in a Time of Crisis*. New York: Random House, 1982.

Rusher, William A. *The Making of the New Majority Party*. New York: Sheed and Ward, 1975.

Viguerie, Richard A. *The New Right: We're Ready to Lead*. Falls Church, Va.: Viguerie Company, 1980.

Warren, Donald I. *The Radical Center: Middle Americans and the Politics of Alienation*. South Bend, Ind.: Notre Dame University Press, 1976.

Whitaker, Robert W. *The New Right Papers*. New York: St. Martin's Press, 1982.

CHAPTER 9

ORGANIC CONSERVATISM AND LIBERTARIANISM

In the 1990s, organic conservatism and libertarianism stand in uneasy alliance as twin pillars—and principal beneficiaries—of the "right turn" in American politics. Both have deep roots in American political thought, but neither has ever found the popular base that would bring it to power—until the rise of populist conservatism. Their current alliance remains fragile, with significant tensions, although some recent developments indicate a potential synthesis.

What organic conservatives and libertarians share is support from the upper-middle class and the business community, their anticommunism, and, most of all, a vigorous opposition to orthodox liberalism. What divides them begins with some fundamental organic conservatives' beliefs: putting the society or community first, a willingness to use government to do what is right for that society, and a skepticism about the economic market's capacity to achieve all that needs to be done for the betterment of the society. Prominent organic conservative voices include columnist-author George Will and William F. Buckley, who founded the *National Review*. In the last decade, they have been joined by a new generation of thinkers—the neoconservatives—such as Irving Kristol, Robert Nisbet, Nathan Glazer, and Michael Novak.

In contrast, libertarians put the individual first. They seek to limit government from any and all interference with that individual's activities, economic and social. They believe that the free market is fully capable of organizing economic life and will produce the full measure of the public interest. Contrary to organic conservatives, government is the problem, never the solution.

Libertarianism came into its own in the 1970s when the desire to "get the government off our backs" spread from economics to the newly important social issues. At that point, many relatively affluent younger people agreed with feminists and civil libertarians on the social issues. They, in effect, merged with the older tradition of antistatist 1890s-style liberalism to end up with an internally consistent laissez-faire libertarianism. Prominent libertarian voices include economist Milton Friedman, philosopher Robert Nozick, and such organizations as the Cato Institute and the Heritage Foundation.

150

To understand the revival of these forms of American conservatism and their current uneasy alliance requires more historical development than is necessary for the other ideologies. Our analysis concludes with a review of the potentially developing synthesis of these two long-standing antagonists.

LINKS TO THE PAST

In the immediate post-World War II period, what Americans called conservatism consisted of two sets of ideas that maintained an arm's length relationship with each other. One set of ideas was an antistatist version of liberalism that emphasized individualism, strictly limited government, and the economic free market. This brand of liberalism, also known as Manchester liberalism after the English school of thought that gave it its clearest expression, was at its height in the 1890s. In the United States it was also associated with social Darwinism. Advocates of social Darwinism held, in essence, that government assistance to disadvantaged people was undesirable because the human species was improved by the struggle to survive.

Antistatist, 1890s liberalism gained support in the postwar years because it warned against the very expansions of government activity that seemed to some to have led inexorably to fascist governments in Germany and Italy or to socialism elsewhere. Freedom, in the sense of freedom from government intervention, was the cornerstone of this brand of liberalism. In particular, the economic free market was held out as a neutral, efficient, and proper allocator of burdens and benefits in the society. Any increase of government functions, particularly in economic affairs, touched off vigorous opposition from this corner as a threat to individual freedom. Today, with the additional concern for keeping government out of the individual's private affairs, this strand of thinking is better called libertarian.

The second set of ideas that made up conservatism in the post-World War II period was descended from the traditional organic conservatism identified with the eighteenth-century English thinker Edmund Burke. This set of beliefs is fundamentally different from liberalism. It does not focus primarily on the individual and his or her needs for fulfillment through various self-seeking activities. Instead, it starts with the society considered as a whole. Its primary concern is the improvement of the civilization represented by that society. The responsibility of leaders is to guide that society in ways consistent with its traditions, natural law, or some other public-interest standard—not to seek favor with necessarily transitory majorities of individuals.

Organic conservatism is concerned with social and cultural dimensions of life, that is, with the moral values and religious or ethical spirit that suffuse the social order and give life meaning. Property rights are important because they assure stability. They also provide opportunity for some to cultivate their intellectual and artistic qualities, thus contributing to the civilization as a whole. Complete economic freedom for individual or corporate self-seeking, however, can be morally or physically damaging to the continued development of the society. The claims of business under 1890s liberalism's laissez-faire principles stand on no higher ground than the claims of individuals for some similar short-term advantages. Organic conservatism always keeps its eyes on long-term goals: appetites must be curbed today so that needs of future generations may be considered.

The position of organic conservatives in the American context has always been awkward. Devoted to the preservation of the society's enduring traditions, they looked to the past for guidance but found only liberalism. Some observers argued that organic conservatism was really another foreign import or a romantic effort to reconstruct the American past and present. Moreover, the basic assumptions of an individualistic society stood squarely in the way of conservatives' efforts to achieve electoral success. One distinguished commentator described conservatism as "the thankless persuasion." Liberals generally dismissed it as a serious factor in American political thinking.[1]

In 1955 the call to arms was sounded by a new conservative journal, which probably did more than any other single factor to unify, expand, and legitimate the new conservative movement. The journal was the *National Review*, and its founder was the uniquely capable William F. Buckley, Jr. Creative thinker, incisive writer, intimidating debater, indefatigable fund raiser, and urbanely witty in the bargain, Buckley is the most important individual figure in the rise of conservatism and perhaps in postwar American political thought. From his first book in 1951, *God and Man at Yale: The Superstitions of "Academic Freedom,"* through *McCarthy and His Enemies*, and a continuing series of other polemics and travelogues, Buckley kept the conservative viewpoint visible, always lively, and on top of every issue.[2]

The *National Review* opened its pages to all brands of conservatism but emphasized anticommunism and the failures of liberalism. It symbolized a decisive shift in the orientation of conservatism, from a defensive posture to an offensive one against the decadent liberal establishment. Conservatism no longer appeared resigned to the dominance of liberalism or to the role of a despairing critic on behalf of an old order. It now took on a much more aggressive approach, offering itself as the prospective replacement of liberalism and talking seriously in terms of achieving the strength to govern and redirect the country.

In a short time, other major publications followed Buckley's. First was Barry Goldwater's *The Conscience of a Conservative*.[3] In it, Goldwater brought 1890s liberalism together with the notion of a powerful government for purposes of fighting communism throughout the world. It served as a rallying point for Goldwater's followers in 1960 and ultimately helped build the movement that achieved his nomination for the presidency in 1964. Another major work was Milton Friedman's *Capitalism and Freedom*, a clear and compelling call for pure laissez-faire and the free market.[4]

In the immediate postwar years, the two strands of conservatism had in common only their defensive posture on behalf of some older American values and the fact that each stood firmly against the mainstream liberal tide. Their critiques of liberalism rested on quite different grounds. However, their apparently shared backward-looking orientation earned them the collective title of the Old Right. They found some mutual support in their opposition to the dominant trend but agreed on little else—until the 1950s. Anticommunism, the cold war, and their shared sense of the need for a powerful American military and political presence around the world provided the initial basis for alliance. This foundation proved to be strong and compelling. Furthermore, it enabled conservatives to draw new support, and not only from the business community.

Now allied, opponents of liberalism could rally others with concerns about the direction that American society was taking. Liberalism was no longer solving problems; it was creating them. As the problems grew, so did the ranks of opponents. Conservatives took considerable pleasure in stressing their differences from liberals.

At first, the antistatist liberals insisted that they were the true liberals. In a way, they were correct. They argued that those in government were misguided egalitarians who had been led to support big government by wrongly blaming the free market for the Depression. Eventually the line had to be drawn. As Milton Friedman's *Capitalism and Freedom*, the leading 1890s liberal tract of the times, declared:

> The liberal will therefore distinguish sharply between equality of rights and equality of opportunity, on the one hand, and material equality or equality of outcome on the other. . . . But [the egalitarian] will defend taking from some to give to others, not as a more effective means whereby the "some" can achieve an objective they want to achieve, but on the grounds of "justice." At this point, equality comes sharply into conflict with freedom; one must choose. One cannot be both an egalitarian, and a liberal.[5]

Traditional conservatives saw the contrast between themselves and mainstream liberals in even more sweeping terms. They complained that liberals wrongly think of the world as a rational, controllable place in which all problems have solutions. A metaphor used by George Will, a leading organic conservative, clearly states the contrast perceived:

> Liberalism is political astronomy—anachronistic astronomy, unaware that even the planets do more wobbling and wandering and banging about than the eighteenth century thought. Conservatism is political biology. It emphasizes the indeterminateness, the complexity of things, and the fact that there is more to a social system than meets the eye.[6]

At some point in the mid-1960s, conservatives of both varieties began to realize that they were not necessarily a permanent minority standing in isolated opposition to an inexorable liberalism. The Goldwater campaign of 1964 is probably the best point from which to date the conservative shift away from a defensive posture. Conservatism was melding the bulk of the business community, the right wing of the Republican party, and new constituents from other sectors into a significant force. To take the offensive, however, requires both the sense that it is possible to become a majority and contend for the right to govern *and* a more positive shared program. It was essential to be *for* some things as well as against many others. It was also important to be against a number of different things for the same reasons and with the same remedies in mind.

Many conservatives were quite self-conscious about this threshold. Organic conservatives began at this point to talk in terms of their own vision of an appropriate welfare state, grounded in a transcendent concept of social justice.[7] The most visible 1890s liberal, Ronald Reagan, regularly used the term *social safety net* to refer to legitimate government protections for disadvantaged people. In looking back at this period from the vantage point of 1983, George Will aptly states the issue that had to be faced:

> For nearly half a century, conservatism was, or felt itself to be, in the political wilderness. . . . Conservatism generally was a doctrine in, and of, opposition. During this period it became cranky and recriminatory. Therefore, a question posed by the coming to power of self-conscious conservatism is this: Can there be conservatism with a kindly face?[8]

The awareness of the potential of majoritarian appeal is itself a powerful force strengthening the synthesis between the two versions of conservatism. Hope for power creates not only strange bedfellows but also more tolerant roommates. It is true that for many the Soviet threat remained alive and dangerous despite its eclipse in official liberal perceptions. Opposition to liberalism was exacerbated by the failure to effectively pursue the war in Vietnam and by apparently unparalleled growth in Soviet military power. But during this period at least three other very important convictions came to be shared with increasing enthusiasm. Each added new layers of strength to the basic foundation already in place.

First, conservatives believed that liberal social engineering and welfarism were undermining absolutely fundamental American values associated with family, religion, and work. For the organic conservatives, such values were deep cultural traditions. They provided the source of the American spirit and the basic social ties that knit the society into an organic unit. They are the values at the very core of the civilization, the essense that conservatism seeks to conserve and enhance.

The 1890s liberals also believed such values were basic building blocks. For them, family, religion, and work were roots of self-reliance and individualism, the essential ingredients of a working free market and good society. All that 1890s liberals opposed most fiercely about governmental intrusion into the realm of personal freedom seemed typified by the substitution of bureaucratic intervention for the roles once played by family and religion in American life.

Second, beginning about 1968, the American economy began to decline; unemployment and inflation became simultaneous problems. None of the liberal remedies celebrated as capable of fine-tuning the economy seemed to work at all. Organic conservatives as well as 1890s liberals began to identify the same causes for these problems: excessive spending, taxes, and regulation on the part of government. Organic conservatives had always believed in a frugal, prudent government of modest size, with a balanced budget and a small deficit. Military needs were one category of priority, but expensive social programs and the taxes required to sustain them were another matter.

The 1890s liberals were even more outraged at the ever-expanding scope of government intervention. They saw mounting levels of spending and taxes as the measures of this expansion. The taxes required to sustain social programs were drawn from an increasingly hard-pressed private economy. The geometrically multiplying regulations added significantly to the cost of doing business. Between taxes and regulations, businesses were neither free nor, in many cases, profitable. Moreover, unbalanced budgets led to inflation and the destruction of predictability in the market economy.

Third, the economy and society were dominated by self-interested behavior on the part of businesses, groups, and individuals alike. Everybody was not only out for themselves but also out to get all they could. This self-aggrandizing took the form of battling over subsidies, concessions, and other supports from government. It had nothing to do with the competition appropriate to a free market situation. There was no regard for a public interest, whether articulated explicitly by government or silently by the automatic workings of the free market.

Both organic conservatives and 1890s liberals saw businesses, particularly big businesses, seeking to avoid competition. Such businesses claimed special favors on the grounds of the widespread public hardship that would otherwise result from their reduced profitability. One of the purest of free market 1890s liberals put the matter this way:

> Although most businessmen publicly proclaim their devotion to the free market, they always do so with a big "but." The "but" is usually followed by some explanation about how their situation is different, about how they are faced with "unfair" competition, or how the "national interest" demands that they receive government help.[9]

Not only businesses but also powerful lobbies and special interest groups were subjected to this criticism. Obviously, none had any concern for the general welfare of the economy as a whole. Liberalism was blamed for encouraging such assertiveness. Furthermore, liberalism had no standards other than relative political power for determining whether a claimant was entitled to help.

Consistent principles were impossible amid these swarming self-seekers. No moral spirit animated either people or business in such a context. Notions of honor, integrity, and other sound principles of social and economic life were lost. In particular, the sense of creativity and satisfaction in capitalist entrepreneurship was missing. Once again, liberalism was to blame for encouraging such a self-interested society in which so many were unwilling to be exposed to the risks requisite to growth and progress. One of the leading publicists of the conservative "return to capitalism" of the early 1980s was George Gilder. In his popular *Wealth and Poverty*, he argued:

> Liberals seems to want wealth without the rich. Yet most real wealth originates in individual minds in unpredictable and uncontrollable ways. A successful economy depends on the proliferation of the rich, on creating a large class of risk-taking men who are willing to shun the easy channels of a comfortable life in order to create new enterprise, win huge profits, and invest them again. . . . They are the heroes of economic life, and those who begrudge them their rewards demonstrate a failure to understand their role and their promise.[10]

In each of these three convictions, the alliance of organic conservatism and 1890s liberalism encountered the happy fact of popular support. People rallied in large numbers to the arguments that the values of family, religion, and work were being undermined; that the government was too big, intrusive, and costly; and that one key cause was excessive self-interest on the part of everybody besides themselves.

Spurred by the realities of popular support and possible power, the two distinct strands of the earlier conservatism moved from strange bedfellows to tolerant roommates and then toward wedded bliss. However, along the way, changes were inevitable. Some values and beliefs allied easily; others merged and became something new; still others struggled for independent survival. Conservatism, in other words, has been going through a process of reconstitution and regeneration. The organic conservative George Will welcomes this development. Speaking of the inevitable and appropriate "clustering" of ideas that, once they take distinct shape, lead to useful labels, Will says:

> There are moments, and this is one, when it is particularly important to suggest alternative clusterings. Specifically, the cluster of ideas that is commonly thought to constitute conservatism should be pried apart and recon-

stituted. . . . My aim is to recast conservatism in a form compatible with the broad popular imperatives of the day, but also to change somewhat the agenda and even the vocabulary of contemporary politics.[11]

Equality and Freedom

Perhaps the traditional value of equality best illustrates the complexity of the emerging conservatism's principles. All conservatives agree that equality should mean only equality of opportunity. Liberalism has done great damage by its incessant efforts to achieve a much-expanded version. For most conservatives, what liberalism seeks is nothing less than equality of outcomes. Further, in seeking such an impossible goal, liberalism has been obliged to create and empower a government of vast and inevitably freedom-destroying scope.

Beyond this point, however, conservative reasoning and remedies begin to diverge in ways that show the synthesis to be still incomplete. For the organic conservatives, the problem caused by the liberal commitment to excessive equality is not the size of the government. The problem is that government authority has been destroyed. For the 1890s liberals, the problem is precisely the government's massive size. It crushes freedom and individual initiative while creating a new kind of inequality in the form of a new class of power holders.

At stake in the continuing tension over definitions of equality and freedom is a newly independent issue—the character and function of government itself. Liberals reach judgments about how the state should be structured and employed from their prior principles about what it should be doing, but conservatives *start* with principles about the power and functions of government. Once again, it is George Will who incisively articulates the organic conservative position. In a few short sentences, he illustrates each of the foregoing points.

> The fundamental goal of modern liberalism has been equality, and it has given us government that believes in the moral equality of appetites. The result is a government that is big but not strong; fat but flabby; capable of giving but not leading. It is invertebrate government. . . . Leadership is, among other things, the ability to inflict pain and get away with it—short-term pain for long-term gain. Liberalism, which is the politics of the pleasure principle, has made government the servant of consumption and, not coincidentally, the enemy of investment, which is the deferral of gratification. The one thing we do not have is strong government.[12]

From the perspective of the 1890s liberal, equality of opportunity is the only version of equality that is consistent with freedom. Every advance beyond it diminishes freedom by exactly the same amount. Many are so adamant about this point that they tend to see any extension of equality of opportunity as amounting to an extreme kind of homogenization of all outcomes and conditions. For some publicists, this may be a deliberate creation of a straw man that can be painted in threatening colors. For others it seems to be a genuine perception. Milton and Rose Friedman have been leading economists and persuasive advocates of the 1890s liberal position for more than three decades. After speaking of the service rendered to the individual by the harmonious relationship of liberty and equality of opportunity, they add:

> A very different meaning of equality has emerged in the United States in recent decades—equality of outcome. Everyone should have the same level of living or of income, should finish the race at the same time. Equality of outcome is in clear conflict with liberty. The attempt to promote it has been a major source of bigger and bigger government, and of government-imposed restrictions on our liberty.[13]

For the 1890s liberals, in other words, *any* expansion beyond the minimal government required to enforce contracts and punish crime is a potential threat to freedom. Vast military expenditures and the government-business establishment that goes with it are necessary but potentially dangerous evils. Underlying such attitudes is the 1890s liberal's complete conviction that only the free economic market can direct resources toward their best use. Only the free market can allocate burdens and benefits in a noncoercive and maximally efficient manner. The market can reward and punish in a way that maintains social harmony, if only government will leave it alone.

Thus, there remains a continuing fissure in conservatism with respect to the appropriate form and function of government. Organic conservatives are willing to use government and even expand it if necessary to assure the kind of social welfare that they consider morally justified in the current context. They want a government capable of doing many things, as we shall see later. The free market is useful when it does its job, but it cannot be left in charge when important goals are at stake. On the other hand, 1890s liberals insist on the free market as the sole allocator of important values in the society. They demand a strictly limited government.

To understand the conservative position with regard to the definitions of equality and freedom, therefore we must be prepared to do two things. First, we must add another value—the scope and power of government and its impact on the free market. Second, we must distinguish between (a) a surface level of agreement between the two major strands on liberalism's errors (for example, in expanding equality and thereby expanding government) and on what equality and freedom should mean and (b) the deeper but divergent reasons behind those positions. This pattern is repeated with respect to other important values. Surface agreement rests on different reasons for a shared position, complicated by tension over the proper form and function of government and its impact on the market.

Individualism

The differences evident with respect to equality and liberty shade directly into some contrasting understandings of the key value of individualism. For the 1890s liberals, the individual is the focus of all concerns. Speaking of the traditional importance of the right and power of individuals to shape their own lives as they wish, the Friedmans say:

> Equality and liberty were two faces of the same basic value—that every individual should be regarded as an end in himself. . . . Equality before God—personal equality—is important precisely because people are not identical. Their different values, their different tastes, their different capacities will lead them to want to lead very different lives. Personal equality requires respect for their right to do so, not the imposition on them of someone else's values or judgment.[14]

This image consists of autonomous individuals seeking satisfaction of their needs, which are harmonized through the free economic market. This, in essence, defines the good society. Equality of opportunity means equality before the law and is thus at once the means of implementing personal equality and an essential component of liberty.[15] All of these values are bound together in one indivisible whole. The consequence, of course, is to place the individual and his or her needs at the center of political thinking and adapt all other definitions and priorities to that first principle.

For organic conservatives, this simply will not do. Let George Will speak one more time:

> Once politics is defined negatively, as an enterprise for drawing a protective circle around the individual's sphere of self-interested action, then public concerns are by definition distinct from, and secondary to, private concerns. Regardless of democratic forms, when people are taught by philosophy (and the social climate) that they need not govern their actions by calculations of public good, they will come to blame all social shortcomings on the agency of collective considerations, the government, and will absolve themselves.[16]

Individualism of the Friedmans' variety is part of the problem that once dominant liberalism has created. A system where everybody puts individual interest foremost has no concept of the public interest, let alone the capacity to implement one if it were found. If individuals are encouraged to think that they should always get whatever they want, they may well come to blame government for not providing it, and organic conservatives see disaffection from government as one of the worst maladies of contemporary society.

Organic conservatives mean something quite distinct by individualism. For them, individuals are important only as members of the community. The individual should be guided toward making contributions to the society's preservation and development. By making such contributions, individuals earn both immediate satisfaction from doing what is right and entitlement to share in the social justice that is appropriate for all in the community. For conservatives, a community implies obligation, where the few with the greatest wisdom teach moral standards and behavior to the multitude of others. Only 1890s liberals (and the bulk of Americans) continue to think of the individual as an isolated social unit whose self-seeking should give the society all its important dynamics and priorities.

Democracy, Property, and Contracts/Law

Most conservatives have little good to say about democracy in its current form in the United States. They see it as giving rise to special interest self-seeking and a set of mounting demands that government simply cannot begin to fulfill. The 1890s liberals are totally committed to the procedural definition of democracy, the more limited the better. The greatest possible room must be left for the free market to control allocations within the society. With their firm sense of a wall of separation between economic conditions and the political world and their devotion to the principle of limited government, they could hardly believe otherwise.

The conservatives' penchant for order and regular procedures is reflected in their endorsement of a central role for contracts and the law. Both strands oppose the proliferation of litigation, which has, in their view, been encouraged by the liberal emphasis on self-seeking claims. Both are certain that liberal judges have taken the courts far too deeply into the social engineering business. Contracts stand on high ground and embody the honor and integrity with which a good society should conduct its affairs. The law is the basis for order. It is the necessary cement for a social system that shows far too many centrifugal tendencies. For organic conservatives law is value-laden and purposeful, whereas 1890s liberals have a sense of the law as a neutral machine not unlike the free market in its workings. In actuality such differences are not very important in the context of essentially full support by each to the established legal system.

The most unequivocal commitment that conservatives share, however, is to the value of property. The right to gain, hold, and use property is the first component of their definition of a good society. For organic conservatives, property is imbued with a moral base. Property gives one a stake in the society. It enables one to act with some responsibility as a citizen, and it allows some members of society the time to develop their talents and wisdom for governing well. The fact that property can be used wrongly or sought too avidly does not detract from its central role in making possible a good society and thus good government.

The 1890s liberal is equally committed to the importance of property rights, but for different reasons. Individual wealth is the necessary and appropriate way to reward risk taking. The society always benefits more than the individual from the activities that produce personal wealth. Incentives are what make the market work effectively. Any effort to tax or otherwise limit wealth derived from economic activities reduces those incentives and warps the market's operation. George Gilder argues that "all the values of advanced culture—equality, bureaucratic rationality, predictability, sexual liberation, political 'populism,' and the pursuit of pleasure"—inspire modern governments to intrude on the free use of property that spells economic growth and progress. He adds:

> Material progress is ineluctably elitist: it makes the rich richer and increases their numbers, exalting the few extraordinary men who can produce wealth over the democratic masses who consume it. . . . Material progress is difficult: it requires from its protagonists long years of diligence and sacrifice, devotion and risk that can be elicited only with high rewards, not "the average return on capital."[17]

PROBLEMS AND POSSIBILITIES

In the 1970s and 1980s the most immediately visible problem for all Americans was that of economic decline. The problem has several facets, changing over time, but all adding up to declining economic growth and general performance when compared with the American past or other industrial countries today. At one point, the problem seemed to be defined by inflation and low productivity; at another, by unemployment and low profitability. At all times, the American economy seemed to be losing the competitive advantages it had so long enjoyed.

The 1890s liberals did not lack for an explanation of what was happening: the problem was excessive government. Too much spending, taxing, regulating, subsidizing, and the like were undermining incentives and work habits and imposing too heavy a burden on business. The Friedmans sum up the situation this way:

> The experience of recent years—slowing growth and declining productivity— raises a doubt whether private ingenuity can continue to overcome the deadening effects of government control if we continue to grant ever more power to government, to authorize a "new class" of civil servants to spend ever larger fractions of our income supposedly on our behalf. Sooner or later—and perhaps sooner than many of us expect—an ever bigger government would destroy both the prosperity that we owe to the free market and the human freedom proclaimed so eloquently in the Declaration of Independence.[18]

Although their immediate concern is with economic freedom as the remedy for economic decline, economic freedom is indivisible from human freedoms. Thus, for the Friedmans, more is at stake in freeing the market from government intervention than merely the rejuvenation of the American economy.

In every decade of the postwar years, however, the threat of Soviet communism has been the perceived problem shared by all conservatives. Anticommunism was the glue holding these twin strands of conservatism together, and it gave them much of their fighting spirit. The Soviet menace was always a clear and present danger, often one for which military preparation and a nuclear "balance of terror" were the essential solutions. With the end of the cold war, the collapse of the Soviet Union into its constituent republics, and their subsequent efforts to reconstruct along free market lines, this external enemy literally disappeared.

Enemies still exist in the world, of course, ranging from the dictator of Iraq to sponsors of terrorism to economic competitors. Military preparation, both for rapid deployment of forces needed to police the world and for shields to guard the U.S. homeland against nuclear threats, remains important. However, none of these have the compelling character of Soviet communism. Even at home, of course, a discredited liberalism was in full retreat. Because the conservative alliance had much less to be *against*, it was in danger of fragmenting into its two basic components.

Perhaps fortunately, in the early 1990s a new enemy was discovered, and a vigorous attack immediately launched. The enemy came in the form of the movement for cultural diversity in the nation's colleges and universities, and it provided new glue. Neoconservatives, organic conservatives, and libertarians (and a few academic liberals) joined in denouncing what they were soon calling "the victims' revolution" and "political correctness."

According to conservatives, women and minority students and faculty have taken over the colleges and universities. As a result, academic standards were lowered, the traditional Western curriculum was replaced with multicultural materials (with consequent loss of academic rigor), and the freedom of speech of resisters to this trend seriously compromised. Affirmative action admissions standards and faculty hiring/retention policies brought low-quality students and faculty onto American campuses. The radicals of the 1960s, now tenured, were moving up the career ladder and substituting their political ideology for true and objective knowledge. Furthermore, administrators were complicitly encouraging resegregation of the races and supinely yielding to the complaints of women and minorities about sexist and racist behavior on campus. A whole new battery of rules and punishments threatened to foreclose free speech and open inquiry.

All of these criticisms were made at length in 1991 in Dinesh D'Souza's *Illiberal Education: The Politics of Race and Sex on Campus*,[19] a major book that rallied all conservatives. D'Souza, a young conservative whose previous work had been a biography of Christian Right leader Jerry Falwell, sounded the alarm on behalf of the endangered American social order.

The academic and cultural revolution on campus is conducted in the name of those who suffer from the effects of race and gender discrimination in America, or from the effects of Western colonialism in the Third World. It is a revolution on behalf of minority victims. . . . Because the revolutionaries view xenophobia, racism, sexism, and other prejudices to be endemic and culturally sanctioned, their project seeks a fundamental restructuring of American society. It involves basic changes in the way economic rewards are distributed, and in the way cultural and political power is exercised.[20]

D'Souza further charges that changes in several disciplines combined with the presence of minority scholars to bring about purported new ways of understanding truth and reality. They actually open the way to mere ideologizing:

The new critics . . . suggest that the very ideal of objectivity is a mirage, and that it is therefore perfectly legitimate for teachers to cast aside pretensions of impartiality and to impose their politically preferred ideas on students. When the traditional norms of scholarship no longer rein in the instinct for activism, license is given for uninhibited ideological proselytizing.[21]

D'Souza concludes by asserting that many colleges and universities will have taught their students

that all rules are unjust and all preferences are principled; that justice is simply the will of the stronger party; that standards and values are arbitrary, and the ideal of the educated person is largely a figment of bourgeois white male ideology; that individual rights are a red flag signalling social privilege, and should be subordinated to the claims of group interest; that all knowledge can be reduced to politics and should be pursued not for its own sake but for the political end of power; that convenient myths and well-intentioned lies can substitute for truth; that double standards are acceptable as long as they are enforced to the benefit of minority victims . . . what many American students are getting is an education in closed-mindedness and intolerance. . . . If the university model is replicated in society at large . . . it will reproduce and magnify in the broader culture the lurid bigotry, intolerance, and balkanization of campus life.[22]

A wide variety of essays and articles from a broad spectrum of conservatives mirrored D'Souza's attack. Echoes included a commencement address at the University of Michigan by President George Bush. Even some academic liberals joined in, condemning the changes being made under the banner of cultural diversity, preferential recruitment, and multicultural curricula. The distinguished historian C. Vann Woodward, for example, asked:

How are our universities ever to pull out of the resegregation, the blatant tribalism, and competitive racial chauvinism they have inflicted upon themselves or permitted to grow and take over within their walls? How are they to encourage students not to substitute politics for learning? How can they weed out curricular nonsense, restore free speech, and revive standards?[23]

How the rising generation will be taught and what principles they will acquire is of paramount importance to the guardians of the dominant culture, which is pretty much how conservatives see themselves. Thus, colleges and universities are political arenas of great importance and perhaps the last redoubt of a fading liberal dominance. As conservatives see it, only the full recapture of the educational system, from top to bottom, can make permanent the recent "right turn" in American politics.

Paralleling the attack on "political correctness" in higher education, the 1990s saw a renewed emphasis on the individual responsibility of African-Americans to compete unaided in the economic and social marketplace of American life. Simply stated, the argument was that blacks should drop their group-conscious victim mentality and internalized self-doubts, stop blaming white racism for their problems, and take personal responsibility for their own advancement as individuals.

Several black conservatives spearheaded this effort to turn political thinking in a conservative direction. They ranged from Judge Clarence Thomas to the academics Steven Carter (*Reflections of an Affirmative Action Baby*)[24] and Shelby Steele (*The Content of Our Character: A New Vision of Race in America*).[25] The careers and views of all these men were prominently featured in the major media. However, the comprehensiveness and style of Steele's arguments earned him the greatest visibility.

Steele premises that blacks who seek power or entitlements as a group do so only in the role of victims. Such a victim mentality makes them passive and unable to assert themselves individually, the only road to real advancement. Race must not be a source of advantage or disadvantage to anyone. Otherwise, all those blacks who do achieve in white society will be suspect in the eyes of whites—*and in their own eyes as well*. He argues that racial identity

> corrupts the greatest source of power and strength available to blacks—the energy latent in our personal desires. . . . In the 1990s, we blacks are more than ever in a position where our common good will best be served by the determined pursuit of our most personal aspirations.[26]

Steele particularly criticizes blacks who avoid personal confrontation with the standards and competition required for achievement in integrated American society. For example, the term *African-American* avoids the confrontation with self-doubts that *black* requires. The same avoidance is visible, he says, in blacks' "tendency to minimalize or avoid real opportunities, to withhold effort in areas where few blacks have achieved, and to self-segregate in integrated situations."[27] He attacks affirmative action as

> an escapist racial policy that offers entitlements, rather than development . . . teaches no skills, instills no values . . . makes color a passport. But the worst aspect of racial preferences is that they encourage dependency or entitlements rather than on our own initiative.[28]

Steele insists that blacks must push their collective identity out of their individual space ("a skin that needs shedding," in his words).[29] They must rely upon their individual effort within the American mainstream. Steele challenges a wide range of governmental standards and programs, generalizing broadly from his own experience and observations of black students' difficulties in his own university. Whether well grounded or not, his arguments certainly fill a major need on the part of conservatives to deal with the great American problem of race relations in a fresh manner.

Another major problem is one that particularly concerns organic conservatives: the loss of authority in government as a result of too much democracy and rampant self-interest. A serious consequence is that government is simply unable to define, and act decisively on behalf of, the long-term good of the society as a whole. In some ways this is a problem inherent in the American polity, a problem to which conservatives acknowledge there is no real solution. One of the best recent statements of this dilemma is Samuel Huntington's *American Politics: The Promise of Disharmony*.[30] Huntington argues that the United States is distinguished by a set of values (essentially those we have identified as the basic American values) so strongly held as to constitute a creed. Instead of ranking these values, Americans simply endorse them all and expect them all to be fully realized. The problem is that governing institutions can never live up to such ideals. There will always be a gap between the aspirations of the creed and the realities of power. If the creedal values are actually sought, then the result is necessarily an attack on the (essential, and constitutionally provided) power and autonomy of governing institutions.

Huntington interprets American history in four cycles of "creedal passion," of which the 1960s and 1970s are the latest example and the Populist-Progressive era the last before that. During such periods, Americans seek realization of their creed with special moralistic vigor and end up reducing the power of government. Huntington sums up the results of the 1960s and 1970s in this way:

> In the 1960s, when Americans became concerned about the gap between their political ideals and their political institutions, they began to eviscerate the political and governmental institutions that had been developed to deal with foreign enemies. . . . The S&S Years [the sixties and seventies] thus left the United States with a more equitable society, a more open politics, a more cynical public, and a less authoritative and effective government. They left the American people confronting foreign and domestic challenges that required the exercise of power, yet still unwilling to legitimize power.[31]

This loss of government power and authority is a recurrent problem in the United States. In European societies, conflicting ideologies are common, and each finds primary expression in one set of governing institutions. Confidence and support are retained for *some* governing institutions no matter the stage of the cycle of change. In the United States, however, broad sharing of basic values means much less conflict between groupings of them. Instead, we have periods of "creedal passion," in which all are avidly sought at once, followed by periods of quiescence. We pay the price in loss of support for *all* governing institutions. Much of our politics consists of antigovernment belief and action:

> In the United States the gap between the political ideal and political reality is a weapon always available for use by social groups against those who control the state. The dominant political creed constitutes a standing challenge to the power of government and the legitimacy of political institutions. Political authority is vulnerable in America as it is nowhere else.[32]

In other words, the problem is acute, distinctively American, and probably insoluble without fundamental change in the essence of American values and beliefs. In this pessimistic attitude, Huntington faithfully represents the characteristic organic conservative resignation to the imperfectability of humankind.

Possibilities

The organic conservatives' concern for restoring authority in government has been spelled out in some detail and yet may be the kind of goal that nobody really expects to achieve. George Will, among others, has suggested what a government should be like:

> The best government exists to frame arrangements in order that they may, over time, become matters of trust. . . . [that] does conduce to an increasingly comfortable fit between institutions and the public, which, like a flowing river, is both a shaper of and shaped by the institutional "banks" between which it flows. A river does not chafe against its banks, except in flood, when it is deformed by unnatural forces. Indeed, a river without banks is incomprehensible; it is a contradiction in terms; it is a lake or a swamp. A river is made by, defined by, whatever keeps it to its course.[33]

Huntington warns us, however, that popular support and trust are not a likely prospect. Americans must first learn to live with "the agony and the promise" of the conflict between the liberal ideal and the institutional reality, our distinguishing cleavage. They can only try "to reduce the gap between their ideals and their institutions, accepting the fact that the imperfections of human nature mean the gap can never be eliminated."[34]

George Will's answer is that politics itself must first be restored so that it can be rescued "from the stale, false notion that government is always and only an instrument of coercion, making disagreeable (even when necessary) excisions from freedom. . . ."[35] He argues that we have "lived improvidently off a dwindling legacy of cultural capital . . . that legacy is a renewable resource, but it will not regenerate spontaneously. Regeneration is a political choice, a political chore." Will's use of the word *choice* has quite different implications from the Friedmans', suggesting instead of free market analogies a conscious and continuing effort at "cooperation" and "collaboration" to bring about a return to civility.[36] It seems clear that if the organic conservatives were to solve their problem of governmental authority, they might well encounter determined resistance from their current allies, the 1890s liberals.

This tension with the libertarians was very much on the mind of the most prominent organic conservative, William F. Buckley, as he wrote *Gratitude: Reflections on What We Owe to Our Country*.[37] In it he articulates a program for the restoration of civic virtue in the United States. However, Buckley's concern is almost as much for maintenance of the alliance between right-thinking conservatives as it is for justifying the noncoercive national service he advocates. In actuality, the dean of organic conservatism has begun to make the case for a synthesis with libertarianism.

Buckley wants Americans to acknowledge their heritage, recognize the blessings given them, and demonstrate their gratitude to their community by helping each other. Acknowledging that his ideas will equally disturb some conservatives and some liberals, he argues there are shared principles underlying both organic conservatism and libertarianism. These principles will justify teaching civic virtue in the way he seeks. Citing the popularity of environmentalism as an illustration of this convergence, Buckley writes:

> About our debt to the planet there is nowadays a considerable consciousness. . . . This perception is that the past is alive in the present . . . The movement, in politics, that has ramified from that radical perception is, I maintain, conservatism. The conservative movement perceives connections between the individual and the community beyond those that relate either to the state or to the marketplace. That is the point, the primary rationale, of this essay. And one need not be a conservative in other particulars to respect it.[38]

Buckley goes on to credit the early liberal, John Stuart Mill, with "this essentially conservative insight." He cites approvingly Mill's belief in the obligation of citizens to act out their gratitude for the benefits of their community in the form of their actions toward their fellow citizens. Buckley's goal is to design a program enabling and encouraging citizens to act out their gratitude without violating "the libertarian presumption against rendering to Caesar any power Caesar does not need, and in any case ought not to want."[39] In a chapter entitled "Anticipating the Libertarian Argument," he uses Adam Smith and George Washington to advance his case for libertarian acceptance of noncoercive ways to build civic consciousness and virtue into the rising generations of Americans.

Buckley envisions a citizenry in which individuals recognize and voluntarily act to demonstrate their obligations to each other and to their community. This is at once the fulfillment of the organic conservative image and, Buckley hopes, of the libertarian's vision of a good society.

IMPLICATIONS AND PROSPECTS

For decades, anticommunism was the "glue" that held the contending strands of conservatism together. Suddenly, in the early 1990s, communism almost literally disappeared. The fragile alliance had no common enemy—and, seemingly, no way to hold the alliance together. The paramount question was whether conservatism would fragment into its three major components, or find some new way to maintain common cause.

Conservatives immediately recognized the implications; some began to stake out new positions consistent with their distinctive perspectives. Pat Buchanan, for example, reminded his readers that the "new god called democracy" was less important than "the character of the people." This is a test of public morality which the United States (in his judgment) fails today.

> But if communism is passé, so, too, is anticommunism—the great solvent that held together Ronald Reagan's coalition—the animating passion in the political life of so many conservatives. . . . We know that crime, corruption, decadence, bankruptcy, and race conflict can go hand-in-hand with democracy. Before we tell (others) how to find their way to the good society, perhaps we ought to retrace our own steps. For we, too, seem to have lost the way.[40]

Between its antielitism and its commitment to the social issues, the populist Christian Right seems likely to antagonize both organic conservatism and libertarianism. The class basis of populist conservatism itself might be enough to keep it in tension with those much less majoritarian ideologies.

No such class-based division exists, however, between the other two forms of conservatism, organic conservatism and libertarianism. Indeed, well before the collapse of communism, tentative steps toward synthesis were already being taken. One of the most interesting developments of the 1990s, and one with profound significance for the possible reconstruction of the American political spectrum, is the beginning of a shared conceptual perspective between organic conservatives and libertarians.

In addition to William F. Buckley, several leading thinkers began to put equal emphasis on the individual *and* the community, linking the two to make them mutually dependent. The virtues of the individual (personal responsibility, hard work, the pursuit of happiness) are meaningful and capable of realization only in a supportive community. Similarly, the community exists as families and neighborhoods of linked individuals, through which the society becomes the focus of conscious individual obligation. The most comprehensive effort at such a synthesis is Charles Murray's recent work, *In Pursuit: Of Happiness and Good Government.*[41]

In his acknowledgments, Murray explicitly declares his debt to two leading libertarians (Friedrich Hayek and Milton Friedman) and two leading organic conservatives (Russell Kirk and Robert Nisbet). His effort at synthesis rests on the premise that

> Jeffersonian democracy is still the best way to run society, including the society in which we find ourselves today. . . . On certain fundamental questions of government, Jefferson and his colleagues were right more universally than they knew. In particular, they understood that the vitality of communities and the freedom of individuals are intertwined, not competitive.[42]

Murray proposes to establish and justify a new and better standard for the evaluation of public policy and the actions of government generally. This standard involves the following question: Have people been better enabled to pursue their own happiness? To put it another way, have the enabling conditions for the pursuit of happiness (which cannot actually be provided by government) been furthered?

Murray distinguishes between the (good) private person and the (bad) public person in ways that deliberately parallel the American Founding Fathers:

> Man acting in his private capacity—if restrained from the use of force—is resourceful and benign, fulfilling his proper destiny; while man acting as a public and political creature is resourceful and dangerous, inherently destructive of the rights and freedoms of his fellowmen.[43]

Because he understands the United States to be founded on the affirmation of the private person and with "profound pessimism" about the public person, Murray believes public policy should maximize opportunities for individuals to respond to challenge, risk, and reward. Central solutions are unworkable because there are too many constituencies to be served with too many conflicting "happinesses." Central solutions ultimately result in denial of democracy because there is too much opportunity for some to decide what the others should want and get.

What does work, in Murray's eyes, is a kind of medical mode. Government becomes the healer, thinking "in terms of solutions that permit a naturally robust organism to return to health."[44] Murray argues such an approach will work because it will release "natural and deeply embedded responses" and "tap dynamics which will naturally occur if you let them."[45]

The vision lying behind these principles is one of individuals embedded in communities, associated with others in what Murray calls (citing the great conservative Edmund Burke) "little platoons" of social relationships. Here is the essence of the possible synthesis of organic conservatism and libertarianism, necessarily quoted at length:

> Strongly bound communities, fulfilling complex public functions, are not creatures of the state. They form because they must. Human beings have needs as individuals that cannot be met except by cooperation with other human beings.

> To this degree, the often-lamented conflict between "individualism" and "community" is misleading. The pursuit of individual happiness cannot be an atomistic process; it will naturally and always occur in the context of communities. The state's role in enabling the pursuit of happiness depends ultimately on nurturing not individuals, but the associations they form. . . . I will be using the image of the "little platoon" to represent the essential relationship of social organization to the pursuit of happiness and, by extension, the relationship of the state's social policy to the pursuit of happiness. We each belong to a few "little platoons." . . . The enabling conditions have to be met—in a properly constructed society, people must have access to material resources, safety, self-respect, and intrinsic rewards. But the little platoons of work, family, and community are the nexus.[46]

Murray is convinced that the release of vital individual initiative can be achieved only in the context of these little platoons within which people live. His favorite preliminary phrase—"unless impeded"—is utterly libertarian. "Unless impeded" by government, that is, individuals can pursue happiness, but the context for that individual pursuit of happiness is the community, an utterly conservative concept. The enabling conditions are assured by effective social policy.

In this way, Murray has built a base for possibly developing a synthesis between organic conservatism and libertarianism. However, there are many centrifugal forces at work, and a relatively small upper-middle-class social base from which to proceed. In all probability, the future of conservatism will be determined by the beliefs and actions of the populist Christian Right and its followers.

ADDITIONAL READINGS

Buckley, William F., Jr. *Gratitude: Reflections on What We Owe to Our Country*. New York: Random House, 1990.

Carter, Stephen L. *Reflections of an Affirmative Action Baby*. New York: Basic Books, 1991.

Friedman, Milton. *Capitalism and Freedom*. Chicago: University of Chicago Press, 1962.

Friedman, Milton, and Rose Friedman. *Free to Choose*. New York: Harcourt Brace Jovanovich, 1980.

Gilder, George. *Wealth and Poverty*. New York: Basic Books, 1981.

Hacker, Andrew. *The End of the American Era*. New York: Atheneum, 1971.

Huntington, Samuel P. *American Politics: The Promise of Disharmony*. Cambridge, Mass.: Belknap Press, 1981.

Laxalt, Paul, and Richard S. Williamson. *A Changing America: Conservatives View the 1980s from the United States Senate*. South Bend, Ind.: Regnery/Gateway, 1980.

Miles, Michael W. *The Odyssey of the American Right*. New York: Oxford University Press, 1980.

Nash, George H. *The Conservative Intellectual Movement in America since 1945*. New York: Basic Books, 1976.

Steele, Shelby. *The Content of Our Character: A New Vision of Race in America*. New York: St. Martin's Press, 1990.

Sullivan, William M. *Reconstructing Public Philosophy*. Berkeley and Los Angeles: University of California Press, 1982.

Will, George F. *Statecraft as Soulcraft: What Government Does*. New York: Simon and Schuster, 1983.

PART V

THE RECONSTRUCTION OF THE AMERICAN POLITICAL SPECTRUM

CHAPTER 10

ENVIRONMENT, ECOLOGY, GREENS, NEW OPTIONS: "BEYOND LEFT AND RIGHT"

Environmentalism has probably had more visible impact on American life from the 1960s to the present than any other set of beliefs. Environmentalism is a broad and general term that encompasses a wide range of applied concerns about damage to the natural setting of human life. The concerns range from air, land, and water pollution to depletion of increasingly scarce resources to overpopulation. In a short three decades, environmentalists have added the phrase *environmental crisis* to the American vocabulary, mobilized quite effective political power, accomplished substantial changes in American public policy, and even modified some aspects of personal life-styles.

Not surprisingly, there are significant differences among environmentalists that have to do with scientific grounding, world view, and the choice of goals and tactics. One basic distinction to be made at the outset has to do with the relationship of environmentalism to ecology, the branch of biological science that focuses on the organism and its habitat and serves as the intellectual source of all versions of environmentalism.

Most ecologists are mainstream biologists (or chemists or physicists) who employ the familiar tools of Enlightenment science to warn of the destruction of aspects of nature by human practices. They see nature as a set of resources that should be better employed by human beings, to serve quality of life and long-term needs, whether by restoration, conservation, or other improved actions. When their work is applied by or as environmentalism, it usually fits comfortably within the liberal or reform liberal framework; that is, it does not challenge basic American values or the structure of the economic system.

However, some ecologists have gone beyond the mechanistic traditions and assumptions of Enlightenment science and see nature quite differently. They argue that because human beings are only one species among many in a living biosphere, they must learn to live in and with nature in a transformed manner requiring vast changes in values and in social and

175

economic practices. When their ideas are applied by or as environmentalism, the changes involved are so drastic that they simply do not fit on any current political spectrum—and often quite unusual political claims and behavior follow as well.

THE ECOLOGY-ENVIRONMENTALISM CONNECTION

This tension within ecology, carried forward into distinctive world views and political activity by environmentalists, serves as the basis for the first part of our analysis. Subsequently, we identify different subgroups within this context, which will better enable us to assess their prospects.

The mainstream of environmentalism is primarily single-issue oriented reform liberalism, well grounded in American history and comfortably middle class in its popular base. Its great success is a classic illustration of how middle-class money and organizational skills can make use of the American political style of publicity, lobbying, and litigation to gain high visibility for an issue, produce new legal standards for public and corporate behavior, and promote widespread changes in individuals' everyday practices.

With the "right turn" in policymakers' priorities in the 1980s, some momentum was lost. Nevertheless, the environmental movement remains rooted in middle-class support and retains much of its power in the 1990s. It is well represented by such groups as the Sierra Club, the Audubon Society, the Natural Resources Defense Council, and the Wilderness Society. It is readily communicated through the works of Rachel Carson, Barry Commoner, Paul Ehrlich, Herman Daly, William Ophuls, and many others.

The reconstructive side of environmentalism flowing from the transformative science of some ecologists actually parallels mainstream environmentalism in some respects. Fundamentally, however, it represents an alternative approach to understanding nature that has always been in tension with mainstream environmentalism.

Reconstructive environmentalists see human beings as only one of many living organisms that make up one holistic, interdependent system. All life is inextricably integrated with nature and its processes on earth. The obligation of human beings is to understand nature in ways that are neither human centered (anthropocentric) nor domination oriented. The latter principle flows from an ecological critique of science itself, which holds that contemporary science was socially created during the seventeenth-century Enlightenment and (innocently, but destructively) aimed at dominating and exploiting nature to achieve humankind's economic goals.

The issue posed by these ecologists is deceptively simple: whether human beings are *of* nature, or *above* nature. If they are of nature, as they argue, there follows a distinct humility, perhaps even a spirituality, with respect to nature—and a felt need to preserve or restore nature purely for its own sake. If they are above nature, as most ecologists and environmentalists conceive themselves to be, there follows a view of nature as a vast storehouse of resources for human use—a storehouse which needs only to be kept reasonably full to serve human needs into the future. It is this latter attitude, the reconstructive ecologists and environmentalists say, that leads the mainstream environmentalists to settle for piecemeal reforms and modest limits on human exploitation of nature.

What sets the reconstructive advocates apart from more mainstream ecologists and environmentalists is thus two-fold: a view of humankind as one of many living components of nature not entitled to exploit its other organisms or its resources, and a self-conscious critique of science itself as serving the goal of human domination of nature. For the reconstructive ecologists, the task is to reconstruct our science and our values so that we can more truly understand and live in harmony with nature.

Neither belief system fits neatly on the traditional political spectrum, which (as we have noted) is based on the distribution of wealth and income and expressed as social class. Both emphasize noneconomic matters that do not seem to be included on that spectrum. Nevertheless, because reform environmentalism never strays far from the status quo, its beliefs can be embraced by most of the traditional American ideologies without great difficulty.

The reconstructive world view, however, calls for a transformation in basic values and, most importantly, in our ways of scientific thinking and knowing reality. It is this call for a transformation that sets this minority component of ecology and environmentalism apart. It has also helped to attract a number of adherents as well as to give rise to a number of newly active groups such as the deep ecologists, Gaians, social ecologists, ecofeminists, Greens, and the New Options movement. Such authors and activists as Aldo Leopold, Wendell Berry, Carolyn Merchant, Donald Worster, James Lovelock, Brian Tokar, Murray Bookchin, Mark Satin, and Gary Snyder testify to the lively diversity among the environmentally oriented today.

In the analysis that follows, we highlight two key distinctions, or thresholds, as suggested in the summary shown in Figure 10.1. The first is the difference between the reconstructive ecology-environmentalism and that of the mainstream versions. The second is the threshold between thought and action, in which reform environmentalism appears to give rise to relatively familiar forms of politics while the more transformative orientation encourages unorthodox political behavior such as direct action and civil disobedience. From the analysis, we shall see the implications of these new ideas for the reconstruction of the American political spectrum, which is the primary focus of this chapter.

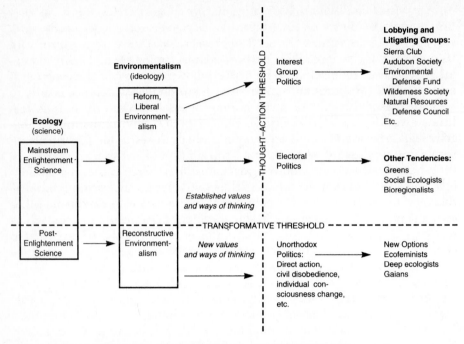

Figure 10.1   Ecology, Environmentalism, and Political Action

ENVIRONMENTALISM AS REFORM LIBERALISM

Environmentalism has its roots in the conservation movement, which began in the mid-nineteenth century with the work of Henry David Thoreau and John James Audubon. Conservationists were concerned primarily with the efficient management of natural resources for the benefit of humankind. Their interest in preventing waste and preserving resources for the future led to such projects as the development of national parks; programs for long-term yields in forests and grasslands; and management of river water for flood prevention, irrigation, and the production of electricity.

While they valued nature far more than most of their contemporaries, conservationists saw nature essentially as a storehouse of resources for human use—a storehouse that required tending and replenishment but which would then yield needed resources for the benefit of humankind forever. Much of contemporary environmentalism follows this principle: so that future generations of human beings may enjoy the same quality of life as their ancestors, nature should be restored and maintained and its "carrying capacity" preserved against overpopulation.

Conservationism was transformed into its modern successor—environmentalism—with the publication of Rachel Carson's *Silent Spring*[1] in 1962. By calling attention to the unintended polluting consequences of pesticides, Carson set in motion a major movement of groups and individuals concerned with the chemistry of air, land, water, and particularly food. Carson had significant predecessors, such as Fairfield Osborn, Bill Vogt, and Aldo Leopold, whose 1948 works led to efforts to deal with alleged overpopulation; problems of food production and distribution; and depletion of resources, particularly energy.

In its early stages, the environmental movement was often quite apolitical. Litter cleanup, scenic plantings, a simpler and more aesthetic lifestyle, the symbolic Earth Days, and other forms of rejection of the consumer society seemed to be things that could be done by individuals. By the 1970s, however, several well-funded groups were actively campaigning for specific new legislation, such as clean-air and clean-water acts and the new enforcement body, the Environmental Protection Agency. The energy crises of the 1970s gave added impetus to the notion of an environmental crisis, as did such publications as the Club of Rome's *The Limits to Growth*[2] and Paul Ehrlich's *The Population Bomb*.[3]

By the late 1980s, an environmental historian could review this experience and see environmentalism crystallizing as an ideology. Robert Paehlke argues that, once past the "single-issue negativism" of the 1970s and early 1980s, environmentalism

> has the potential to become the first original ideological perspective to develop since the middle of the nineteenth century. . . . It can be developed into an ideology able to see the developed countries through the transition to a post-industrial society, much as liberalism, conservatism, and socialism saw us through the formation of a new society during the Industrial Revolution . . . A full development of environmentalist ideas—an environmentalist ideology—becomes possible only when environmentalism is seen as neither "left" nor "right."[4]

Paehlke proceeds to make a persuasive case for a revised set of values and concerns that would constitute this new ideological environmentalism. He does not reject the basic liberal values as we have understood them; indeed, he embraces them and, in effect, merely adds a gloss of new concerns. In the thirteen "central value assertions" of environmentalism that he presents, shown here as Figure 10.2, he has also reached about as far as reform liberals can toward the reconstructive world view.

Paehlke recognizes that environmentalism in some respects challenges liberalism's acceptance of the economic market and that it will be necessary to find new ways to justify much more government intervention. He acknowledges that there is a gap between environmentalism and liberalism, insists that it must be bridged, and declares that "environmentalists have no choice" but to try to do so.

> What is at stake here is the meaning of progress. Liberalism, perhaps ideology itself, was born with the notion of progress, and throughout the long history of liberal democracy, progress has driven society both politically and eco-

Figure 10.2   The "Central Value Assertions" of Environmentalism

1. An appreciation of all life forms and a view that the complexities of the ecological web of life are politically salient.
2. A sense of humility regarding the human species in relation to other species and to the global ecosystem.
3. A concern with the quality of human life and health, including an emphasis on the importance of preventative medicine, diet, and exercise to the maintenance and enhancement of human health.
4. A global rather than a nationalist or isolationist view.
5. Some preference for political and/or population decentralization.
6. An extended time horizon—a concern about the long-term future of the world and its life.
7. A sense of urgency regarding the survival of life on earth, both long-term and short-term.
8. A belief that human societies ought to be reestablished on a more sustainable technical and physical basis. An appreciation that many aspects of our present way of life are fundamentally transitory.
9. A revulsion toward waste in the face of human need (in more extreme forms, this may appear as asceticism).
10. A love of simplicity, although this does not include rejection of technology or "modernity."
11. An aesthetic appreciation for season, setting, climate, and natural materials.
12. A measurement of esteem, including self-esteem and social merit, in terms of such nonmaterial values as skill, artistry, effort, or integrity.
13. An attraction to autonomy and self-management in human endeavors and, generally, an inclination to more democratic and participatory political processes and administrative structures.

SOURCE: Robert C. Paehlke, *Environmentalism and the Future of Progressive Politics* (New Haven, Conn.: Yale University Press, 1989), p. 144–145.

nomically. Environmentalism, however, suggests that our idea of progress is too linear, even arrogant. Growth in GNP is not progress. Nor is bigger better. Progress must be redefined as *meeting real needs more efficiently.*[5]

Thus, reform environmentalism becomes a better way of accomplishing traditional goals. The political methods that Paehlke endorses are, in his words, uniformly "moderate." Nevertheless, Paehlke sees environmentalism as a potential replacement for liberalism as the "progressive" ideology of the future.

ECOLOGY-ENVIRONMENTALISM: THE RECONSTRUCTIVE THRESHOLD

Ecology has always been interwoven with environmentalism and recognizes many of the same seminal thinkers in its heritage. The concept of ecology was defined in the work of George Perkins Marsh in 1864 as the "study of the interrelationships between organisms and environment." John Muir and Aldo Leopold also were early antianthropocentrics who were concerned about the human tendency to selfishly exploit nature for short-term benefit—with destructive consequences for fragile ecosystems and resources. Models of behavior, in their eyes, were provided by native Americans' ability to live lightly on the land without scarring or despoiling it.

Reconstructive environmentalists also claim Rachel Carson as one of their own, emphasizing not her extensive evidence about pollutants but her more intuitive and experiential sense of wonder about nature. They cite her conclusion to *Silent Spring*, in which she says:

> The "control of nature" is a phrase conceived in arrogance, born of the Neanderthal age of biology and philosophy, when it was supposed that nature exists for the convenience of man.[6]

The reconstructive perspective insists that humankind is and must understand itself as part of nature, with the obligation to preserve and restore natural conditions insofar that is as possible. All other living organisms, and indeed all natural objects, have entitlements equal to that of human beings because they are all part of the overall system that is nature. Carolyn Merchant describes the human-nonhuman relationship in nature as follows:

> Nonhuman nature, therefore, is not passive, but an active complex that participates in change over time and responds to human-induced change. Nature is a whole of which humans are only one part. We interact with plants, animals, and soils in ways that sustain or deplete local habitats. Through science and technology, we have great power to alter the whole in short periods of time. The relation between human beings and the nonhuman world is thus reciprocal. Humans adapt to nature's environmental conditions; but when humans alter their surroundings, nature responds through ecological changes.[7]

The notion of a sustainable society, which permits only such economic growth as can be maintained without net depletion of resources, is central to the views of reconstructive environmentalists.

Today's reconstructivists challenge basic aspects of the scientific way of knowing itself. They argue first that science is socially constructed, in the sense that the concepts and assumptions that underlie it at any given time are products of the history, culture, values, and goals of the society in which the scientists live. In the period of the seventeenth-century Enlightenment (from which today's science derives), notions of hierarchy, patriarchy, and control—over nature, and over other people—were prominent. Therefore, science too sought and promoted human domination and control over nature. Unless such a version of science is replaced with one that is nonanthropocentric, reconstructive ecological goals will be unattainable.

A leading historian of ecological thinking, Donald Worster, describes the science of ecology as a continuing conflict between two sets of moral philosophies. One seeks to discover and preserve the intrinsic values of nature (ecology), while the other seeks to understand and make use of nature as an instrumental world (environmentalism). Worster argues that the choice is not a scientific one but an ethical one: "What we need, quite simply, is a more carefully hedged, skeptical, and humble notion of truth."[8] Worster describes his own notion of science elsewhere as

> an intellectual adventure open to all sorts of people, a democratic, participatory pursuit, which is not exclusionary or clubbish, not aristocratic, but is able to withstand dissent and welcome differences.[9]

In other words, for Worster and perhaps for other ecologists tending toward reconstruction, the search for a better way of understanding nature and reality begins with an ethical judgment about better ways for humankind to live on the planet Earth. And, he would argue, the same essentially ethical choice would lie behind *any* version of science or set of principles about the human relationship to nature. While this may sound highly relativistic, it puts the responsibility for charting the human future squarely on today's generation—and gives them a wide range of choice. How some different groups have begun to make their choices will become clearer as we review their distinctive values and beliefs.

Deep Ecologists

The term *deep ecology* was coined by Arne Naess in 1972 to emphasize the difference between the shallow views of reform-oriented environmentalists and the deeper, more complex and intuitive, ethically generated feelings about nature that were characteristic of his brand of ecologists. Naess elaborated on the values and principles of his version of deep ecology in 1976 in the form of an eight-point platform reproduced here as Figure 10.3. The last point, the imperative of action to implement the other principles, is generally understood to apply to both one's own lifestyle and one's political activity. The overall intent of the platform was to give deep ecologists a means of self-definition and to promote discussion with others.

Some deep ecologists see themselves as moving from the principles of the interrelatedness of all systems of life on the Earth and the need for human self-realization toward a wider evolutionary fulfillment of the liberatory goals of the Enlightenment. Michael Zimmerman, for example, makes the link between new beliefs and the Enlightenment in this fashion:

> To hope for such a transformation means to believe in the possibility of *human evolution* . . . We have to *finish* the job of human liberation, at the same time as we have to tackle the problem of the domination of nature. . . . Deep ecology is

Figure 10.3   A Platform of the Deep Ecology Movement

1. The flourishing of human and non-human life on Earth has intrinsic value. The value of non-human life forms is independent of the usefulness these may have for narrow human purposes.
2. Richness and diversity of life forms are values in themselves and contribute to the flourishing of human and non-human life on Earth.
3. Humans have no right to reduce this richness and diversity except to satisfy vital needs.
4. Present human interference with the non-human world is excessive, and the situation is rapidly worsening.
5. The flourishing of human life and cultures is compatible with a substantial decrease of the human population. The flourishing of non-human life requires such a decrease.
6. Significant change of life conditions for the better requires change in policies. These affect basic economic, technological, and ideological structures.
7. The ideological change is mainly that of appreciating *life quality* (dwelling in situations of intrinsic value) rather than adhering to a high standard of living. There will be a profound awareness of the difference between big and great.
8. Those who subscribe to the foregoing points have an obligation directly or indirectly to participate in the attempt to implement the necessary changes.

SOURCE: Arne Naess, *Ecology, Community, and Lifestyle* (New York: Cambridge University Press, 1989), p. 29.

part of the great liberation movement that culminated in the Enlightenment and now is trying to move beyond the Enlightenment's limitations. . . . It's about freeing all beings from unnecessary kinds of control and exploitation.[10]

Bill Devall, perhaps the most prolific of American deep ecologists, offers a somewhat more mystical version that captures further dimensions of the concept:

The term *deep ecology* refers to finding our bearings, to the process of grounding ourselves through fuller experience of our connections to earth. . . . Deepness is felt in the way we are experiencing our lives. Deepness of thinking means articulating basic priorities, or more or less intuitive beliefs. Deepness means exploring our dreams to recognize our archaic unity with all life and basic symbols. . . . Deepness implies dwelling-in-the-moment, meditating; letting one's own rhythms and perceptual room open up; respecting and including what is there, what comes, involving the flow of actions. . . . Deepness is settling into the stream of things as they are. . . . Deep ecology is ecological realism.[11]

For Devall, the task of deep ecologists is a frankly transformational one—to accomplish fundamental change in the basic values and ways of thinking that are characteristic of the United States. He readily recognizes that this is a long-range task and that many accommodations with reform environmentalists will be necessary along the way.

Gaians

The Gaian belief system is associated with the work of the scientist James Lovelock, who first offered the hypothesis in 1979 that the Earth is a living organism, which he named Gaia after the Greek name for the Earth goddess. Lovelock and his colleagues saw the Earth as physiologically alive, with the biosphere (the immediate surroundings of the earth's crust) consisting of a living atmosphere plus billions of microbes serving as transformers converting cosmic radiations into various forms of energy. This animate biosphere gave the Earth an adaptive capacity so that it may be said to evolve much as any other organism. Instead of inanimate rocks and oceans plus a few living organisms, Lovelock proposes that the evolution of species and their environment are all of one piece and ought to be studied together.

Reconstructive environmentalists interpret this theory as requiring even greater movement away from anthropomorphic thought, and perhaps away from political action entirely. For example, Lovelock says:

> Gaia theory forces a planetary perspective. It is the health of the planet that matters, not that of some individual species of organisms. This is where Gaia and the environmental movements, which are concerned first with the health of people, part company. The health of the Earth is most threatened by major changes in natural ecosystems. . . . It may seem to many readers that I am mocking those environmental scientists whose life work is concerned with these threats to human life. This is not my intention. I wish only to speak out for Gaia because there are so few who do, compared to the multitudes who speak for the people.[12]

Clearly, deep ecology and Gaia theory (as it is often understood in rather mystical ways) have in common a perspective that can remove one from one's immediate terrestrial surroundings and/or the possibility of political action. Much of the burden for implementation is placed in the hands of individuals, whose self-determined actions will be crucial to change. As Lovelock says,

> it all depends on you and me. If we see the world as a living organism of which we are a part—not the owner, nor the tenant; not even a passenger—we could have a long time ahead of us and our species might survive for its "allotted span." It is up to us to act personally in a way that is constructive. . . . If living with Gaia is a personal responsibility, how should we do it? Each of us will have a personal solution to the problem.[13]

Perhaps the most ambitious attempt to date to synthesize deep ecology and Gaian thinking is Jeremy Rifkin's *Biosphere Politics: A New Consciousness for a New Century*.[14] Rifkin claims that "a new political vision" is taking shape in response to unprecedented global environmental problems and beginning to change the thinking and redirect the social behavior of a new generation. He defines *biosphere politics* as follows:

> The term "biosphere" was coined at the beginning of the twentieth century and refers to the thin chemical envelope, extending from the ocean depths to the stratosphere, that sustains all the various forms of life on the planet. The new politics envisions the earth as a living organism, and the human species as a partner and participant, dependent on the proper functioning of the biosphere and at the same time responsible for its well-being.[15]

For Rifkin, biosphere politics unites post-World War II movements for participatory democracy and economic justice—all environmental movements and also the spiritual reawakening and therapeutic consciousness movements of recent years. He sees this vision rooted in local bioregions, naturally-bounded regions that give the ecologically minded a place-connected identity and culture that are already shaping their lives.

Rifkin endorses the notion that human beings have passed through two stages of consciousness. The first involved a oneness with nature in the manner of an infant with its mother; the second involved the separation from and domination over nature. Biosphere politics amounts to a third stage of human consciousness, which can be reached by the self-aware choice of individuals:

> Today, the third great stage of human consciousness opens up before us: to make a conscious self-aware choice to reparticipate with the body of nature. . . . To reparticipate with nature out of an act of love and free will, rather than out of fear and dependency, is what makes the third stage of human consciousness so fundamentally unique. . . . From mother to Mother Earth, from undifferentiated oneness to self-aware reparticipation, from utter dependency to mutually accepted responsibility, the consciousness of the individual and the species reach out from a self-imposed exile to reembrace the earth, secure in the fullness of their grounding inside the biosphere.[16]

Social Ecologists

People who identify themselves as social ecologists do so because they believe that ecological problems (just as all other problems of the world) are caused by social behavior, that is, the actions of the rich and powerful who control the society. Many social ecologists are essentially communitarian anarchists, who see the profit orientation and hierarchical organization of the developed societies as the source of social and ecological problems. Only by reconstructing the power distribution and hierarchical organization of these societies can such combined human and natural problems be solved.

Because they are so sensitive to arbitrary uses of power by people in authority, social ecologists are profoundly troubled by what they see as a dangerously authoritarian tendency among the deep ecologists. Murray Bookchin, former director of the Institute for Social Ecology in Vermont, for example, has mounted an especially vigorous polemic against biocentrism in general and deep ecology in particular:

> What renders this new "biocentrism," with its antihumanistic image of human beings as interchangeable with rodents or ants, so insidious is that it now forms the premise of a growing movement called "deep ecology." "Deep ecology" was spawned among well-to-do people who have been raised on a spiritual diet of Eastern cults mixed with Hollywood and Disneyland fantasies. . . . Reduced to merely one life-form among many, the poor and the impoverished either become fair game for outright extermination if they are socially expendable, or they become objects of brutal exploitation if they can be used to aggrandize the corporate world. Accordingly, terms like "oneness" and a "biocentric democracy" go hand-in-hand with a pious formula for human oppression, misery, and even extermination.[17]

Bookchin sees social ecology faced with narrowing choices between deep ecology on one side and a flawed liberal environmentalism on the other—an environmentalism so tied to the competition and growth imperatives of capitalism that it "must ultimately devour the natural world, just like an untreated cancer must ultimately devour its host."[18] His solution is to focus on the social factors that have unbalanced humankind's relationship with nature and, in particular, to seek an end to the domination of some human beings by others.

Bookchin calls for an egalitarian, decentralized society in which human spontaneity and creativity are released, one in which natural and human evolution can proceed in harmony. This future society can only be achieved by collective social action, not by individuals acting in isolation. He concludes his most recent book, *Remaking Society: Pathways to a Green Future*, as follows:

> Social ecology advances a message that calls not only for a society free of hierarchy and hierarchical sensibilities, but for an ethics that places humanity in the natural world as an agent for rendering evolution—social and natural—fully self-conscious and as free as possible in its ability to make evolution as rational as possible in meeting non-human and human needs. . . . This entails a new form of rationality, a new technology, a new science, a new sensibility and self—and, above all, a truly libertarian society.[19]

Ecofeminism

Many feminists have been attracted to reconstructive ecological thinking because it is so holistic and so consistently critical of socially produced elements in our ways of thinking and knowing. Feminists have insisted for years that patriarchy and associated gender roles are built into American values, assumptions, and ways of thinking at the deepest and most fundamental levels. Feminists who are also reconstructive ecologists find such gender-based assumptions in scientific thinking about nature as a woman to be dominated by men. To end domination (whether of women by men, or of nature by human beings) requires the same kind of reconstruction of values and ways of thinking. Rosemary Reuther says in *New Woman/New Earth*:

> Women must see that there can be no liberation for them and no solution to the ecological crisis within a society whose fundamental model of relationships continues to be one of domination. They must unite the demands of the women's movement with those of the ecological movement to envision a radical reshaping of the basic socioeconomic relations and the underlying values of this society.[20]

Karen Warren argues that making the connection between the oppression of women and the domination of nature requires a new or "transformative" version of feminism. This would see all forms of oppression together, put women's experience into the social construction of knowledge, recognize the similarities in all forms of domination, and develop new concepts of what it means to be human.[21] Clearly, ecofeminism would go well beyond both ecology and one-dimensional versions of feminism.

Some ecofeminists envision a global ecological transformation in which changes in ecology, production, reproduction, and human consciousness would go hand in hand. Carolyn Merchant, for example, believes that such a revolution, perhaps triggered by a global ecological crisis, would take place over a considerable period of time. It would also replace today's mechanistic ways of thinking with an ecological version that would

> reconstruct gender relations between women and men and between humans and nature. The domination of women and nature inherent in the market economy's use of both as resources would be restructured. . . . In opposition to the subject/object, mind/body, and culture/nature dichotomies of mechanistic science, ecological consciousness sees complexity and process as including both culture and nature. In the ecological model, humans are neither helpless victims nor arrogant dominators of nature, but active participants in the destiny of the webs of which they are a part.[22]

Some ecofeminists have been attracted to deep ecology for some of the same reasons, but others have raised a major challenge to it. They ask whether the main ecological problem might not be *"andro*centrism" (*man* centeredness) rather than anthropocentrism, and whether patriarchy might not be the real cause of *both* the destruction of the biosphere and the rise of authoritarian practices.[23]

Extending this point, Janet Biehl notes that humanity is not an undifferentiated whole but rather is sharply divided between male and female, rich and poor, black and white. Moreover, women who have recently come into a new self-consciousness and seek a society in which they can act out that selfhood are not willing to be submerged in a boundaryless, cosmic oneness with men.[24]

The Greens

One of the first efforts to bring together people who hold ecological views and believe in collective political action is the Green movement. Inspired by the early electoral success of Green political parties in Europe, a combination of young activists and veterans of the 1960s struggles began to organize in earnest in 1984. The American Greens have not moved very far beyond their initial committees of correspondence stage, in part because of the bias of the American electoral system against third parties but perhaps more because of differences within the traditional American Left.

The notion of an explicitly Green politics was first brought to the United States through the work of Charlene Spretnak and Fritjof Capra. In *Green Politics: The Global Promise*,[25] the authors used the European Green slogan "We are neither left nor right; we are in front" and attempted in a special section to rally Americans to emulation of the Europeans' successes.

Brian Tokar's *The Green Alternative: Creating an Ecological Future*[26] is the most comprehensive American source on the U.S. Greens to date. Tokar argues that the West German experience demonstrates that a sweeping ecological critique can shift the terms of social and political debate. He defines Green values and beliefs as follows:

> The Greens in West Germany have come to be known by their Four Pillars: ecology, social responsibility, democracy, and non-violence. Greens in the U.S. have generally expanded this list to include an explicit emphasis on decentralization—the need to reorient both politics and economics toward the local community level. There is often a strong link to the feminist vision of a society that guarantees equal rights to all and embodies the need for personal as well as political transformation. Many Greens also emphasize the search for a new ethical and spiritual orientation, one that reaffirms the place of human cultures within the natural world and seeks to heal the cultural rift between people and the earth that our civilization has imposed.[27]

Tokar stresses that the Green vision "is more than just a list of reforms. It is an effort to understand how all the pieces of our great post-industrial crisis mesh together as an intricately interlocking puzzle."[28] Thoroughly reconstructive in its orientation, the Green movement seeks simultaneously to promote democracy (in both politics and economics) and a broad social-justice agenda. In many ways, it is the 1990s embodiment of the 1960s New Left with an ecological premise; it is concerned with all the internal tensions between races, genders, and classes, as well as elitism and absolute democracy that characterized that 1960s movement.

New Options

As the Greens have sought to collect and give direction to reconstructively oriented people who believe in organized political action, so the New Options movement has sought to define a postliberal, postconservative, postsocialist politics for individuals generally. The movement draws its name from the *New Options* newsletter published by Mark Satin from 1984 to 1990, and from his 1991 book, *New Options for America: The Second American Experiment Has Begun.*[29]

Satin was once a 1960s radical and later cofounder of the New World Alliance, an organization committed to being "beyond left and right." In a systematic way, he made it his business to seek out and give visibility to those individuals with new political and economic ideas and programs that were Green, decentralist, diverse, and, most of all, practical. In the process, Satin attracted a considerable audience of New Age and other individuals, won prizes for alternative reporting, and became a spokesperson for a new kind of politics.

Satin sees a "second experiment" underway in shaping an American democracy and focuses on what the attributes and context of individuals should be if they are to further that experiment, which is postliberal, Green, and transformational. He holds little hope for the Democratic party or the Green movement, for economic growth or the welfare state, or any of the traditional ideologies. Only a new kind of individual—the caring individual (as contrasted with the rugged individual of the American past)—can create and sustain a desirable new society.

Satin makes a major effort to find positive elements in new ideas and practices wherever possible. He argues that the second experiment has an "overriding commitment to the human potential and the spiritual health of Americans," and cites with approval the self-esteem movement because "at least it takes our political attention away from ideology and economic growth and *things* and puts it where it should be: on our health and happiness."[30] He takes up and embraces specific policy proposals, such as the idea of a flat income tax with a big personal exemption, where they appear likely to promote a "beyond-left-and-right" version of community—the vital need in America. Consistently, he is a warm supporter of multiculturalism.

> I believe that the multicultural vision is such an attractive one that, sooner or later, multiculturalism will follow environmentalism as our next great social

movement. More than any large idea I know now, multiculturalism has the capacity to inspire vision and idealism.[31]

Summary

Several tendencies within the general rubric of reconstructive environmental thinking have been reviewed here: deep ecology, Gaian thought, social ecology, ecofeminism, Green politics, and the New Options movement of unrelated individuals. All of them share reconstructive ecological premises and a potentially transformative impact on traditional American values and ways of thinking.

Many other themes run through most or all of the tendencies, which are for the most part overlapping rather than mutually exclusive. However, they remain distinguishable, and sometimes even in conflict with each other, in their basic values and beliefs. As we shall see in the next section, some never go beyond thought, but most endorse some kind of action program—in which case, differences again become visible. Identifying these differences will also contribute to our ability to assess the reconstructive impact these new ways of thinking may have on the American political spectrum.

STRATEGY AND TACTICS: THOUGHT AND ACTION

There is wide agreement among all brands of environmentalists that American public policy and personal practice must be changed to conform to environmentally sensitive perspectives and priorities. The great majority of environmentalists and all the ecological tendencies share the conviction that values and beliefs are of fundamental importance, and that new ways of thinking that go beyond left and right are imperative. Where they begin to disagree is on the questions of how drastic the changes must be and how they are to be accomplished.

Most environmentalists are usually pragmatic reformers, and their organizations are masters of the American political process at both national and state levels. By mobilizing their supporters and endorsing cothinkers in primaries and general elections and by assiduous lobbying in legislatures, they assure themselves of a voice at the policy-making level. Litigation and the threat of litigation with respect to such existing requirements as the protection of endangered species and environmental-impact statements offer many opportunities for influence.

Environmentalists have by and large succeeded in setting the terms of debate about environmental matters by establishing that there is a global crisis involving global warming, ozone and resource depletion, acid rain and other air and water pollution, deforestation, desertification, and species extinction. In this effort, they have received unexpectedly strong support from the United Nations-sponsored 1987 report of the World

Commission on Environment and Development entitled *Our Common Future*.[32] The report endorsed the notion of an interlocking global crisis and called for sustainable development and equitable economic relations on a world scale. The commission's proposed legal principles would bind member states to maintenance of an environment adequate to the health and well-being of all human beings, through conservation, sustainability, and preservation of ecosystems and processes essential to the functioning of the biosphere.

Success in shaping the assumptions and terms of debate is no small achievement, and it may be an early step toward changing the reigning ideologies. In order to displace the existing ideologies, however, environmentalists must broaden their horizons to take on a variety of economic, racial, and social issues. Paehlke sees this task clearly, calling it "the transformation of environmentalism from an ideology of limited scope to one of broad scope."[33]

Paehlke considers five major changes essential: integration with the peace movement, development of a environmental-progressive economic program, cultivation of decentralization and an urban environmentalism, reducing work time and increasing productivity ("the greatest political challenge on the environmental agenda"), and "taking seriously the claim that environmentalism is neither left nor right" by appealing to conservatives.[34] This last effort would involve emphasis on fiscal responsibility, individual initiative and responsibility, and restraints on consumer spending. To Paehlke and perhaps other environmentalists, such an expanded ideology would offer the chance to replace progressive liberalism and become the principal alternative to the various contemporary conservatisms.

To many reconstructive environmentalists, however, this would be a typically tepid and reformist response to a real problem and opportunity. The effort to form a Green political party, or at least Green-oriented caucuses within the Democratic party, is one way to develop greater autonomy and purity of principles. The Green committees of correspondence have developed a platform with ten key values (see Figure 10.4) in hopes of clarifying their ideology and attracting members. Presumably, many environmentalists could subscribe to these values and find them better served by an organization devoted uncompromisingly to them.

Much of the hope that the Greens have that "an ecological transformation of society is indeed possible," according to Brian Tokar, rests on "the development of new community-based institutions and experiments in local democracy."[35] He sees the Green movement as "an important vehicle for renewing public activity at the local level" and beginning to "create a genuine counter-power to the influence of established institutions."[36] Indeed, the only electoral successes that Greens have achieved to date have been at the local level, particularly in New England.

A more militantly anticapitalist version of Green politics is offered by the Left Green Network of social ecologists, also primarily from New

Figure 10.4 Ten Key Values of the Green Committees of Correspondence

1. Ecological Wisdom

How can we operate human societies with the understanding that we are *part* of nature, not on top of it? How can we live within the ecological and resource limits of the planet, applying our technological knowledge to the challenge of an energy-efficient economy? How can we build a better relationship between cities and countryside? How can we guarantee rights of nonhuman species? How can we promote sustainable agriculture and respect for self-regulating natural systems? How can we further biocentric wisdom in all spheres of life?

2. Grassroots Democracy

How can we develop systems that allow and encourage us to control the decisions that effect our lives? How can we ensure that representatives will be fully accountable to the people who elected them? How can we develop planning mechanisms that would allow citizens to develop and implement their own preferences for policies and spending priorities? How can we encourage and assist the "mediating institutions"—family, neighborhood organization, church group, voluntary association, ethnic club—recover some of the functions now performed by government? How can we relearn the best insights from American traditions of civic vitality, voluntary action, and community responsibility?

3. Personal and Social Responsibility

How can we respond to human suffering in ways that promote dignity? How can we encourage people to commit themselves to lifestyles that promote their own health? How can we have a community-controlled education system that effectively teaches our children academic skills, ecological wisdom, social responsibility, and personal growth? How can we resolve interpersonal and intergroup conflicts without just turning them over to lawyers and judges? How can we take responsibility for reducing the crime rate in our neighborhoods? How can we encourage such values as simplicity and moderation?

4. Nonviolence

How can we, as a society, develop effective alternatives to our current patterns of violence, at all levels, from the family and the street to nations and the world? How can we eliminate nuclear weapons from the face of the Earth without being naive about the intentions of other governments? How can we most constructively use nonviolent methods to oppose practices and policies with which we disagree and in the process reduce the atmosphere of polarization and selfishness that is itself a source of violence?

5. Decentralization

How can we restore power and responsibility to individuals, institutions, communities and regions? How can we encourage the flourishing of regionally-based culture rather than a dominant monoculture? How can we have a decentralized, democratic society with our political, economic, and social institutions locating power on the smallest scale (closest to home) that is efficient and practical? How can we redesign our institutions so that fewer decisions and less regulation over money are granted as one moves from the community toward the national level? How can we reconcile the need for community and regional self-determination with the need for appropriate centralized regulation in certain matters?

6. Community-based Economics

How can we redesign our work structures to encourage employee ownership and workplace democracy? How can we develop new economic activities and institutions that will allow us to use our new technologies in ways that are humane, freeing, ecological, and accountable and responsive to communities? How can we establish some form of basic economic security, open to all? How can we move beyond the narrow "job ethic" to new definitions of "work," "jobs," and "income" that reflect the changing economy? How can we restructure our patterns of income distribution to reflect the wealth created by those outside the formal, monetary economy: those who take responsibility for parenting, housekeeping, home gardens, community volunteer work, etc.? How can we restrict the size and concentrated power of corporations without discouraging superior efficiency or technological innovation?

7. Postpatriarchal Values

How can we replace the cultural ethics of dominance and control with more cooperative ways of interacting? How can we encourage people to care about persons outside their own group? How can we promote the building of respectful, positive, and responsible relationships across the lines of gender and other divisions? How can we encourage a rich, diverse political culture that respects feelings as well as rationalist approaches? How can we proceed with as much respect for the means as the end (the process as much as the products of our efforts)? How can we learn to respect the contemplative, inner part of life as much as the outer activities?

8. Respect for Diversity

How can we honor cultural, ethnic, racial, sexual, religious, and spiritual diversity within the context of individual responsibility to all beings? While honoring diversity, how can we reclaim our country's finest shared ideals: the dignity of the individual, democratic participation, and liberty and justice for all?

9. Global Responsibility

How can we be of genuine assistance to grassroots groups in the Third World? What can we learn from such groups? How can we help other countries make the transition to self-sufficiency in food and other basic necessities? How can we cut our defense budget while maintaining an adequate defense? How can we promote these ten Green values in the reshaping of global order? How can we reshape world order without creating just another enormous nation-state?

10. Future Focus

How can we induce people and institutions to think in terms of the long-range future, and not just in terms of their short-range selfish interest? How can we encourage people to develop their own visions of the future and move more effectively toward them? How can we judge whether new technologies are socially useful—and use those judgments to shape our society? How can we induce our government and other institutions to practice fiscal responsibility? How can we make the quality of life, rather than open-ended economic growth, the focus of future thinking?

SOURCE: Charlene Spretnak and Fritjof Capra, *Green Politics: The Global Promise* (Sante Fe, N.M.: Bear & Company, 1986), pp. 229–233.

England. This group's strategy is summed up in this one paragraph of their 1989 manifesto:

> We hold the concept of "Green" to be explicitly radical, inherently anti-capitalist, and completely wedded to the New Left's commitment to participatory democracy. We believe the Green movement should carry forward the anti-hierarchical and anti-authoritarian themes of the New Left, while advancing a social-ecological perspective as the basis for a new independent political movement.[37]

As the tone suggests, this version of Green politics would probably be much less attractive to moderate environmentalists. Indeed, one of the problems that many Green sympathizers see with the movement is its factional character, along with failure to include people from minority races, women, and lower classes in adequate numbers.

For many people who hold strong reconstructive convictions and a sense of urgency about the global ecological crisis, both liberal environmentalist efforts and the Green movement seem too slow and too uncertain. They seek something that they can *do* right now, in small groups of like-thinking others or by themselves, to defend the biosphere and act out the ecological transformation to their lives. Less orthodox forms of politics appeal to them, including civil disobedience in front of nuclear installations and/or direct action techniques, such as spiking trees or sabotaging power lines.

The most visible group committed to these actions probably is Earth First!, cofounded in 1980 by David Foreman and Bill Haywood. Based on Edward Abbey's novel *The Monkey Wrench Gang*,[38] the group devised tactics for a variety of forms of sabotage, particularly of logging operations, in order to save the forests from despoiliation. These tactics are described in a book edited by Foreman and Haywood entitled *Ecodefense: A Field Guide to Monkeywrenching*.[39] The rationale, according to Abbey, is that

> representative democracy in the United States has broken down. Our legislators do not represent those who elected them but rather the minority who finance their political campaigns and who control the organs of communication that have made politics a game for the rich only. Representative government in the USA represents money not people and therefore has forfeited our allegiance and moral support. . . . The wilderness is our true home, and if it is threatened with invasion, pillage, and destruction—as it certainly is—then we have the right to defend that home, as we would our private rooms, by whatever means are necessary.[40]

With only a relative handful of participating members, but with broad sympathy among deep ecologists, Earth First! has proved to be a highly controversial means of focusing attention on ecological issues. As always, the willingness of a few to break laws on behalf of their values and beliefs forces others to take their positions more seriously.

Far less dramatic, but undoubtedly engaging many more people, are the efforts of the thousands of local groups that play diverse roles in what Mark Satin calls the second American experiment. What they share is a concern for personal well-being of men, women, and children, new ways of addressing old issues, and "such Green values as decentralism, deep ecology, global responsibility, and voluntary simplicity."[41]

The central building block of the second American experiment, according to Satin, is the caring individual. Gone are the rugged individual (who, in the Republican model, makes money at the expense of the community and the environment) and the collective individual (who, in the Democratic model, is a follower with an identity that comes from the group to which he or she belongs). Emerging today is the caring individual, who cares deeply about self *and* others. In Satin's words, "They identify with their jobs and interest groups, but also—and more profoundly—with all humanity or Earth as a whole."[42] This caring individual is produced chiefly by the will of individuals to change themselves, to go "beyond ideals, beyond politics" to reach a new level of "love, intimacy, and generativity."[43]

The point is not that such individual self-absorption takes people away from the kind of politics with which we are familiar, although that is certainly what it does. Rather, the point is that perhaps millions of people in the rising generations are seeking *something* that does not seem to be provided by our present ideology and politics. There may be a vast constituency out there, groping for some new way of understanding and acting in our society. And environmental-ecological concerns appear to be an important part of their views of the world.

IMPLICATIONS AND PROSPECTS

It seems clear that environmental-ecological concerns have worked their way into the terms of public debate and the structure of public policy, and that they have to some extent changed the pattern of American values and beliefs. These changes are quite evident in individual life-styles and practices, such as participation in recycling programs, litter cleanup, pollution control, and packaging of consumer products. They are much less evident when the environmentally correct practice would cost money or jobs or impose regulation on corporate or personal freedoms. Moreover, the march of environmental progress appears to have stalled, or perhaps to have reached a plateau, and turned to defense against the inevitable reaction and counterattack.

The impact of environmentalism on the basic American values seems to be modest, more additive than fundamentally altering. Individualism may be moderated by a new sensitivity to natural conditions, and the notion of property rights limited by a new set of concerns. The main body of liberal values and the centrality of the economic market remain with us much as before; we have essentially added environmental protection to the list of "good things" to stir into the public stew.

The transformative potential of the ecological world view—though clearly articulated in the reconstructive imperatives of basic value change and new ways of knowing and being—has not yet had much effect. Whenever in direct conflict with economic needs and priorities, all environmental thinking seems to give way. It may be that until ecological needs become more compelling and/or take an economic form, they will remain peripheral to the real or operational ideological spectrum.

The impact of environmentalism on American politics up to the present time thus seems to have been broad but shallow, exactly what the deep ecologists accuse the environmentalists of being. The advocates of reconstruction have so far had little transformative effect at the deeper levels they claim as their own. The American political economy and its cultural base have rolled and absorbed these new beliefs without a basic change of character or course.

This is not to say that, given fundamentally changed economic circumstances or future convergence with other new belief systems, a transformative environmentalism could not serve to reconstruct the American political spectrum. If there are ideologies with such capability, reconstructive ecology and feminism are certainly among them. It is simply to point out that the slogan "beyond left and right" may be descriptive of new ideas, but it is not yet of a visible, ongoing transcendence of the long-standing American ideological context.

ADDITIONAL READINGS

Biehl, Janet. *Rethinking Ecofeminist Politics*. Boston: South End Press, 1991.

Bookchin, Murray. *Remaking Society: Pathways to a Green Future*. Boston: South End Press, 1990.

Devall, Bill. *Simple in Means, Rich in Ends*. London: Merlin Press, 1990.

Diamond, Irene, and Gloria Orenstein, eds. *Reweaving the World: The Emergence of Ecofeminism*. Washington, D.C.: Sierra Club Books, 1991.

Ehrlich, Paul R. *The End of Affluence: A Blueprint for Your Future*. New York: Ballantine, 1974.

Foreman, Dave, and Bill Haywood, eds. *Ecodefense: A Field Guide to Monkeywrenching*. Tucson, Ariz.: Ned Ludd, 1987.

Lovelock, James. *The Ages of Gaia: A Biography of Our Living Earth*. New York: Oxford University Press, 1989.

Merchant, Carolyn. *Ecological Revolutions: Nature, Gender, and Science in New England*. Chapel Hill: University of North Carolina Press, 1989.

Ophuls, William. *Ecology and the Politics of Scarcity*. San Francisco: Freeman, 1977.

Paehlke, Robert C. *Environmentalism and the Future of Progressive Politics*. New Haven, Conn.: Yale University Press, 1989.

Porritt, Jonathan, and David Winner. *The Coming of the Greens*. London: Fontana, 1988.

Rifkin, Jeremy. *Biosphere Politics: A New Consciousness for a New Century*. New York: Crown, 1991.

Satin, Mark. *New Options for America: The Second American Experiment Has Begun*. Fresno: The Press at California State University at Fresno, 1991.

Schell, Jonathan. *The Fate of the Earth*. New York: Alfred A. Knopf, 1982.

Tokar, Brian. *The Green Alternative: Creating an Ecological Future*. San Pedro, Calif.: R. & E. Miles, 1987.

Worster, Donald. *Nature's Economy: A History of Ecological Ideas*. New York: Cambridge University Press, 1985.

CHAPTER 11

AMERICAN IDEOLOGIES AND THE NEW POLITICS OF THE 1990s

The new global economic and political context as well as the expressed preferences of the American people would appear to encourage—even compel—significant change in terms of ideological and political debate in the United States. Some new ideologies have attracted support and introduced a new dynamism to American politics in the last decades. However, despite wide agreement that the old ideological labels are outdated and that there is a need to get "beyond left and right," not much tangible progress has yet been made in doing so.

A number of constraints have operated to slow the process of change in the impact of these ideologies, and, at most, they have only begun to revise the American political spectrum. American politics seems to be stuck somewhere in the 1960s; it seems to offer only frustration and resentment to constituents and participants alike. As any number of observers have noted, the revival of democracy around the world has been paralleled by its decline at home.

In this chapter, we first briefly survey the many factors in our current context that seem to encourage or compel ideological change. Then we assess the responsiveness (the strengths and weaknesses in the new context) of each active ideology and the constraints that appear to hold them back from making more dramatic impact. Next, we develop a revised two-dimensional map of the American ideological spectrum today, as a means of seeing where we may be headed. Finally, we speculate about the ideological changes and principles that are most likely to inspire and mobilize Americans and eventually to reshape our politics.

THE NEW GLOBAL CONTEXT

There is a remarkable consensus among informed observers and advocates that the liberal-conservative-socialist belief systems of the industrial era are no longer relevant to the conditions and needs of the present age. E. J. Dionne's widely acclaimed *Why Americans Hate Politics* is only the most strident in attributing the American distaste for and withdrawal from politics to the "false choices" presented by liberals and conservatives.[1] All across the spectrum, from ecologists to populists to libertarians, people resonate to feelings such as these expressed by two radical democrats from Vermont in a recent proposal to decentralize government in that state:

> First of all we believe the liberal/conservative definition is a black hole in the universe of ideas. . . . The new movement afoot in America is neither Left nor Right, liberal nor conservative, Democratic nor Republican. It is an ideological bridge to a new future. On this bridge one will find people whose politics have differed—many of them combatants in the past—who now seek together a global society of just, peaceful, and dutiful human communities.[2]

Of all the most fully agreed-upon slogans in politics, this must surely rank with "balance the budget" and "cut the waste in Washington" as far more easily said than done. Why is this so? This chapter is an effort to answer that question. The staying power of traditional values, beliefs, and symbols, supported by electoral tactics and apathy, is not to be underestimated. Even as we review the apparently encouraging components of our new context, for example, we see that it includes obstacles to change.

Ideologies and Elections

It seems clear that the traditional ideologies no longer speak to the issues that concern most Americans. As we saw in Chapter 1, the New Deal electoral coalition that sustained liberalism in power for thirty years fractured irretrievably in the late 1960s. The reaction against the advancement of blacks, life-style changes, feminism, and the anti-Vietnam War movement raised what we have called the social issues to the fore. Urban ethnics, blue-collar workers, and southerners—all key members of the old New Deal coalition—began to move toward the Republicans and one or another form of conservatism.

We have also seen that the conservative coalition is inherently unstable. The upper-middle-class organic conservatives and libertarians vigorously disagree over the proper uses of government, and neither one is great enough in number to gain power. Their mass base, the populist conservative-Christian Right, emerging from the lower-middle and working classes, endorses positions and methods quite at odds with the organic conservatives and the libertarians. The only grounds for an electoral coalition are antipathy to liberalism, anticommunism, or a charismatic leader such as Ronald Reagan.

With the absence of Reagan and the decline of the cold war, such a conservative coalition can be mobilized only by an attack on 1960s liberalism, whether that is a relevant target or not. Dionne refers to this as a "false polarization" in which the "cultural civil wars" (his term for what we have been calling social issues) of the 1960s are refought again and again. Electoral victory for conservatives, in other words, depends on keeping the focus on the ideological battles of the thirty-year past. Similarly, liberals have found it rewarding for decades to run against the memory of Herbert Hoover and in favor of long-outdated economic remedies.

In both cases, perceived electoral advantages result in preserving old categories. Dionne says:

> Since the late 1980s, American politics has been held hostage to conservatism's impasse and liberalism's past failures. The result has been immobility in government, an increasing harshness in politics, and a lack of substance in electoral campaigns.[3]

Thus, in Dionne's eyes, the various liberalisms and conservatisms are all flawed; none offers solutions or even approaches to present problems. They endure because they *work* as symbols that energize enough voters to win elections, even if many other voters are so disgusted that they withdraw from politics entirely. Political scientist John White summarized this phenomenon in the title of a recent book, *The New Politics of Old Values*.[4]

Popular Preferences

The most salient feature of American political behavior in the last decades has been the steady decline in voter participation at all levels. While black participation rates climbed during and after the civil rights years, the white working class has been withdrawing from voting in growing numbers for four decades. In the 1990s a significant portion (perhaps 25 percent or more) of the population is simultaneously low in income-producing skills, increasingly squeezed out of government services, *and* withdrawn from politics as well.

Confidence in public institutions and leaders also fell steadily from the 1960s to the present, with special dips after the Vietnam War and after the Watergate scandal and the subsequent resignation of President Nixon. Many reasons for this decline are noted in Chapter 1, and probably all have played some part. However, the factor of special importance that is relevant to this discussion is frustration at the failure of popular preferences to be debated and acted upon in our politics.

Dionne argues that there are ideas that unite rather than divide Americans today ("the perfectly obvious preferences of the American people"[5]) that do not get expressed in our politics because of the dominance of liberal/conservative false choices. In his judgment,

> what is required to end the popular hatred of politics . . . is the creation of a new political center. What I have in mind is not a bland centrism, but a coalition for social reform that could command broad support in the middle class.[6]

While Dionne offers no evidence in support of any particular "perfectly obvious preferences" or the nature of a potential middle-class "coalition for social reform," there is considerable evidence tending in this direction available from recent public opinion surveys. One major national study making use of several different methods that combined surveys with in-depth interviewing was published in 1991 with the title, *The Day America Told the Truth*.[7] Important findings included the conviction that new leadership is needed to make the American political system supply clear choices and a growing impatience with individual greed and failure to invest in the productivity of the American economy.

The authors sought to find principles on which the largest number of respondents would agree and for which they would be willing to sacrifice by paying extra taxes (usually "as much as it takes") or by volunteering significant blocks of their own time. What emerged was a people's national agenda featuring educational, environmental, and children-centered programs, in this order:[8]

1. Drastic improvement in the education system.
2. Elimination of illiteracy.
3. Permanent protection of the environment.
4. Prevention and help for child-abuse problems.
5. Doing something meaningful about homelessness.
6. Fighting a realistic war on poverty.
7. Effectively combatting drug abuse.

Moreover, the authors reported that there was a high level of recognition of national problems, great impatience to get to work on them, and readiness for dramatic efforts such as a set of "crusades." Once again, the people seem readier to move decisively in new directions than are their leaders or their mainstream ideologies.

Problems: The Agenda of the Future

The problems filling the public agenda of the 1990s are far removed from those that the traditional ideologies were designed to address when they first crystallized in the mid-nineteenth and early twentieth century. They involve qualitatively distinct global, ecological, economic, bureaucratic, technological, and human relationships that the earlier categories cannot be stretched to cover. We shall consider only three in illustration.

The newest major item on the American agenda is that of defining the new world order and the American role in it. For almost the entire twentieth century, and with particular intensity since 1945, the United States has felt threatened by and stood firmly against communism and the Soviet Union. With almost blinding speed, this threat has been removed, or at least greatly altered. A whole new world system is quickly taking shape, and the American role in it (once resolved) will fundamentally shape our national politics well into the twenty-first century. Moreover, it is an interdependent world with quite unprecedented needs for mutual understanding and cooperation.

The second item, probably the most important problem of all and the one that always rises to eclipse whatever fad threatens to claim the momentary ideological stage, is that of the American economy. Americans have been accustomed to steady growth, relative affluence, and broad distribution of income and services, all of which are threatened in the present global context. The challenge is to restore the U.S. economy to something like long-term competitive levels in the midst of new ecological, human-resource, and international constraints.

Working to derail or deflect efforts to solve these first two problems, however, are the social issues, or "cultural civil wars" remaining from the 1960s. The United States must find ways to mute or transcend the moral absolutes in the present ideological discourse. Race relations, feminism and family issues, and basic questions of the moral quality and purpose of American society must be somehow made into subjects of mutually tolerant and respectful community discussion. Until this is accomplished, the society will continue to be divided between a relatively affluent upper two-thirds of the population and an increasingly impoverished and inert underclass.

THE IDEOLOGIES: DEAD, DYING, AND DYNAMIC

Which ideologies—if any—of those currently contending for acceptance in the United States have the capacity to mobilize a mass base of support among the American people? The apparent answer is none. A better question might be, which aspects of which ideologies offer the potential to mobilize people under favorable future conditions? As we review the current status of each ideology, however, we shall see not only specific dynamic elements in some of today's ideologies, *but also* that there *may be* one current ideology with the capacity to reconstruct our politics.

Dead or Dying

Those ideologies that appear to have lost (or never had) the capacity to mobilize millions and become something like a popular movement include liberalism, neoliberalism, neoconservatism, organic conservatism, and progressive populism. The flaws of the traditional liberalism of the New Deal and immediate postwar world have been exhaustively analyzed, and it has been thoroughly discredited from Right and Left. The most telling charges against it are its association with the Vietnam War, its integral link to centralized big government, and its unequivocal and unselective commitment to economic growth. Its reputation alone is fatal.

Neoliberalism has never generated much interest and has little or no constituency. It is too technocratic, too managerial, and too lifeless as a set of fighting principles. Furthermore, it involves too much use of centralized government management of the economy for most Americans.

Neoconservatism was a much livelier set of allegations and exhortations, and it was presented in such a vigorous style that it always made good media headlines. It served the purpose of establishing intellectual respectability for the Reagan presidency very well. However, it was never more than a small coterie of anxious intellectuals, and it always exaggerated its enemies' transgressions so greatly that it strained credulity, sounding precious and self-absorbed in the process. Without its favorite liberal targets, neoconservatism has neither a focus, function, *nor* mass base.

Organic conservatism has something to say and deserves better of its American audience. However, it is appealing only to a fastidious few, and too much of everyday life repels the genuinely upper-class sensitivities of organic conservatives. Organic conservatism's future is as a welcome but miniscule voice on behalf of the long-term traditions and needs of the American enterprise.

We include progressive populism in this category of dead or dying not because its beliefs and programs are unattractive to Americans, but in spite of their undeniable popularity with sectors of the population. The problem with progressive populism (barring total economic collapse) is that its components are locked in continuing conflict with each other, a conflict for leftover fragments of status and power that they are simply unable to transcend. Economic radicalism, minority politics, trade union organization, feminism, community activism, and all the other special interests that are attracted to progressive populism are in fact drawn by their distinctiveness, not by what they share with others. Each insists upon recognition of its special importance, and only the most temporary and fragile coalitions are possible in the context of American history and circumstances.

Dynamic

The ideologies with dynamic elements capable of mobilizing at least substantial numbers of Americans today include ecology/environmentalism, feminism, libertarianism, the Christian Right, and (our mystery contender for reconstruction of our politics) a version of reform liberalism.

We have just seen that environmentalism is a broadly attractive set of principles for great numbers of Americans, perhaps just because it does not challenge basic values at great depth. One brand of ecology/environmentalism in particular has reconstructive potential because it seeks not only changes in basic values but also an entirely new way of thinking and knowing. However, it must come to an accommodation with needs for economic growth and effective distribution.

Feminism too has entered the mainstream of evolving American beliefs and cannot now be dislodged. The data from *The Day America Told the Truth* establish that women are increasingly looked to for the kind of leadership that Americans are seeking. Although it has a considerable way to go to encompass a full range of problems and issues, feminism has already begun to extend beyond gender relations to include the workplace, the family, and several child-centered issues.

Libertarianism is perhaps the major winner from the ideological conflicts of the 1980s and seems to have established at least a beachhead among the baby-boom generation and the middle class. Individualism, freedom in the sense of the absence of governmental restraint, and decentralization are very powerful appeals in the American context of values. What libertarians have not yet done is to reach out to the less-advantaged sectors of the population and exhibit compassion for those less successful than themselves.

The Christian Right remains a significant factor in American politics, even though anticommunism appears to be losing its mobilizing power. For many Americans, religion comes first, and/or morality in society is an enduring motivator. Secular humanism remains a visible threat, particularly as libertarianism gains ground.

The populist conservative side of the Christian Right remains a question mark, depending chiefly on the status of the economy. Indeed, the great bulk of populist potential, progressive or conservative, rests substantially on how well the economy is growing and distributing its rewards to the lower half of the social pyramid. Populism is a highly volatile set of beliefs, as we have emphasized, and in hard times there is likely to be a substantial movement on behalf of government action and redistributive policies. At other times, populism may be relatively quiescent.

Our mystery contender for a possible future role as the new mainstream of American ideology is a special version of reform liberalism. We offer three basic reasons for nominating it to a possible future role, and we define the content of that "special version" in the final section, after summarizing our image of the American political spectrum in the 1990s.

First, some brand of liberalism is inevitable in a country so fully imbued with the values of individualism, property first among individual rights, freedom as limited government, and the economic market. Even European social democracy (the model for all the aspiring newly democratic societies of the industrial world) seems out of reach for the United States. The constraints imposed by the bedrock values cannot be exaggerated: it is more likely that the whole notion of ideology itself is out of date, than that the basic American values will be substantially altered in the near future.

Second, Americans generally dislike the prospect of substantial change and always want to preserve the basic outlines of the essentially favorable status quo in the country that they genuinely love. This may be another way of saying that the United States is a middle-class country, both in the distribution of wealth and income and in the way that the people think of themselves. Property rights and established procedures are both compelling forces. Without broad support in the middle classes, there is no real prospect of any kind of change achieving political success.

Third, the form of change in the United States is thus *reform*, specifically reform led by the middle class with a decent regard for, and mass support from, the populist working classes, including most minorities. Populists aspire to the middle class and are most comfortable following its lead when it is not elitist in rhetoric or practice. Populists of both progressive and conservative inclination will support the economic revitalization programs of reformers and accept other kinds of reform as well. *The key is to synthesize the reform liberal and libertarian agendas*, an accomplishment that is prefigured by the writers featured in several previous chapters and summarized in the final section of this chapter.

THE REVISED AMERICAN POLITICAL SPECTRUM OF THE 1990s

A visual presentation of a political spectrum is intended to show relationships between different sets of beliefs. Because beliefs differ in many ways, the presentation of a spectrum involves first the choice of what sorts of relationships are important enough to be emphasized.

In Chapter 3 we note that the traditional spectrum displayed attitudes toward the distribution of wealth and income. Historically, this paralleled the makeup of social classes, conceptions of human nature, and definitions of key values such as freedom and equality. The enduring character of both the straight-line spectrum and social class as the principal cue to received ideology led us, despite stated reservations, to organize our analysis of American ideologies in traditional Left-Right terms and to emphasize their social-class origins.

We also saw that evidence from the 1970s showed the effects of the rise of the social issues and their effects in creating a four-cell matrix. In that matrix, populist and libertarian belief systems were seen together with the more familiar liberal and conservative ideologies. Clearly, the spectrum was changing in several ways that could only be unraveled after we had examined various American belief systems in some detail.

Now, however, that four-cell matrix seems inadequate to represent the full range of important differences in American ideological debate. In its place, we suggest the image presented in Figure 11.1. On the horizontal axis is the original and continuing core relationship: Left-Right contrasts in regard to distribution of wealth, income and power, and the social-class origin and base of each position. This remains the essential basis for understanding ideologies, because it is the most important issue in our politics.

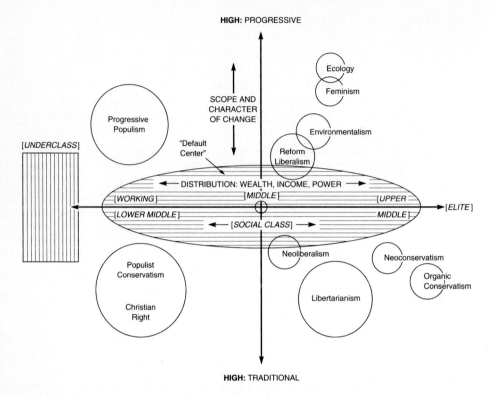

Figure 11.1   A Revised American Political Spectrum, 1990s

The social issues, however, are not the only additional factor to be added to the Left-Right-plus-social-class relationship. Somehow, we need to try to reflect several different vectors of change—the social issues *plus* other issues and problems of salience to American ideologies today.

We have done so by adding a vertical axis to measure the scope and character of change sought by various ideologies. At both extremities, the scope of change sought is high; at the origin, the scope of change sought is low or nonexistent. The character of change, however, is in contrast: at the top, the change is progressive, or toward newer values and goals; at the bottom, the change is traditional, or toward older and/or previous values and goals.

As can be seen, each ideology examined in this book is portrayed on this two-dimensional figure in terms of *both* their redistributive and class appeals and the nature of the change that they seek. For example, libertarianism (a relatively large and appealing ideology) draws upon a middle-class base and seeks substantial change in a generally traditional direction. Populisms of the Left and Right, quite numerous in their support, draw from a similar class base but tend toward contrasting kinds of change. Neoconservatism, neoliberalism, and organic conservatism, on the other hand, are quite small numerically and all reflect a middle- or upper-middle-class origin.

Two other important features of contemporary American politics are reflected in this figure. One is the detached and inert nature of the American underclass, shown by the vertically hatched block at the far left of the figure. This underclass, made up chiefly of poor, minority, and women-headed households, is more or less permanently excluded—partly by the workings of the political system and partly by their own actions—from participation in American politics.

The other feature is the wide-ranging nonideological and often apathetic middle stratum, shown by horizontal hatching. This large group, perhaps half of all Americans, represents a kind of "default center" in American politics. They are not particularly interested in ideological debates and avoid all extremes. Instead, they cling to essentially traditional beliefs and centrist practices, waiting for others to take the initiative. In our view, this great centrist body will provide a good share of the support for whatever version of reform liberalism appears viable and capable of solving problems.

PROSPECTS: A NEW REFORM LIBERALISM?

What would be the leading characteristics of this magic new "special version" of reform liberalism? Essentially, it would be a synthesis of reform liberalism and libertarianism, with primary emphasis on economic revitalization and individual opportunity in an environmentally and gender-sensitive framework (and undoubtedly with a new and attractive label that nevertheless would sound quite traditional). Many authors from as many different perspectives have contributed one or more central values or programs, which we now briefly summarize.

One major component of the new synthesis would be the return of moral purpose to social life—the notion of a common good, citizenship, virtue, and social obligation—all the ingredients of community now distinguished by their absence from American life. A second component would be reliance upon individual responsibility and personal initiative, with rewards for work and merit—principles that reflect the market and the desire to keep government's role limited. A third would be decentralization and the new politics of place—the local community, or the bioregion of the ecologists' imagery. Finally, the new synthesis would surely have to stress the mutual respect and tolerance that can accept the disagreements that are inevitable among democratic citizens.

This possible new communitarian-individual democracy begins to sound a lot like Thomas Jefferson's ideal system of two centuries past. Indeed, many of the advocates who endorse parts of this set of principles explicitly invoke Jefferson in support: he was, after all, simultaneously individualist, communitarian, republican, and democratic. If this should be our version of "back to the future," it would be both traditional in rhetoric and yet unprecedented in practice—just the kind of combination that Americans seem to prefer. It is an image that, in contrast to worries about the national debt or the recurring annual budget deficits, might have the capacity to mobilize the best impulses among millions of Americans.

ADDITIONAL READINGS

Bryan, Frank, and John McLaughry. *The Vermont Papers: Recreating Democracy on a Human Scale*. Post Mills, Vt.: Chelsea Green Publishing Company, 1989.

Dionne, E. J., Jr.: *Why Americans Hate Politics*. New York: Simon & Schuster, 1991.

Edsall, Thomas Byrne. *The New Politics of Inequality*. New York: Norton, 1984.

Ferguson, Thomas B., and Joel Rogers. *Right Turn: The Future of the Democratic Party and American Politics*. New York: St. Martin's, 1985.

Halberstam, David. *The Reckoning*. New York: Simon & Schuster, 1986.

Kemmis, Daniel. *Community and the Politics of Place*. Norman: University of Oklahoma Press, 1990.

Murray, Charles. *In Pursuit: Of Happiness and Good Government*. New York: Simon & Schuster, 1988.

Patterson, James, and Peter Kim. *The Day America Told the Truth*. New York: Prentice Hall Press, 1991.

Phillips, Kevin. *The Politics of Rich and Poor: Wealth and the American Electorate in the Reagan Aftermath*. New York: Random House, 1990.

NOTES

PREFACE

1. Robert A. Dahl, *Dilemmas of Pluralist Democracy* (New Haven: Yale University Press, 1982), p. 3.
2. E. J. Dionne, Jr., *Why Americans Hate Politics* (New York: Simon & Schuster, 1991).
3. Ibid., p. 11.

CHAPTER 1

1. Dionne, *Why Americans Hate Politics*, pp. 11–13.
2. Cornel West, "Race in America," *Tacoma News Tribune*, September 20, 1991, p. A17.
3. Dionne, *Why Americans Hate Politics*, p. 345.
4. Frank Bryan and John McClaughry, *The Vermont Papers* (Post Mills, Vt.: Chelsea Green Publishing Company, 1989), p. 6.
5. West, "Race in America," p. A17.
6. Betty Friedan, *The Second Stage* (New York: Dell Publishing, 1981), pp. 332–333.

CHAPTER 3

1. Donald I. Warren, *The Radical Center: Middle Americans and the Politics of Alienation* (South Bend, Ind.: University of Notre Dame Press, 1976).
2. William Maddox and Stuart Lilie, *Beyond Liberal and Conservative* (Washington, D.C.: Cato Institute, 1984).

CHAPTER 4

1. Louis Hartz, *The Liberal Tradition in America* (New York: Harcourt Brace, 1955).
2. Paul Hawken, James Ogilvy, and Peter Schwartz, eds., *Seven Tomorrows: Toward a Voluntary History* (New York: Bantam, 1982), p. 222.
3. Ibid., p. 225.
4. Ibid., p. 228.

CHAPTER 5

1. Irving Kristol, "What Is a Neoconservative?" *Newsweek*, January 19, 1976, p. 87.
2. Midge Decter, quoted in *The Weekly* (Seattle, Wash.), November 16, 1983, p. 12.

3. Irving Kristol, *Two Cheers for Capitalism* (New York: Basic Books, 1978), p. 178.
4. Ibid., p. 179.
5. Nathan Glazer, *Affirmative Discrimination: Ethnic Inequality and Public Policy* (New York: Basic Books, 1976).
6. Decter, quoted in *The Weekly*, p. 13.
7. Samuel P. Huntington, "The United States," in Michael J. Crozier, Samuel P. Huntington, and Joji Watanuki, *The Crisis of Democracy* (New York: New York University Press, 1975). The same essay appears in the bicentennial edition of *The Public Interest*, Nathan Glazer and Irving Kristol, eds., *The American Commonwealth—1976*.
8. Robert Nisbet, *The Twilight of Authority* (New York: Basic Books, 1972).
9. Michael Novak, *The Spirit of Democratic Capitalism* (New York: Simon and Schuster, 1982).
10. Kristol, *Two Cheers for Capitalism*, p. 171.
11. Peter Steinfels, *The Neoconservatives: The Men Who Are Changing America's Politics* (New York: Simon & Schuster, 1979), p. 56.
12. Novak, *Democratic Capitalism*, p. 31.
13. Ibid., pp. 359–360.
14. Paul Tsongas, *The Road from Here: Liberalism and Realities in the 1980s* (New York: Alfred A. Knopf, 1981), p. xiii.
15. Robert B. Reich, *The Work of Nations: Preparing Ourselves for 21st Century Capitalism* (New York: Alfred A. Knopf, 1991).
16. Paul Tsongas, *A Call to Economic Arms: Forging a New American Mandate* (Boston: Foley, Hoag and Eliot, 1991).
17. Charles Anderson, *Pragmatic Liberalism* (Chicago: University of Chicago Press, 1990).
18. Charles Peters, "A Neoliberal's Manifesto," *Washington Monthly*, May 1983, p. 10.
19. Ibid., p. 12.
20. Ibid., p. 13.
21. Ibid., p. 18.
22. Ibid., p. 10.
23. Tsongas, *Economic Arms*, p. 11.
24. Tsongas, *Road from Here*, p. 90.
25. Reich, *Work of Nations*, passim.
26. Tsongas, *Economic Arms*, p. 5.
27. Lester Thurow, *The Zero-Sum Society* (New York: Basic Books, 1980), p. 194.
28. Ibid., p. 206.
29. Robert Reich, quoted in *The New York Times Magazine*, August 28, 1983, p. 63.
30. Peters, "Neoliberal Manifesto," p. 17.

CHAPTER 6

1. Martin Luther King, Jr., "Letter from Birmingham City Jail" (Philadelphia: American Friends Service Committee, 1963).
2. Angela Davis, *Women, Culture, and Politics* (New York: Vintage Books, 1986), pp. 7–9.
3. Manning Marable, "Black History and the Vision of Democracy," in Harry C. Boyte and Frank Riessman, eds., *The New Populism: The Politics of Empowerment* (Philadelphia: Temple University Press, 1986), pp. 205–206.

4. Cornel West, "Populism: A Black Socialist Critique," in Boyte and Reissman, *The New Populism*, p. 208.
5. Susan Faludi, "Blame It on Feminism," *Mother Jones*, September/October 1991, p. 26.
6. Betty Friedan, *The Second Stage* (New York: Dell Publishing, 1981), p. xvi.
7. Ibid., p. 60.
8. Faludi, *Feminism*, p. 28.
9. Friedan, *Second Stage*, p. xxv.
10. Carolyn G. Heilbrun, *Hamlet's Mother and Other Women* (New York: Ballantine Books, 1990), p. 3.
11. Mary Field Belenky et al., *Women's Ways of Knowing: The Development of Self, Voice, and Mind* (New York: Basic Books, 1986).
12. Carol Gilligan, *In a Different Voice: Psychological Theory and Women's Development* (Cambridge, Mass.: Harvard University Press, 1982).
13. Belenky et al., *Women's Ways*, p 8.
14. Reprinted in "Works in Progress," Olympia, WA, August 1991.
15. Ellie Smeal, "Why I Support a New Party," *Ms*, January/February 1991, p. 73.
16. Marianne Means, "NOW's Plan Could Damage Cause of Women's Rights," *Seattle Post-Intelligencer*, September 27, 1991, p. A12.
17. Ibid., p. A12.
18. Friedan, *Second Stage*, p. 30.
19. Bolenky et. al., *Women's Ways*, p. 8.
20. National Conference of Catholic Bishops, *Economic Justice for All* (Washington, D.C.: United Catholic Conference, 1986), pp. ix–xi.
21. Paul Savoy, "Toward an Economic Bill of Rights," *The Nation*, June 17, 1991.
22. Irving Howe, "New Styles in 'Leftism'," in *Steady Work: Essays in the Politics of Democratic Radicalism, 1953–1966* (New York: Harcourt, Brace and World, 1966), p. 78.
23. Ann Ferguson, *Sexual Democracy: Women, Oppression, and Revolution* (New York: Cambridge University Press, 1991), p. 135.
24. Matthew Rothschild, "For a New Party," *Peace and Democracy News*, Summer 1991, p. 14.
25. Allan Bloom, *The Closing of the American Mind* (New York: Random House, 1986).
26. E. D. Hirsch, Jr., *Cultural Literacy* (New York: Basic Books, 1985).
27. Rick Simonson and Scott Walker, eds., *Multicultural Literacy: Opening the American Mind* (St. Paul, Minn.: Graywolf Press, 1988), p. x.
28. Ibid., p. xiii.
29. Flora Lewis, "Idealism Is No Excuse for Thought Control," *Seattle Times/Post-Intelligencer*, July 14, 1991, p. D3.
30. Eric Foner, Review of the Smithsonian's "The West as America," in *The Nation*, July 29–August 5, 1991, p. 163.

CHAPTER 7

1. Tom Harkin, "The Making of a Democratic Populist," in Harry C. Boyte and Frank Reissman, eds., *The New Populism: The Politics of Empowerment* (Philadelphia: Temple University Press, 1986), p. 237.
2. Kevin Phillips, *The Politics of Rich and Poor: Wealth and the American Electorate in the Reagan Aftermath* (New York: Random House, 1990).

3. Jack Newfield and Jeff Greenfield, *A Populist Manifesto: The Making of a New Majority* (New York: Warner Paperback Library, 1972), p. 9.
4. "Founding Statement of the Campaign for Economic Democracy." Appendix in Tom Hayden, *The American Future: New Visions beyond Old Frontiers* (Boston: South End Press, 1980).
5. Martin Carnoy and Derek Shearer, *Economic Democracy: The Challenge of the 1980s* (White Plains, N.Y.: M. E. Sharpe, 1980).
6. See *An Economic Strategy for the 1980s* (Washington, D.C.: Full Employment Action Council and National Policy Exchange, 1982). The Full Employment Action Council is an umbrella organization of more than eighty trade union, civil rights, religious, and other organizations.
7. Herbert Gintis, "A Socialist Democracy for the United States," in Stephen Rosskamm Shalom, ed., *Socialist Visions* (Boston: South End Press, 1983), pp. 12–13.
8. Jeremy Brecher and Tim Costello, eds., *Building Bridges: The Emerging Grassroots Coalition of Labor and Community* (New York: Monthly Review Press, 1990), p. 9.
9. Ibid.
10. Mike Miller, "Populist Promises and Problems," in Boyte and Reissman, *The New Populism*, p. 139.
11. Jim Hightower, "Kick-Ass Populism," in Boyte and Reissman, *The New Populism*, p. 241.
12. Ibid., p. 242.
13. Ibid.
14. Martin Carnoy, Derek Shearer, and Russell Rumberger, *A New Social Contract: The Economy and Government after Reagan* (New York: Harper & Row, 1983), pp. 1–2.
15. See Sec. 2(1) and Title I, Sec. 101.
16. Carnoy, Shearer, and Rumberger, *New Social Contract*, pp. 1–2.
17. Full Employment Action Council, *Economic Strategy for the 1980s*, p. 51.
18. Carnoy, Shearer, and Rumberger, *New Social Contract*, p. 2.
19. Joshua Cohen and Joel Rogers, *On Democracy* (New York: Penguin, 1984), p. 169.
20. Many good examples of applied scholarship may be found in the journal *democracy*.
21. Gintis, "Socialist Democracy," pp. 13–14.
22. Barry Bluestone and Bennett Harrison, *The Deindustrialization of America: Plant Closings, Community Abandonment, and the Dismantling of Basic Industry* (New York: Basic Books, 1982).
23. Miller, "Populist Promises," p. 132.
24. Barbara Mikulski, "A Populist, a Feminist, and a Progressive," in Boyte and Reissman, *The New Populism*, p. 257.
25. Carnoy, Shearer, and Rumberger, *New Social Contract*, p. 2.
26. Gar Alperovitz, "Toward a Tough-Minded Populism," in Boyte and Reissman, *The New Populism*, p. 169.
27. Full Employment Action Council, *Economic Strategy for the 1980s*, p. 36.
28. Alan Wolfe, *America's Impasse: The Rise and Fall of the Politics of Growth* (Boston: South End Press, 1981), p. 239.
29. Ibid., p. 246.
30. Michael Harrington, *Decade of Decision: The Crisis of the American System* (New York: Simon and Schuster, 1980), p. 301.

31. Michael Ansara and S. M. Miller, "Democratic Populism," in Boyte and Reissman, *The New Populism*, p. 148.
32. Elizabeth Kamarck Minnich, "Toward a Feminist Populism," in Boyte and Reissman, *The New Populism*, p. 192.
33. Harkin, "Making of a Democratic Populist," in Boyte and Reissman, *The New Populism*, p. 238.
34. Hightower, "Kick-Ass Populism," p. 244.
35. Ibid.

CHAPTER 8

1. Paul Weyrich, quoted in Richard A. Viguerie, *The New Right: We're Ready to Lead* (Falls Church, Va.: Viguerie Company, 1980), pp. 59–60.
2. Patrick J. Buchanan, *Right from the Beginning* (Washington, D.C.: Regnery Gateway, 1990), p. 91.
3. Ibid., pp. 95, 99.
4. Viguerie, *New Right*, is the best historical source and is used throughout this chapter unless otherwise noted.
5. Viguerie, *New Right*, pp. 54–55.
6. Kevin P. Phillips, *Post-Conservative America: People, Politics, and Ideology in a Time of Crisis* (New York: Random House, 1982), p. 47.
7. William A. Rusher, *The Making of the New Majority Party* (New York: Sheed and Ward, 1980).
8. Viguerie, *New Right*, pp. 66–71.
9. Phillips, *Post-Conservative America*, p. 49.
10. Phyllis Schlafly, "America's Great Religious Document," *Phyllis Schlafly Report*, July 1982, p. 4, cited in Rebecca E. Klatch, *Women of the New Right* (Philadelphia: Temple University Press, 1987), p. 23.
11. Pat Robertson, "The Family and the Law," speech at Family Forum II conference, July 1982.
12. Buchanan, *Right from the Beginning*, p. 342.
13. Ibid., p. 337.
14. Sara Diamond, *Spiritual Warfare: The Politics of the Christian Right* (Boston: South End Press, 1989), p. 138.
15. Bob Wiener, 1985 radio address, cited in ibid., p. 45.
16. Tim LaHaye, *The Battle for the Mind*, cited in ibid., p. 85.
17. Phyllis Schlafly, cited in Klatch, *Women of the New Right*, p. 60.
18. Ed McAteer, cited in Klatch, ibid., p. 58.
19. Samuel T. Francis, "Message from MARS: The Social Politics of the New Right," in Robert W. Whitaker, ed., *The New Right Papers* (New York: St. Martin's, 1982), pp. 68–69.
20. Robert J. Hoy, "Lid on a Boiling Pot," in ibid., p. 98.
21. Buchanan, *Right from the Beginning*, p. 357.
22. Phyllis Schlafly, cited in Diamond, *Spiritual Warfare*, p. 109.
23. Paul M. Weyrich, "Blue Collar or Blue Blood? The New Right Compared with the Old Right," in Whitaker, *New Right Papers*, p. 60.
24. Editorial, *Conservative Digest*, November 1978.
25. Buchanan, *Right from the Beginning*, p. 354.
26. Phyllis Schlafly, cited in Klatch, *Women of the New Right*, p. 130.

27. Buchanan, *Right from the Beginning*, p. 365.
28. Ibid., p. 374.

CHAPTER 9

1. Clinton Rossiter, *Conservatism in America: The Thankless Persuasion* (New York: Alfred A. Knopf, 1962).
2. William F. Buckley, Jr., *God and Man at Yale: The Superstitions of "Academic Freedom"* (Chicago: Regnery, 1951) and *McCarthy and His Enemies* (Chicago: Regnery, 1954).
3. Barry Goldwater, *The Conscience of a Conservative* (Shepherdsville, Ky.: Victor, 1960).
4. Milton Friedman, *Capitalism and Freedom* (Chicago: University of Chicago Press, 1962).
5. Ibid., p. 195.
6. George F. Will, *Statecraft as Soulcraft: What Government Does* (New York: Simon and Schuster, 1983), p. 156.
7. Ibid., p. 131.
8. Ibid., p. 130.
9. Bruce R. Bartlett, *Reaganomics: Supply-Side Economics in Action* (New York: Quill, 1982), p. 207.
10. George Gilder, *Wealth and Poverty* (New York: Basic Books, 1981), p. 245.
11. Will, *Statecraft as Soulcraft*, p. 12.
12. Ibid., pp. 158–159.
13. Milton Friedman and Rose Friedman, *Free to Choose* (New York: Harcourt Brace Jovanovich, 1980), pp. 119–120.
14. Ibid.
15. Ibid., p. 123.
16. Will, *Statecraft as Soulcraft*, p. 45.
17. Gilder, *Wealth and Poverty*, p. 259.
18. Friedman and Friedman, *Free to Choose*, p. xx.
19. Dinesh D'Souza, *Illiberal Education: The Politics of Race and Sex on Campus* (New York: Free Press, 1991).
20. Dinesh D'Souza, "Illiberal Education," *The Atlantic*, March 1991, p. 55.
21. Ibid., p. 76.
22. Ibid., p. 79.
23. C. Vann Woodward, Review of D'Souza, *Illiberal Education*, in *The New York Review of Books*, July 15, 1991, p. 36.
24. Stephen L. Carter, *Reflections of an Affirmative Action Baby* (New York: Basic Books, 1991).
25. Shelby Steele, *The Content of Our Character: A New Vision of Race in America* (New York: St. Martin's Press, 1990).
26. Ibid., p. 30.
27. Ibid., p. 49.
28. Ibid., p. 90.
29. Ibid., p. 172.
30. Samuel P. Huntington, *American Politics: The Promise of Disharmony* (Cambridge, Mass.: Belknap Press, 1981), p. 258.
31. Ibid., pp. 40, 220.

32. Ibid., p. 42.
33. Will, *Statecraft as Soulcraft*, p. 96.
34. Huntington, *American Politics*, p. 261.
35. Will, *Statecraft as Soulcraft*, p. 22.
36. Ibid., p. 165.
37. William F. Buckley, Jr., *Gratitude: Reflections on What We Owe to Our Country* (New York: Random House, 1990).
38. Ibid., p. 19.
39. Ibid.
40. Patrick J. Buchanan, Editorial, *The Seattle Post-Intelligencer*, August 28, 1991, p. A7.
41. Charles Murray, *In Pursuit: Of Happiness and Good Government* (New York: Simon & Schuster, 1988).
42. Ibid., p. 13.
43. Ibid., p. 164.
44. Ibid., p. 233.
45. Ibid.
46. Ibid., pp. 260–261.

CHAPTER 10

1. Rachel Carson, *Silent Spring* (Boston: Houghton Mifflin, 1962).
2. Donella H. Meadows et al., *The Limits to Growth* (New York: Universe Books, 1972).
3. Paul R. Ehrlich, *The Population Bomb* (Rivercity, Mass.: The Rivercity Press, 1975).
4. Robert C. Paehlke, *Environmentalism and the Future of Progressive Politics* (New Haven, Conn.: Yale University Press, 1989), p. 3.
5. Ibid., p. 211.
6. Rachel Carson, *Silent Spring*, cited by Bill Devall, *Simple in Means, Rich in Ends* (London: Merlin Press, 1990), p. 20.
7. Carolyn Merchant, *Ecological Revolutions: Nature, Gender, and Science in New England* (Chapel Hill: University of North Carolina Press, 1989), p. 8.
8. Donald Worster, *Nature's Economy: A History of Ecological Ideas* (New York: Cambridge University Press, 1985), p. 347.
9. Ibid., p. ix.
10. Michael E. Zimmerman, "Introduction to Deep Ecology," Interview in *In Context*, Summer 1989, p. 24.
11. Devall, *Simple in Means*, pp. 11–12.
12. James Lovelock, *The Ages of Gaia: A Biography of Our Living Earth* (New York: Oxford University Press, 1989), p. xvii.
13. Ibid., p. 236.
14. Jeremy Rifkin, *Biosphere Politics: A New Consciousness for a New Century* (New York: Crown, 1991).
15. Ibid., p. 3.
16. Ibid., p. 326.
17. Murray Bookchin, *Remaking Society: Pathways to a Green Future* (Boston: South End Press, 1990), pp. 12–13.
18. Ibid., p. 15.

19. Ibid., p. 204.
20. Rosemary *Reuther, New Woman/New Earth* (New York: Seabury Press, 1975), p. 204.
21. Karen Warren, "Feminism and Ecology: Making Connections," *Environmental Ethics*, 9:1 (Spring 1987), p. 3.
22. Merchant, *Ecological Revolutions*, pp. 269–270.
23. Zimmerman, "Introduction to Deep Ecology," p. 24.
24. Janet Biehl, "It's Deep, But Is It Broad? An Ecofeminist Looks at Deep Ecology," *Kick It Over* (Toronto, Ont., n.d.), n.p.
25. Charlene Spretnak and Fritjof Capra, *Green Politics: The Global Promise* (Santa Fe, N.M.: Bear & Co., 1986).
26. Brian Tokar, *The Green Alternative: Creating an Ecological Future* (San Pedro, Calif.: R. and E. Miles, 1987).
27. Ibid., p. 3.
28. Ibid., p. 56.
29. Mark Satin, *New Options for America: The Second American Experiment Has Begun* (Fresno, Calif.: The Press at California State University at Fresno, 1991).
30. Ibid., p. 2.
31. Ibid., p. 126.
32. World Commission on Environment and Development, *Our Common Future* (New York: Oxford University Press, 1987).
33. Paehlke, *Environmentalism and the Future*, p. 235.
34. Ibid., p. 236.
35. Tokar, *The Green Alternative*, p. 147.
36. Ibid.
37. Left Green Network, "Call for a Left Green Network," Lebanon, N.H., 1989, p. 2.
38. Edward Abbey, *The Monkey Wrench Gang* (New York: E. P. Dutton, 1983).
39. Dave Foreman and Bill Haywood, eds., *Ecodefense: A Field Guide to Monkeywrenching* (Tucson, Ariz.: A Nedd Ludd Book, 1987).
40. Ibid., p. 8.
41. Satin, *New Options*, p. 224.
42. Ibid., p. 184.
43. Ibid., p. 251.

CHAPTER 11

1. E. J. Dionne, Jr., *Why Americans Hate Politics* (New York: Simon & Schuster, 1991), p. 11.
2. Frank Bryan and John McLaughry, *The Vermont Papers: Recreating Democracy on a Human Scale* (Post Mills, Vt.: Chelsea Green Publishing Company, 1989), p. 6.
3. Dionne, *Why Americans Hate Politics*, p. 15.
4. John C. White, *The New Politics of Old Values* (New York: Praeger, 1983).
5. Dionne, *Why Americans Hate Politics*, p. 15.
6. Ibid., p. 27.
7. James Patterson and Peter Kim, *The Day America Told the Truth* (New York: Prentice Hall Press, 1991).
8. Ibid., p. 231.

GLOSSARY

The glossary presents in classic form the major isms in the American experience. Here we use the language of political theory, whereas in the text we follow ordinary American usage. There are some important differences between the two, as we shall see. *Liberalism, capitalism*, and *democracy* are discussed first because they had the greatest impact on our nation's history and still dominate our political thought. Challengers, both historical and prospective, follow.

LIBERALISM

Liberalism comes first because that is where the United States starts and, some would add, very nearly ends. Its basic components are described in Chapter 2 as the basic elements of the American political belief system. The defining characteristics of liberalism are individualism; natural rights, with particular emphasis on property rights; and the contract as the source of social order. Despite their strength and depth in the United States, this particular combination of principles did not just happen to come together on the North American continent. It arose out of the transformation of English feudal society into what would ultimately be recognized as capitalist society.

Under feudalism, the great land-owning families effectively ruled. Most people were born into the status of serf or peasant on a lord's manor. They owed that lord fealty and service for their entire lives; the lord owed them protection and work. The king and the church "owned" vast tracts of land and claimed fealty and service from the lords and nobles. However, in realistic terms, a system of varying degrees of influence reigned. Parochial, predictable, and stable, this world was understood by most people to be one organic whole with a proper place and role for everyone.

Into this ordered (and agricultural) world, the Protestant Reformation introduced the notion of individual responsibility for salvation. At the same time, some people began to trade and sell fabricated goods. However, those people involved in trade, finance, and early manufacture had no traditional status. They were neither serfs nor lords, but a class between the two. The church frowned on, even regulated or restrained, their commercial activities. Their earnings were subject to confiscation by any king's or lord's arbitrary action. Their property was often even in danger from mobs of propertyless serfs and peasants. Thus this rising commercial middle class needed both a personal justification and protection for the property it was earning through commerce. The Protestant notion of individual responsibility and rights rooted in natural law met these needs.

By the late seventeenth century, the new middle class found its fullest expression in the writings of John Locke. In his *Second Treatise on Government*, Locke set forth a complete version of a society and government organized by individuals voluntarily coming together for that purpose. Locke argued that individuals are originally in a state of nature. Each individual possesses freedom and certain natural rights as well as the reason necessary to know them. Individuals also possess any property with which they have mixed their labor. However, possession is insecure; some individuals use superior force to infringe on others' rights—and most particularly, the right to the fruits of their labor, their property. Therefore, reasonable individuals *contract* to create a social and governmental order, ceding to it some of their natural rights, powers, and freedom in return for its protection of all the others. The basis of such social order rests with the individuals who compose it. It derives all its authority from their transfer of powers to it. Finally, and as a safeguard, if the government fails in its fundamental protective duty, those same contracting individuals have the right to change it.

In seventeenth-century England, all this was highly controversial. It stood in stark contrast to previous beliefs and practices. Instead of an organic social whole with everyone in a divinely ordained place, individuals were assumed to be paramount and became the source of the society's entire existence. Furthermore, individuals were not only free to seek property through commerce but also were encouraged to do so. They could even rise in wealth, power, and prestige until they rivaled members of the aristocracy themselves. Possessed of the reason capable of deciding when their government had violated their natural rights, these individuals were potentially subversive of all established authority. They were willing to take upon themselves the decision of when to replace one government with another. Locke's work was published just after the Glorious Revolution of 1688, in which the British Parliament had removed one line of kings and installed another. On the surface, Locke's work appeared to be a justification of that revolution.

In England, Locke's notions met stern resistance from a still dominant aristocracy. On the American continent, the state of nature was all too obvious, and Locke's assumptions fit perfectly with a living reality. People did in fact contract with each other to create churches and governments. The new world was predominantly populated by entrepreneurs, merchants, and others of the new middle class—or people who aspired to the middle class through the new possibility of land ownership. Few aristocrats in the English sense chose to emigrate. Some came briefly to Virginia or Maryland or served as royal governors, but few stayed. Similarly, there were no serfs or peasants. Indentured servants came the closest, but their labor was contracted for only a limited number of years. They, too, aspired to the readily available land ownership that distinguished the developing society.

The special features of the United States' birth established liberalism as not so much the predominant belief system as the *only* belief system. In his famous *The Liberal Tradition in America,* historian Louis Hartz argues that liberal tenets are so pervasive that Americans have lost the sense of their distinctiveness. With no significant challenges from other classes, middle-class American liberalism reigned supreme. Liberalism was tempered elsewhere by conservatism grounded in a former aristocracy and by socialism emerging from the lower classes. Such challenges were simply missing from the American scene. By now, liberalism is self-evident and often unrecognized. Hartz's analysis helps to explain why the debates within the American political belief system have been over definitions and priorities associated with shared values and assumptions. We are all liberals, Hartz says, of marginally different kinds.

CAPITALISM

The United States is unique among nations of the world in the strength of capitalism as a popular belief system. The powerful appeal of capitalism rests on its congruence with the very same values that are fundamental to liberalism. Individualism, property, and contract already served as the foundation of a moral social and political order. Capitalism merely gave them a more specifically economic expression. Essentially, capitalism means private ownership of the means of production. It normally includes a profit-seeking system with unlimited exchange of goods and services. The closely associated notions of the free market and laissez-faire again connect with liberal faith in the free, economically oriented individual.

The economic system preceding capitalism was mercantilism. Under mercantilism, economic activity was meant to serve national interests as defined by the state. This had the effect of restricting the expansion and profitability of private enterprises. Leading governments, such as that of Great Britain, simply drained colonial wealth into the national treasury. Favored companies were granted monopoly trading rights. Royal or semipublic corporations were allowed to develop the high-profit opportunities. National governments strictly enforced taxes, restricted trade, and centrally managed the currency and credit—all to their own advantage. Many would-be entrepreneurs, particularly on the American continent, saw profitable opportunities denied them by these mercantilist policies.

Their resentment was well represented in the powerful arguments of the Scottish philosopher Adam Smith. In the *Wealth of Nations* (1776), Smith argued for the elimination of all governmental restrictions on private business. He claimed that the dynamism thus released would generate much greater wealth. An unrestricted market system would harmonize the demands of buyers with the supply produced by profit-seeking sellers. Thus, all members of the society would be satisfied. The nation as a whole would benefit because the country's resources would be fully employed with the greatest efficiency. Americans were eager to develop and profit from a richly endowed continent. Chafing under mercantile restrictions, they found Smith's argument utterly compelling.

With the liberal foundation firmly in place, the new U.S. Constitution assured an open national market. No obstacles remained to capitalist economic development. What the country seemed to need most was a multitude of willing risk takers. A large number of speculators and entrepreneurs were more than ready to participate. As both capital formation and industrial techniques became more sophisticated in the early nineteenth century, capitalism thrived. Science and technology seemed to be in harness with nature to generate progress and prosperity, at least for some and perhaps soon for all. Although the road might be hard at times, America was indeed the land of opportunity. Individuals who worked hard and took risks would prosper. Capitalism and liberalism were precisely the right combination of beliefs and practices, in the right place at the right time. As America flourished and grew more powerful, so did they.

DEMOCRACY

Our discussion in Chapter 2 of the ways that Americans have understood democracy has wide applicability beyond the United States. Originally a derogatory term, *democracy* now carries a broad and powerful appeal in all Western countries. Equally common is the conflict between procedural and substantive versions. Its very universality makes the concept extremely difficult to pin down. To associate it with one author, as can be done with Lockean liberalism or Adam Smith's capitalism, is impossible. We must try to distill from general aspirations some essential values.

Literally, *democracy* means "government by the people." The American version—"government of the people, by the people, and for the people"—is attributed to Abraham Lincoln. That succinct phrase does capture the variety of possibilities in the concept of democracy. *Of the people* implies that office holders, rulers, governors, and so forth, should come from the ranks of the population, the commoners. *For the people* means that government policies should benefit the majority, or as close as possible to the totality, of the nation's population. The crucial preposition is *by*. Fulfilling the intention behind *of the people* and *for the people* is possible without participation by the citizens at large. However, *by the people* suggests that people generally are capable of making and should participate in those decisions that affect their lives. Fundamental to democracy is the promise of some degree of *control* of the conditions of one's existence.

Left unanswered by the basic definition, of course, is the crucial question of just how "the people" are to govern. A very substantive aspiration becomes a procedural puzzle. In a large country with many citizens, the direct participation of all people in all public decisions appears impossible. How to limit the nature of participation and which questions shall be open to public control provoke immediate disagreement. Some argue that participation and decision-making powers must be very broad if democracy is to have any real meaning. Others, also self-proclaimed democrats, believe participation and decision making need to be limited in keeping with the dictates of practicality. Furthermore, certain areas of life, such as personal liberties or economic activities, should be off limits to popular preferences. Obviously, there can be any number of variations on the democratic theme.

For our purposes, the crucial fact is that liberalism was firmly grounded and capitalism was taking shape on the same foundation *before* democracy gained acceptance in the United States. Thus, the dominant understanding of democracy eventually would have to conform to liberal-capitalist values and practices. Remaining from the founding period was the distrust of democracy as mob rule. The belief that the greatest danger to democratic government was the "tyranny of the majority" persisted. By the time democracy became generally accepted, the notion of "majority rule, minority rights" was taken for granted. Constitutionally erected barriers to popular majorities and protection of minority rights (particularly property rights) went unquestioned. This is, of course, the beginning of *procedural* democracy. Many social and economic dimensions of life are placed beyond the reach of public action—until substantive democracy claims the right to enter the arena.

The greatest problem in using classic labels to understand the evolution of American ideas is grounded, fittingly enough, in the transformation of 1877 to 1920. The basic liberal-capitalist belief system essentially split in two under the pressure from the substantive democratic claims of the era. One part moved toward acceptance of the new role of government; the other held strongly to the classic version of liberalism (see the following discussion of "true" conservatism). The *new* liberalism agreed with the democrats that government had an obligation to soften the hardships from which people were suffering, and it held that the new large corporations should be limited in order to protect the well-being of all. Though adopting some of democracy's goals, this new belief system retained the liberalism label throughout the Progressive era. Later versions are variously known as "corporate liberalism" or "welfare liberalism." The *old* liberalism became known as "conservatism," even though it stands for exactly what all liberals stood for before the period of transformation, and substantive democracy faded away into the new liberalism's definitions and procedures.

For the American political spectrum, of course, the result has been a vigorous debate between one form of liberalism and another. To Americans, it appears as if great issues are at stake. To some other observers, it looks like the proverbial tempest in a teapot. This suggests that the American political spectrum, as discussed in the text, is a specially narrow version of the range of possibility. Neither the character nor the evolution of American political thinking can be understood without recognizing how naturally Americans have come to cluster around the capitalist-liberal middle. Radical substantive democracy has been made to seem far more threatening than its genuine roots in a continuing tradition actually justify. Other possibilities, both Right and Left, must be fully understood in order to gain perspective on the American liberal myopia. If our spectrum widens in the present era of transformation, one or more of these challenges may powerfully affect our future.

HISTORICAL AND PROSPECTIVE CHALLENGERS

Some of the classic isms to be defined and developed briefly in this section do not fit comfortably on a Left-Right political spectrum. It should also be understood that any American version would have specially American features appropriate to our times and circumstances. "True," or organic, conservatives posed the greatest challenge to liberalism historically. They were, after all, replaced by it. In the United States, organic conservatives often have been misunderstood as irrelevant or as adaptive liberals, but their critique is worth exploring. After looking at organic conservatism, we turn to the more likely challengers—socialism, communism, Marxism, American socialism, anarchism, corporatism, fascism, and totalitarianism.

Conservatism

Perhaps the greatest contrast between ordinary American usage and classic definitions lies in the understanding of conservatism. To Americans, *conservative* usually means a highly individualistic and strict laissez-faire doctrine. This is essentially a very pure version of a late nineteenth-century form of liberalism. Sometimes known as "Manchester liberalism," it was never confused elsewhere with conservatism.

The essence of classical conservatism was articulated in the eighteenth century by the British leader Edmund Burke. He held an organic image of society as an independent entity with a life and needs apart from the individuals who happen to make it up at any given time. Conservatives strive to achieve the preservation and improvement of the civilization represented by this society. They believe, in contrast to liberals, that most people are not in fact reasonable or able to decide what is best for themselves. Certainly ordinary people are not capable of deciding what is best for the society by means of some majority vote. Instead, conservatives believe in the necessity of government by the relatively few people who have the talent and wisdom to discharge such functions.

The conservative principle of government by the talented few means opposition not only to majority rule but also to any special role for business corporations or economic elites. Conservatives have a profound respect for property, but for different reasons from liberals. Property is needed to give people a sense of being rooted, of having a stake in the society's future. Moreover, property allows some people the necessary time to study the history of the society so as to make the correct decisions regarding its future. Profit is not the end of property ownership; wisdom and stability are. The mere achievement of wealth or corporate position does not entitle anyone to claim the right to govern. Too often businesspeople, capitalists, have a short-term attitude, an orientation toward current gratification and profits. They overlook the real long-term needs of the society. In particular, this common capitalist attitude leads to an avoidance of the sacrifices necessary to benefit the society as a whole in the long run.

Conservatism is not at all a status quo doctrine. History never stops; societies must adapt to survive. However, changes must be made consistent with the traditions and experience of the society. They must be changes for which the society is ready. Conservatives imagine a long line extending from the past through the present into the future, a kind of partnership of generations past, present, and yet unborn. Today's members are only transitory, in a sense irrelevant. They will be replaced tomorrow, as a new combination will reflect all births and deaths. As temporary beneficiaries, individuals have an obligation to further their *society's* needs so that the quality of the civilization will steadily improve.

Conservatism is not unwilling to make use of governmental powers for appropriate ends. Purposeful use of government to shape and direct the society is a major conservative tenet. Obviously there are many fundamental differences between "true," or organic, conservatism and what Americans mean by *conservatism*. Some early New England Puritans and even a few of the framers of the Constitution had significant conservative principles. It was the vestiges of American organic conservatism that spoke out against the appalling working conditions, squalid tenements, and general destructiveness of early industrialism. However, later experiences were so exclusively liberal and capitalist that conservative ideas began to disappear. When organic conservatives look back to see what long-lived traditions should be conserved, all they find are liberal-capitalist practices.

Though organic conservatives can mount a critique of liberal capitalism, they have been and are few in number in the United States. With the exception of literary versions of "a plague on all your houses," organic conservatives are probably irrelevant to the present era of transformation. More likely possibilities arise from the remaining isms to be discussed.

Socialism, communism, and Marxism share a similar foundation while differing in important respects. We first consider the commonalities and then discuss each separately, describing some of their differences. There are two commonalities in particular. First, all three focus on the mode of production. The way in which a social order produces its material means of survival is a crucial influence on the social, political, and cultural worlds. Spheres of activity are not, cannot be, separated. Like a prism, these spheres are reflections of each other around a fundamental core, the economic system. Therefore, prescriptions and political activity of these isms focus on a change in the ownership of at least the major means of productive activity.

Second, all three are based on a notion of a *social* world. This is not society as the unit of analysis, with needs and demands of its own, above and beyond the individuals that compose it at any one time. Similarly it is not the self-serving, isolated individual as the primary unit. The individual is assumed to be a social animal whose full development as a human being requires positive interaction with other human beings. For each of these three isms, an individual does not and cannot exist alone, in isolation. A human being only fully develops in concert with others. This does not mean, however, that the community or social world takes precedence over the individual. It means that the community and the individual should fit together. When it comes to the specific mix of community/individual and the relationship of that community/individual mix to the social/economic/political order, differences emerge among the three isms.

Socialism

Socialism derives its name from an underlying assumption that human beings are social beings. Full personal development can only take place within a healthy community. A primary prerequisite is material security and well-being for each member of the social order. In American terms, substantive equality in the economic conditions of life precedes the possibility of individual freedom and development. This does not mean that everyone is the same or even that everyone is entitled to the same. But it does mean that everyone is entitled to the basic means of survival and to a healthy life situation. The material well-being of each citizen is not only a proper object of government concern but should be actively promoted.

In order to accomplish widespread material security and to remove economic coercion of individuals, at least the major units of the economy should be publicly owned. Private ownership of the means of production, for the purpose of private profit, can only lead to an unhealthy environment, useless production, and degradation of working people. Socialism would leave small units of production in private hands. Private property, especially in the sense of personal possessions, is accepted. However, large and overwhelming economic concentrations are not permissible. Social ownership of the major means of production, for the public good and social welfare, is a tenet of socialism.

Communism

Pre-Marxist and pre-Soviet-bloc communism has roots reaching at least as far back as early Christian communities. Many groups of people throughout the centuries have lived communally. In all that time, classic communism has changed very little. Though each community or utopian experiment devised its own adaptations, certain fundamentals remained.

Communism implies the common ownership of property or material goods. Substantive equality is much more widespread; material goods are equally distributed. The slogan "from each according to ability, to each according to need" summarizes Communist aspirations. In this view, private property is the source of all exploitation and conflict between human beings, and the state itself functions to maintain this coercive situation. Should private ownership and profit seeking be abolished, all other unnatural distinctions among human beings would disappear. Peace on earth would prevail.

Marxism

Socialism and communism preceded Karl Marx as political visions. However, Marx authored the systematic analysis and prescription that forever afterward underlay in some way most versions of socialism and communism. He devoted his life to development of the philosophical base and analytical method appropriate to these isms. Americans tend to lump them all together: anything anticapitalist is Marxist. In one sense, this is true; in another, it is completely false.

Marx begins with a notion of "species being," of human beings as social, productive, creative beings. For them to reach their full development as a species, they need a healthy social world in which their productive and creative capacities can be freely used. What makes human beings distinctive is their ability to creatively produce. Capitalism deprives human beings of this capacity. When human beings sell their labor, they turn their productive activity into a commodity. This alienates them from one of the most basic facets of their personalities. Equally important, liberal individualism alienates humans from each other. Therefore, individualistic capitalism prevents human beings from reaching their true nature as species beings.

Second, private ownership of the means of production for private profit, besides alienating workers from their true being, creates a class society. Class is a crucial analytic unit in Marxist thought. Some own the means of production—the bourgeois. Some do not—the proletariat. History is the story of the change in the underlying mode of production and thus in class relationships. Capitalism will be overthrown by the proletariat, the working (nonowning) class, once it becomes conscious of itself as a class, a class for itself. Following the proletariat revolution, the proletariat will run the state for the benefit of the working class. Once all have reached the same class level, or communism, the state will wither away.

More important than Marx's conclusions, perhaps, is the method he developed to arrive at them. *Scientific materialism* is a method for analyzing a social order through study of the means and relationships of production. Furthermore, *dialectics* enables one to see the world in motion. It assumes contradictions inherent in all things or processes, contradictions that will be overcome and transcended. Scientific materialism encompasses the empirical, tangible processes of the world. Dialectics encourages exploration of the multiple potentialities in that world, the many possible futures, even while recognizing the dominant tendencies.

Marxism is not really an ism in the same way the term has previously been used. Colloquially, *Marxism* is used to cover any ism that is anticapitalist, anti-individualist, proworking class, or revolutionary; that proclaims itself to be Marxist; or that is claimed to be so by the United States. When used in this way, it loses all meaning. When specifically connected to one author, Marxism is a respected philosophical system. As a rigorous analysis and alternative vision to liberal capitalism, it is unmatched.

Thus, socialism and communism could be said to be variants of Marxism, whether Marx is given credit or not. Marxism could also be said to be the philosophical base of most versions of socialism and communism, in spite of their vast variety (and sometimes they are only very distantly related).

The Essence of Marxism Few sets of ideas have had as much impact or been so variously understood as the principles developed by Karl Marx. Since the 1850s, American socialists have wrestled with the problem of adapting Marx's ideas to the specific realities of the American social experience. Some have tried to make direct applications in almost literal fashion. Others have made so many modifications that their Marxism has not seemed distinguishable from standard American reform liberalism.

In this section, we briefly indicate some of the concepts and methods that Karl Marx contributed to the current versions of democratic socialism in the United States. By now, most democratic socialists perceive these basic analytic principles as a matter of common sense rather than as specifically Marxist in origin. They do, however, provide democratic socialists with a common core of ways of thinking about social life.

Marx was first and foremost a *comprehensive* thinker. He sought to grasp the entirety of a social order as it moved from one form through the present toward another form. Each new form was both old and new, a synthesis of past and future. If a society did not adapt to its changing environment in this way, it would not survive. Marx was specifically writing about industrial societies like those of Europe in the mid-nineteenth century. He believed capitalism to be a necessary prerequisite to the higher forms of socialism and communism.

Capitalism was in turn a higher form than feudalism because it generated improved material conditions. It possessed the productive capacity to raise everybody's standard of living far beyond the stage where people had to struggle for survival. However, capitalism also produced greed, destructive competition and wars, and irrational abuse of natural resources; it denied people the opportunity to realize their innate potential as *human* beings. The profit motive compelled people to exploit each other. Capitalism, in turn would create the economic conditions and social pressures that would transform it into socialism.

However, Marx never believed the transition to socialism to be inevitable, mechanical, or necessary in the sense of being preordained. It was a highly desirable possibility, essential, in fact, if the world were to survive and progress. On the other hand, capitalism would not be the first social order to perish because of failure to change when conditions required it. Every society, like any complex situation, contains within it several possible futures.

Marx always emphasized the potential that situations or societies had for becoming something that they were not yet but could be. The purpose of philosophy was to find ways to bring about the better, more desirable potential. Socialism was important to Marx because it would create the conditions under which human beings could realize their true potential.

The essential factor was what human beings did with their opportunity to shape their future. Human agency determines which of several potential futures will actually come about, constrained only by the range of the possible set by surrounding historical conditions. In Marx's world, the historical agency of change was the working class. It would determine whether capitalism served as a prelude to socialism or to barbarism and eventual human extinction after a period of rigidification, fascism, war, and the like. Marx saw class conflict as the source of change that led to the establishment of capitalism. The shift to socialism, the next possible and desirable form of social order, would only occur if that great opposition class, the working class, came to a consciousness of both the social imperative of forcing the change and its own strength and capacity to do so.

Marx's concept of class had both objective and subjective dimensions. Objectively, the working class was defined by its dependent relationship to the major means of production owned by the few capitalists. It was the capitalists whose ideas and power dominated the society. In other words, all those who had no way to earn their living except by selling their labor power were objectively one class. Furthermore, their interests were opposed to those of the capitalists whether they realized it or not. When economic and social conditions made it possible, workers would become aware of their shared interests, conscious that such interests were irreconcilable with those of the capitalists, and would become determined to act on their own behalf. At this point, the subjective dimension of class would be reached. The working class would be *class conscious* and ready to fulfill its role as the historical agent of change to socialism.

Marx never underestimated the power of the ruling ideas within capitalist society. He was aware of their effectiveness in preventing workers from understanding their own true interest in forcing the change to socialism. He saw all people as *socially produced* in the sense that their language, values, concepts, ways of thinking, and even their personal identities were shaped by the society in which they were raised. People would see and understand their world as that world wanted. Wherever they looked, they would find confirmation of the rightness, inevitability, and permanence of its particular distribution of wealth and power. Only dramatic changes in economic and social conditions would break the grip of the dominant ideology. At that point, knowledgeable socialists and a working-class political party should be ready to help the class take power in the state. Only then could the working class as a whole begin to implement socialist reconstruction of the society, a process that would be long and arduous.

Marx emphasized thinking and acting in terms of a desirable future that was only a potential, neither predetermined nor inevitable. He was impatient with utopians, by which he meant those who imagined and sought to bring about future societies that were not historically possible under existing conditions. Marx was always concerned with the range of the possible set by current economic and social circumstances. However, he always viewed those circumstances flexibly—in the light of what they would permit and could become, rather than what they were or how they might prevent change. This led him to intensive studies of contemporary conditions. He looked for the contradictions within them, the things that capitalism was doing that would lead to internal conflicts or opposition. His search was always for the openings and opportunities that might allow for socialist advances.

With such a perspective, Marx was more interested in and optimistic about the prospect of social change than most other people in Western societies. Particularly in the United States, people tended and still tend to see the world exclusively in terms of tangible, measurable facts about its current situation. Any thoughts about change generally focus on one or two factors, with everything else perceived as remaining fixed. Far-reaching changes in the basic structures of the society thus seem both impossible and undesirable. It is hard for Americans to understand why Marxists do not like capitalist society. More important, it is difficult to believe things could ever be different from what they are today.

When recession or depression brings unemployment and hard times, however, many people become more receptive to Marx's advocacy of a more egalitarian and stable economic system. His most famous work, *Capital*, is a detailed critique of capitalism that contains explanations for many of the processes and results that regularly occur. At first, this was the only major work that socialists had as a source for understanding his ideas. Marx's earlier publications, *The Economic and Philosophical Manuscripts of 1844* and *The German Ideology*, became widely known to Americans only after World War II. From these, it was possible to piece together Marx's humanism and his comprehensive image of the process and purpose of change. With so much more to go on, however, socialists began to disagree more. In addition, the experiences of successful socialist movements in other countries soon added to the principles that had to be considered, as well as to the resistance to Marxist ideas in the United States.

The Marxism that American democratic socialists employ is a synthesis around an economic core, thoroughly adapted to American realities. However, it is composed of many strands rather than a single agreed content. Academic and other economists have kept Marx's economic analysis of capitalism alive by applying it to explain downturns in the business cycle. Others have concentrated on merging Marx's methods and humanistic purposes with psychology and existentialism to produce a cultural critique of American society.

American Socialism

Before the Civil War, socialism was essentially grounded in moral rejection of capitalism's practices—its greed, selfishness, sharp dealings, and, particularly, its treatment of workers. Long hours, low pay, and unsafe and authoritarian working conditions led many to look for alternatives; some embraced socialism. At this point, it meant public ownership of the means of production and an egalitarian sharing of both the burdens and benefits of the new industrial capacities. Some socialists sought to act out their beliefs in the form of experimental cooperative communities. For many reasons these were short lived, but ever since their sponsors have been known as utopian socialists.

As industrialization proceeded, the contrast in the way owners and workers were affected by it led to a growing sense of two classes whose interests were directly opposed. Many workers were immigrants, and among them were Germans who had knowledge of Marx's writings and had experience with socialist political activities. Socialism began to focus on building a mass working-class organization grounded in the developing labor movement. From the beginning, socialists were divided by controversies over tactics and routes to be followed.

The Socialist Labor Party (SLP), formed in 1877, represented one major position. It was highly critical of the labor movement for being too ready to cooperate with capitalism. While led by Daniel DeLeon, an aristocrat of Spanish descent who joined the party in 1889, the SLP stood for an all-or-nothing transformation of the society. A particular target was the American Federation of Labor (AFL) under Samuel Gompers. However, the AFL remained the largest labor union and adhered to reformist goals in the characteristic manner of American interest groups.

A much more flexible position was maintained by the greatest of the early socialists, Eugene V. Debs, of Indiana. Debs was originally a railroad union leader and was involved in several bitter strikes of the 1890s. He became a socialist while in jail for his part in the Pullman strike of 1894. Debs believed in bringing together as many workers as possible to work for immediate improvements. In the process, he hoped that they, too, would come to see the necessity of socialism. He was a thoroughgoing democrat, and this was reflected in the Socialist party, which he was instrumental in forming in 1901. In part because of its pragmatic radicalism, the Socialist party enjoyed much greater electoral success than the SLP ever did.

Another major issue dividing socialists in this period was the form of labor organization that would best serve the goals of building a working-class political base for socialism. One group wanted to work within the AFL. Hoping to rise to power in the trade union movement, they believed they could eventually bring the workers to socialism. The AFL was organized on the basis of distinct skilled crafts, however. This meant not only that its members had greater leverage against employers than did unskilled workers but also that they were better paid and, hence, less receptive to radical political programs.

Others wanted to form their own socialist unions and bring workers into them. Usually this meant organizing *industrial* unions, or a union of all workers in a given industry, from the most skilled to the ordinary laborers. Debs was committed to industrial unionism as the only way to effectively get socialism on the agenda of the trade union movement. He was initially a supporter of the International Workers of the World (IWW), a group dedicated to organizing the many workers in seasonal, migrant, and other hard-to-organize occupations. Despite some real successes, the IWW finally alienated many socialists with its violent rhetoric and sometimes violent practice.

Prior to World War I, American socialism was predominantly a democratic educational enterprise devoted to electoral efforts to build its strength. Debs and others often denounced the violence of some anarchists and IWW followers. In 1912, probably the high point of socialism in the United States, more than 1,200 elected public officials were socialists. That year socialists also made up almost one-third of the delegates at the AFL convention and hotly contested Gompers's reelection. Its own leadership elections repeatedly demonstrated socialism's commitment to racial and sexual equality.

Then came World War I. Socialist parties in Europe abandoned international workers' solidarity to vote support of their respective capitalist governments' war efforts. Millions of workers literally fought each other. American socialists sought to preserve international working-class solidarity, vehemently opposing American involvement in the war. They called a convention in April 1917 and passed a resolution declaring the war "a crime against the people of the United States." They pledged that "in support of capitalism we will not willingly give a single life or a single dollar." At almost the same moment, the U.S. Congress declared war against Germany.

In the fall of that year, as part of its opposition, the Socialist party ran several municipal and state candidates on peace platforms. Many of them did well, which seemed to promise a continuing effective socialist opposition to the war. However, socialism was promptly overwhelmed by patriotic nationalism and forced on the defensive. New federal laws prohibited opposition to the draft. Local police and vigilantes joined in harassing socialists, and the Immigration and Naturalization Service investigated and deported thousands of socialists as "alien agitators."

The success of the Bolsheviks in the Russian Revolution greatly complicated the situation for American socialists. Some socialists wanted to
defend everything the Soviet Union did. This meant they had to suddenly
reverse themselves and support the war against Germany so that the
Soviets would be free to proceed with their experiment. More important,
to many Americans it made the threat posed by American socialists seem
greater. The U.S. government redoubled its efforts to jail, deport, and
silence socialists. After the armistice, a major campaign was mounted to
eliminate socialism as a force in American life.

Under these pressures and beset by internal disagreements, socialism
began to dissolve. In 1920, although once again in jail, this time for
speaking out against the war, Debs ran for president for the sixth time. In a
remarkable individual tribute, he received nearly a million votes. However, socialism generally ceased to be a significant factor in American
politics. Ever since, except for a short period in the depths of the depression of the 1930s, socialism has not approached its earlier role as an
organized opponent of capitalism in the United States. It remains to be
seen, of course, whether its current renascence can change this situation.

Anarchism

Anarchism focuses on domination, whether it be by capitalists, the state,
bureaucrats, socialists, communists, or Marxists. People are assumed to be
naturally good, cooperative, even harmonious. The imposition of social
institutions destroys this natural order and creates the very problems
supposedly solved. Domination of any sort, not only in productive terms,
alienates individuals from their free, unfettered creative self.

Anarchism can be either individualist or community based, depending
on the specific emphasis given to the characteristics of human nature.
According to both versions, all institutional barriers to individual development need to be removed. The versions differ on whether individuals then
will be spontaneously communal or individualistic. In any event, spon-
taneous creativity is the answer to institutional domination.

This is one of the European isms with a peculiar force and history in the
United States. In the early 1900s, a unique blend of communal solidarity
and rugged individualism developed and found expression in the anarcho-
syndicalism of the International Workers of the World. This was especially
true among the frontier workers in the mines and logging camps of the Far
West. More generally, the individualist version of anarchism naturally
appeals to a country in which individualism is taken for granted. Liberal
individualism, pushed to its limit, can lead to a version of anarchy in
which the only free individual is the totally undominated one. The totally
free individual always lurks beneath the surface as the American ideal.

Socialism, communism, Marxism, and anarchism view the world from
the bottom up, so to speak. They begin with the working class or the

oppressed and alienated individual. Capitalism, and the bureaucratic and social institutions necessary to sustain it, is the enemy. Corporatism, fascism, and totalitarianism view the world the other way around, from the top down. Among these three isms, too, there are some basic commonalities, with variance in degree. Each of these three isms is based on the notion of a partnership among the major social, economic, and political units of the system. Large economic units and a centralized and powerful state apparatus are accepted, even encouraged. The majority of the population maintains private activity. If not working directly for the major economic units, they are almost irrelevant, as long as they do not threaten the large and powerful economic base in any way. In general, the state's purpose is to maintain the profitability and growth of the economic sector, regardless of the social cost. Differences between corporatism, fascism, and totalitarianism arise out of the terms of the partnership and the degree of rigor imposed on the underlying population.

Corporatism

Corporatism appears to be a true partnership between big government and big business. Other major corporate bodies, such as labor or even consumers' organizations, are encouraged. Bigness is a fact of life that must be accepted. Each individual should be a member of some corporate body. Corporatism is almost feudal in that identity and power are connected with a larger corporate unit. Bigness is assumed to be efficient, as is private ownership and private profit. Therefore, bigness is accepted, even applauded and encouraged, in the belief that eventually everyone will benefit with a generally stable and affluent system.

Fascism

Fascism carries a more negative connotation. Though usually assumed by Americans to apply solely to Nazi Germany and Mussolini's Italy and the horrors associated with them, its application is in fact more general. Though sometimes equated with demagogic democracy, that is not the core of classic fascism. The base is the partnership between the major economic units of the system and a centralized state apparatus whose business is to protect and maintain those units. Other major units, however, such as labor or the church, are discouraged. The state takes on the job of managing the population, usually in troubled economic times, in order to maintain the private profit structure. Managing the population includes rousing patriotic and nationalistic appeals, calls to sacrifice for the good of the nation. It implies an adept use of symbols to manipulate a gullible, sheeplike citizenry. Though the population may be engaged in the beginning, skillful manipulation of crises, economic and political, gradually leads to almost religious patriotic fervor. Suppression of any dissent becomes increasingly oppressive, though still within procedural, legal limits. Eventually, all necessary roads are taken to maintain the governing partnership.

Totalitarianism

Totalitarianism, as its name implies, is total state control. It can be of either the Right or Left. In other words, the major economic units may remain in private hands, although they will be closely tied to members of the state, or the state and the economy may be one and the same. The defining characteristic of totalitarianism is the total lack of private space for the individual. The state has complete control of all facets of people's lives—religious, educational, social, cultural, familial, not to mention economic livelihood. It is obviously a heavy police state. In order to manage an entire population, the state must also be skilled in terror. There is a strong and large secret police and little pretense of any legal, procedural forms. Only fear prevails: the bottom fears the top, while the top fears the bottom.

INDEX